Creativity and Giftedness in Culturally Diverse Students

Perspectives on Creativity
Mark A. Runco (ed.)

Reclaiming the Wasteland: TV & Gifted Children
Bob Abelman

The Motives for Creative Work
Jock Abra

Remarkable Women: Perspectives on Female Talent Development
Karen Arnold, Kathleen Noble, and Rena Subotnik (eds.)

Creativity and Giftedness in Culturally Diverse Students
Giselle B. Esquivel and John Houtz (eds.)

Investigating Creativity in Youth: A Book of Readings on
Research and Methods
*Anne S. Fishkin, Bonnie Cramond, and Paula Olszewski-
Kubilius (eds.)*

Enhancing Creativity of Gifted Children: A Guide for Parents
and Teachers
Joe Khatena

Style and Psyche
Pavel Machotka

Unusual Associates: Essays in Honor of Frank Barron
Alfonso Montuori (ed.)

Creativity Research Handbook Volume One
Mark A. Runco (ed.)

The Young Gifted Child: Potential and Promise—An Anthology
Joan F. Smutny (ed.)

forthcoming

Critical Thinking and Reasoning: Current Research, Theory
and Practice
Daniel Fasko, Jr. (ed.)

Critical Creative Processes
Mark A. Runco (ed.)

Theories of Creativity Revised Edition
Mark A. Runco and Robert S. Albert (eds.)

Creating Conversations: Improvisation in Everyday Discourse
R. Keith Sawyer

Creativity and Giftedness in Culturally Diverse Students

edited by

Giselle B. Esquivel
John C. Houtz

Fordham University

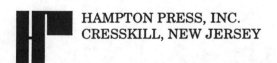

HAMPTON PRESS, INC.
CRESSKILL, NEW JERSEY

Printed in the United State of America

Library of Congress Cataloging-in-Publication Data

Creativity and giftedness in culturally diverse students / edited by Giselle B. Esquivel, John C. Houtz.
    p. cm. -- (Perspectives on creativity)
  Includes bibliographical references and index.
  ISBN 1-57273-224-5 -- ISBN 1-57273-225-3
    1. Gifted children--Education--United States. 2. Children of minorities--Education--United States. 3. Creative ability in children. I. Esquivel, Giselle B. II. Houtz, John. III. Series.

LC3993.2 .C74 1999
371.95--dc21

                                   99-051492

Hampton Press, Inc.
23 Broadway
Cresskill, NJ 07626

In Memory of Armando
In Honor of Daniel and Kristen

and

To all the children in our lives

Contents

**PART 3: IDENTIFICATION AND ASSESSMENT OF
GIFTED AND CREATIVE ABILITIES IN
CULTURALLY DIVERSE STUDENTS**

PART 4: EDUCATIONAL INTERVENTIONS AND PROGRAMS

Foreword

Laura M. Hines

Perhaps the best way to introduce this volume is to say that the importance of such a work cannot be overstated.

As early as 1981, when the then Secretary of Education, T.H. Bell, created the National Commission of Excellence in Education, it was evident that a widespread public perception was that there were serious problems in our educational system. The perception was well founded, and the Commission proceeded to produce some recommendations for reform. In *A Nation at Risk,* the Commission recognized that its finding and recommendations would be a beginning; that educators, psychologists, and other specialists would build on its recommendations; and that our nation need no longer be at risk.

In preparation for this textbook, the authors conducted a thorough search of the literature for references and appropriate materials dealing with identification and educational intervention of giftedness among culturally diverse populations. Finding very little, they assembled an excellent body of knowledge that will fill the void and provide the impetus for significant changes in the education of an increasingly larger population of linguistically, culturally diverse, gifted children.

The book is composed of 11 chapters. Each one is written by a scholar or scholars engaged in an ongoing research in the areas mentioned. Their combined expertise makes this text a unique one that should be useful for psychologists, educators, clinicians, teachers, and students.

Acknowledgments

We wish to acknowledge all those who contributed to the development of this book. First of all, we thank our respective mentors (Abbie Salny, Laura Hines, Judith Kaufman, and John Feldheusen), whose own giftedness and sensitivity to diversity and the needs of children and youth, have been a source of inspiration in our work. In turn, we thank our own students, giving special recognition to Fern Sandler and Susan McCann Brown for their chapter contributions, and to Kristen Peters for her efforts in the final stages of preparation. We are proud of and grateful to our past graduates (Emilia Lopez, Sara Nahari, and Mario Martorell), who have made their own professional mark as reflected in their chapter contribution. We are indebted to all of the colleagues who authored chapters and to each other for our abiding collaboration and friendship. We thank our respective mother/parents for fostering within us the gifts of love and creativity and our spouses for their love and support through this process. Foremost, we thank the children in our lives and all those who have touched our lives with unique gifts of the heart and the creative spirit.

About the Editors

Giselle B. Esquivel is professor, director of the bilingual school psychology specialization, and current chair of the Division of Psychological and Educational Services, in the Graduate School of Education at Fordham University.

John C. Houtz is professor, director of the Creative Studies Masters Program, and a past chair of the Division of Psychological and Educational Services, in the Graduate School of Education at Fordham University.

Part 1

Creativity and Giftedness Within a Cultural Context

Chapter 1

The Culturally and Linguistically Diverse School Population in the United States

Angela Reyes-Carrasquillo
Fordham University

Demographic changes in the U.S. population have brought a significant number of linguistically and culturally diverse students to public and private schools. Cultural and linguistic diversity in the school population is a reality in almost every classroom in the United States. This diversity poses the need for educators to accept the cultures and languages from which language-minority students come and to embrace the imperative to work through that understanding to help these students to ease their way into a new language and culture, while still retaining their own. Through an understanding of cultural and linguistic diversity, schools can contribute to the elimination of stereotyping or indifference toward these students that influence the way students are perceived, assessed, and ultimately instructed. Culturally and linguistically diverse students, if properly guided and instructed, produce unique strengths and talents such as bilingualism, multiculturalism, and cognitive development, which are unique attributes to these diverse school populations.

Historically, language-minority students' programs and instruction have been positively affected by political and social pressures in creating federal educational policies and programs on students' behalf. Although these educational policies and programs have helped to academically move students to achieve, based on their strengths and talents, culturally and linguistically diverse students still face many social and educational challenges. Reactionary attempts are made to underestimate linguistic and cultural diversity and to keep schools at a distance from providing challenging and quality instruction and learning for all children and youth, including the culturally and linguistically diverse.

The theme of this chapter is that culturally and linguistically diverse students enrich the U.S. educational system, but at the same time their unique educational characteristics and needs present many challenges to educators, policymakers, as well as parents. The chapter is divided into four areas: (a) the demographic changes of the school population in the United States, (b) national educational policies that have prompted educators to recognize linguistically and culturally diverse students' educational rights and needs, (c) students' strengths, and (d) social and educational challenges. The terms or labels *culturally and linguistic diverse* and *language minority* students are used interchangeably throughout this chapter to refer to students who come from a culture and language other than the Anglo/White American population.

DEMOGRAPHIC CHANGES OF THE SCHOOL POPULATION

The U.S. population projects to reach 275 million in the year 2000, and it is projected to grow from 252 million in 1991 to 383 million in the year 2050, a 50% increase. The U.S. Census Bureau data show that Black, Asian, and Hispanic populations are growing faster than the White/Anglo population. The Census Bureau has projected that an increase in births among women living in the United States, coupled with massive immigration, will add more people to the nation's population during the 1990s and the first part of the next century than any other time since the baby boom decade of the 1950s. By the middle of the 21st century, virtually half of the population will consist of African Americans, Hispanics, Asians, and Native Americans. Therefore, the current terminology of *majority* and *minority* will become meaningless because there will not be one majority group, but rather several ethnic groups that will make up a significant percentage of the U.S. population. The African American group will continue to be a strong group in terms of the numbers, followed by the Hispanic group, the Asian group, and the American Indian. These changes are the result of fertility rates (more new born children, almost two births per woman), illegal immigration and legal migration, and legislation that will continue to allow more legal immigrants into the country.

The United States has absorbed immigrants from all corners of the world, who have brought with them different cultural values, religious beliefs, and languages. The United States is and has been the destination of about half the world's immigrants who seek permanent resettlement. Minority and immigrant women have more children than White women. In addition, they have their first children earlier and therefore will probably have babies for a longer period of time. The number of immigrants in the United States increased after 1965, when amendments to immigration legislation eliminated quotas and reduced emphasis on accepting immigrants with high levels of skills and education. In addition, the increase in the number of refugees and the political turmoil in Central America and Southeast Asia increased the number of immigrants into United States. The projections, which in the last decade assumed about 500,000 immigrants into the country each year, in the 1990s included over a million people a year (National Center for Education Statistics, 1993).

It is projected that while the immigrant population grows, the Anglo/White population decreases. The Anglo population (a person having origins in any of the original peoples of Europe) would slowly grow from 191 million in 1992 to 208 million in 2029, then slowly decline in 2050. The percentage of the White population in 1992 was about 75. It will be 72% in 2000, 68% in 2010, 60% in 2030 and 50% in 2050 (United States Bureau of the Census, 1992). Table 1.1 summarizes the U.S. population projections.

By the year 2000, the population of the United States will show the following characteristics: (a) a big decrease in the White/Anglo population, (b) about 13% of the population will be African American, (c) 11% will be Hispanic, (d) 5% of the population will be Asian, and (e) almost 1% of the population will be Native American. By the year 2050, the U.S. population will comprise 16% African American, 21% Hispanic, 11% Asian and 1% Native American.

Culturally and linguistically diverse students in the United States are predominantly Hispanic, Asian, Native Americans, as well as Haitians, Arabs, and Russians (recent European immigrants). These ethnic groups are briefly described in the following sections.

Table 1.1. Percentage Distribution of the U.S. Population.

Ethnic Group	1990	2000	2030	2050
White	75.7	71.6	60.2	52.7
African American	11.8	12.3	13.8	15.0
Hispanic	9.0	11.1	17.2	21.1
Asian	2.8	4.2	8.4	10.1
Native American	0.7	0.8	1.0	1.1

Source: U.S. Bureau of the Census, 1992.

Hispanic Students

Hispanic students are those students who are Mexican, Puerto Rican, Cuban, Central, and South American or from other Spanish language or origin. The Hispanic population in the United States is expected to rise from 24 million in 1992 to 31 million in the year 2000, to 39 million in 2010 to 59 million in 2030 and 81 million in 2050. Hispanics have emerged as one of the fastest growing population groups in the United States and can be found in almost every region. The major concentration of Hispanics can be found in nine states and Puerto Rico, including California (7.6 million), Texas (4.3 million), New York (2.2 million), Florida (1.5 million), Illinois (0.9 million), New Jersey (0.74 million), Arizona (0.68 million), New Mexico (0.57 million), and Colorado (0.42 million). In 1995, the Hispanic population was estimated to be between 23 to 24 million which constituted 9% of the United States population. There is a belief that Hispanics were under counted by 5.9% in the 1990 census. Although, in 1993, Hispanics composed 9% of the U.S. population, the projections indicate that by the year 2000, Hispanics are likely to represent 11% of the population (United States Bureau of the Census, 1992).

The Hispanic population is a young, diverse, and dynamic group that is experiencing rapid growth in the United States. The Hispanic population is a community of first-, second-, and third-generation immigrants, who have uprooted their families and left homes, friends, and relatives for economic, political, professional, ideological, and educational reasons.

Hispanic students have a broad range of language and cultural characteristics and needs that impact on their academic and cognitive development. The cultural patterns of Hispanic students are reflective of those created by their parental heritage, by the length of time their families have been in the United States, and by the socioeconomic level they have achieved in the United States (Baruth & Manning, 1992; Carrasquillo, 1991). There are general experiences shared by many Hispanic families in the United States such as the Spanish language, family structure and characteristics, and Hispanic culture. Spanish language, religious beliefs, family structures, and general customs are enhanced among Hispanics. But, at the same time, Hispanic students represent a diverse group within a group in a country that does not value diversity, but instead values uniformity through a common language, culture, and race.

Hispanic students and their families face many challenges to their survival and development in the United States. For example, a significant percentage of Hispanic students are poor. The 1993 Census reported the poverty rate of Hispanics at 29.3% compared to 18.0% for the entire U.S. population (United States Bureau of the Census, 1993). The low-status occupations and high unemployment rates among Hispanics translate into low incomes and high levels of poverty. In spite of these challenges, Hispanic students show the desire to learn and their parents show the desire to provide them with the best moral, spiritual, educational, and material support. These goals are achieved in a greater or lesser degree due to Hispanics' precarious experience in the United States.

A significant number of Hispanic students perform poorly in school. There is considerable variation among Hispanic students in academic achievement related to socioeconomic and other contextual factors. For example, Hispanic students who arrive in the United States after several years of schooling in Latin America appear to have better academic prospects than Hispanic students born in the United States (Cummins, 1991).

Although much has been said about Hispanic students' lack of educational achievement, not too much is known about their learning and cognitive styles. The following characteristics have been listed, although they do not include all Hispanic students: (a) stand closer, (b) like to work in groups rather than independently, (c) avoid eye contact while listening or following directions, (d) prefer contact and individualized attention, and (e) rely on authority figures to solve problems. More research is needed in the area of identifying the cognitive and learning styles of Hispanic students. Better understanding of learning styles can be an excellent means of improving Hispanics' learning performance. By taking advantage of Hispanic students cognitive and learning strengths, educators can facilitate their learning and increase their motivation to learn.

Asian Students

Educators, especially teachers and school counselors, must understand the educational values of Asian people in order to develop a strategic plan to deal with their cultural and educational diversity in the most beneficial way. Asian students comprise children and youth from more than two dozen different countries of Asia and the Pacific Islands, which include countries such as Cambodia, China, Korea, India, Japan, Laos, Philippines, Samoa/Tonga/Guam, Thailand, and Vietnam, to mention a few. Asian students do not share a common language, a common religion, or a common cultural background. The Asian population is expected to continue to be one of the fastest growing groups, rising from 9 million in 1992 to 13 million in the year 2000, to 17 million in 2010, 29 million in 2030, and 41 million in 2050. New York City, for example, contains the largest Chinese community in the United States and the second largest Korean community after Los Angeles.

There is no single Asian-American ethnic group. Each group mentioned has its own distinct history, culture, language, art, religion, traditions, customs, values demography, and lifestyles. They represent diverse cultural, racial, educational, and occupational backgrounds, and like their children they encountered a different assimilation process and various problems. Each group wishes to retain its respective ethnic communities where ethnic culture, values and virtues are perpetuated and enriched. All of these groups, although living in the United States, maintain their language, culture and life styles. They tend to stay together by settling in the same neighborhood or community. Asian Americans are highly concentrated in the western region of the United States. The majority of Asians live in metropolitan areas with about equal numbers living in central cities and suburbs. Half of them live in the following metropolitan areas: Honolulu, Los Angeles, Long Beach, San Francisco, Oakland, New York, Chicago, and San Jose (United States General Accounting Office, 1994). Chinatowns throughout the United States have their economic base, and legitimate residents often profit from them. Chinatowns have become political power bases in dealing with the outside world. They are also the center of social and cultural life.

Most Asian children have been raised in a very rigid, disciplined, and sheltered environment (Peterson, 1983; Yao, 1985). Asians see the goal of education as the training of people to obtain the skills and required degrees or diplomas to be fully employed. For this reason Asian students are pushed to excel in school. The traditional role of tests in achieving promotion or academic progress has placed a tremendous emphasis on examination preparation. For many parents the most important subjects are reading, writing, and mathematics. Parents make sure that when their children are at home they are practicing these subjects. Asian students use experience in practice, memory, and drilling until they become proficient on the subject. Asian parents have a great respect for scholastic work. Degrees and diplomas are valued. One reason that a degree is so valued is that in most countries in Asia there are far fewer universities to satisfy the demand for higher education, and a university education is for the academic elite. Therefore, the competition to enter universities is intense, and examinations are the keys for university acceptance. Such intense pressure has resulted in sending students to tutorial training and other test preparatory courses.

Asian students are less verbal and expressive at social occasions than other U.S. students. They need reinforcement from teachers, and they work efficiently in a well-structured, quiet learning environment in which definite goals have been established for them. They seldom reveal their opinions or their abilities voluntarily or dare to challenge their teachers. Even when they know the answer to the teacher's question, they may not respond by raising their hand, choosing instead to sit quietly as if they are lost (Yao, 1985). Older students who are accustomed to structured and passive learning conditions may perform well in rote memorization and mathematics operation but may do poorly in creative writing and analytical commentary (Peterson, 1983, Yao, 1985). In general, Asian students perform academically well in U.S. schools.

Native American Students

Native American ("original Americans" or "American Indians") students have special needs that warrant educators' understanding: unique language and cultural characteristics, familiar traditions, and learning problems that present schools with special challenges. Although some common characteristics emerge when studying Native American students, one must use caution not to oversimplify or ignore individual differences. Native American students are those whose origins are found in any of the original peoples of North America and who maintain cultural identification through tribal affiliation or community recognition. Projections on Native Americans indicates that their numbers are growing, although not as fast as the previous groups mentioned. Approximately one half of the Native American population resides on Native American lands, whereas the other half lives outside of urban and metropolitan areas. States with the greatest population of Native Americans include

California, Oklahoma, Arizona, New Mexico, and Washington. Of the federal reservations, the Navajo Nation Reservation is the largest. Other states with reservations comprising large land holdings include South Dakota, Wyoming, and Montana. Native Americans speak about 2,200 different languages (Baruth & Manning, 1992; Carrasquillo, 1995). Wide-scale differences exist in the Native American ability to speak English. Some speak English well, but a significant number of American Indians lack proficiency in English.

Native Americans have not had an easy life in the United States. Settlement by Europeans meant the elimination of the Indian land. Revenge against Native Americans came when the Indians confronted the European settlers. By the end of the 19th century Native Americans were confined to reservations, managed and controlled by the Bureau of Indian Affairs. Poor living conditions and diseases in the reservations caused many deaths among Native Americans. Reservations brought other problems such as unemployment, alcoholism, lack of housing, and lack of educational opportunities, which depended in many instances on federal government subsidies.

Nearly all literature on Native American education alludes to the vital importance of addressing Native American cultural differences in education. Each of the Native American/Indian cultures developed its own religious system; no single, unified "Indian religion" exists. Nevertheless, certain features are common to other religions traditionally practiced by Native Americans. One of these beliefs is in a supreme spiritual force, sometimes called the "great spirit." Another common belief is the need to search for one's own guiding spirit, a spiritual being who will seek greater contact with the spiritual world through fasting, meditating, dancing, or using certain natural drugs (Baruth & Manning, 1992).

Most Native Americans have become increasingly concerned about the teaching of Native American languages and cultures in schools. Of the approximately 155 Native American languages still spoken regularly, only 20 have children who speak the language (Baruth & Manning, 1992). Although schools alone cannot save Native American languages, it will be very difficult for most Native American groups to do so without the schools' assistance. In addition, schools in general are not meeting the academic needs of Native American students; they are performing poor in measures of academic achievement.

The Native American culture plays a major role in the shaping of children and adolescents, and societal and cultural beliefs and traditions of the Native American people influence children's evolving identities. General characteristics of children may include:

(a) consideration of the ability and willingness to share to be most worthy; (b) tendency to patience and passive temperament, as they are taught to be patient, to control emotions, and to avoid passionate outburst; (c) tendency to lower their voices to communicate anger; (d) deep respect for the rights and dignity of individuals; and (e) ability to work collaboratively toward a common goal.

Other Ethnic Groups

U.S. schools have received an influx of other immigrant students in addition to those already mentioned. Among these, Haitian, Russian, and Arab students are represented in the U.S. school population; for example, Haitians are found in great numbers in the Northeast. Having come from an authoritarian society, Haitian students need extensive orientation to life in the United States. As with most immigrant groups, language difficulties present numerous problems. These problems are compounded for those Haitians who are illiterate and without school experience (New York State Education Department, 1987).

The Arab student population is also growing. The Arabs are made up of several different people who live in the North of Africa and Western Asia (the Middle East) and share a common culture. Because a growing number of Arabs are Muslims, it is important to respect their religion in the classroom and to make the other students acknowledge it as well. Educators need to be familiar with these students' religious and lifestyle practices.

U.S. classrooms are populated with students from diverse European backgrounds, especially from the eastern and northern parts of Europe. Most of these families emigrated to the United States because of uncertainty in their own countries due to rapid political and economic changes. These immigrant students speak more than 100 different languages and have different cultural and religious practices as well as lifestyles. A group that is rapidly growing in the northeastern part of the United States is the Russian population, representing various political and religious orientations. European students in the United States need to adjust to a new language, a new lifestyle, new cultural values and attitudes, and they need to learn to live with other Europeans who may have different styles, religious practices, and political points of view.

Educational Implications

Educators in the United States are becoming aware of the changes in the racial and ethnic composition of the nation's public school population. Cultural diversity as well as linguistic diversity present challenges to school districts and policymakers. Failure to understand diverse student cultures often hinders effective teacher-student communication. The elementary and secondary school population is constantly increasing. In 1990, African Americans, Latinos, Native Americans, and Asians made up 32% of the total public school enrollment in the nation. Thirty-three percent of the largest school districts had an enrollment of over 50% ethnic- and language-minority students (National Center for Education Statistics, 1993). The elementary school population (ages 5 to 13) will increase by more than 4 million during the 1990s to over 36 million by the year 2000. The high school population (ages 14 to 17) will increase from 13.4 million in 1991 to 15.7 million in the year 2000 and 16.9 million in 2010 (United States Bureau of the Census, 1992). Therefore, educators will be challenged to educate a higher percentage of students that is less homogeneous and ethnically and linguistically more diverse, and that will require a different approach to learning and teaching. Bilingual/ESL (English as a Second Language) learners are one of these students' groups.

BILINGUAL/ENGLISH AS SECOND LANGUAGE LEARNERS

Bilingual/ESL learners, commonly known as limited English proficient (LEP) students, are those individuals who have a primary language other than English and who are learning English as a second language. In the United States they are usually immigrants from other countries who have adopted the United States as their second home, or they may have been born in the United States and raised in a non-English-speaking environment in which their parents may have little understanding of English. Also, chances are they have been living in the country for only a short period of time.

Second language learners vary not only in terms of location and purpose for learning English but in terms of individual differences. They represent a wide range of language variations with varying levels of literacy and proficiency in their first as well as in the second language. There are second language students who show linguistic deficiencies relative to their age in both the primary and the second language. Other students come to the second language classroom with the ability to analyze and reformulate materials in their native language. In other words, they show a high level of proficiency in their respective native language. In addition, the organization and analysis of knowledge may differ from culture to culture. These factors, therefore, play an important role in planning for the development of linguistic and cognitive skills in English.

Although in this chapter we refer to these students as bilingual/ESL learners, federal and state agencies refer to them as "limited English proficient students." Currently, no nationally accepted definition of "limited proficient English" (LEP) exists, and consensus is lacking on the criteria for determining limited proficiency in English (United States General Accounting Office, 1994). The United States Department of Education (1993) warns that "the lack of standardization across the country can affect estimates of the size and characteristics of the national LEP student population. Presumably, if the methods and standards were changed, in some large school districts, the estimates of the numbers and characteristics of the LEP population might also change" (p. 6). This lack of consensus is particularly true regarding the level of language skills that constitutes limited proficiency in English. Following the definition used by the Congressional Research Service when it employs census data to estimate the LEP population, the United States General Accounting Office defined as LEP all persons aged 5 to 17 living in families whom the Census reported as speaking English "not well" or "not at all." Current estimates by the U.S. Department of Education (1993), the Council of Chief State School Officers (1990), and other sources place the number of total school-age LEP students between 2.3 and 3.5 million. However, observers believe that this figure underestimates the actual number of LEP students enrolled in public schools as well as in non-public schools and suggest that the number is more than 4 million students. Despite the divergent methods used to define the LEP population and the varied estimates they yield, this group is growing at a significantly faster rate than the overall student population. For example, federally funded programs (such as Title VII, and Chapter 1) serve only a small proportion of LEP students. Figures available are usually gathered from surveys of states' reports to the Office of Bilingual Education and Minority Language Affairs (OBEMLA), but only states receiving Title VII funds are required to report such data. Federal aid is intended to supplement state and local funding to promote educational equity. Therefore, it is not likely that there are many more LEP students than those reported to OBEMLA.

Nationally, LEP enrollments increased by 56% between 1985 and 1992 (Hopstock & Bucaro, 1993; United States Department of Education, 1993). From 1985 to 1993, the LEP student population increased at an average of 9.2% per year. By contrast, the overall student population increased by approximately 1% annually (Hopstock & Bucaro, 1993). Spanish speakers are in the majority

(73%) followed by speakers of Asian languages (12%). Although Hispanics and Asians and Pacific Islanders form the largest segments of the non-native-speaking students, the number of native speakers of Arabic, Armenian, Polish, Haitian Creole, and Russian increased considerably (United States Department of Education, 1993). The result is a diversity of languages and cultures in U.S. classrooms. By the end of the century, language-minority students will comprise close to 42% of the total public school enrollment (Carrasquillo, 1995; Fleschman & Hopstock, 1993).

INFLUENTIAL EDUCATIONAL LAWS AND COURT CASES

Historically, culturally and linguistically diverse students' education have been positively influenced by court and federal legislation. The Civil Rights Act, *Lau vs. Nichols*, The Bilingual Education Act, and the Lau Remedies are the most influential ones. A brief description of each follows.

Title VI of the Civil Rights Act of 1964

Title VI of the 1964 Civil Rights Act prohibited discrimination on the basis of race, color, or national origin in federally assisted programs and activities and imposed on grant-making agencies responsibilities for ensuring compliance. To enforce Title VI compliance, the Office of Civil Rights (OCR) was established in the Department of Health, Education and Welfare (DHEW). In 1968, DHEW issued general Title VI guidelines that held educational systems responsible for assuring that students of a particular race, color, or national origin were not denied the opportunity to obtain the education generally available to other students in the system.

In 1970, the director of the Office of Civil Rights followed up on the 1968 general guidelines with a memorandum providing specific information on responsibilities to school districts whose national origin minority enrollments exceeded 5%. Specifically, it directed school districts to take affirmative steps to rectify the language deficiency in order to open its instructional program to students who had the inability to speak and understand the English language.

Lau vs. Nichols

Lau v. Nichols is the name of a class-action suit by the parents of nearly 3,000 Chinese pupils in the San Francisco public school system, who were not provided an equal educational opportunity compared to that of their English-speaking peers. In the San Francisco Public School System approximately one third of the Chinese students received supplemental instruction in the English language; the remainder received no special instruction. The plaintiffs alleged that the school district's conduct violated both the 14th amendment of the Constitution and Title VI of the Civil Rights Act of 1964. The Court found the San Francisco educational system in violation of Title VI by denying the Chinese-speaking students a meaningful opportunity to participate in the educational program.

The Lau Remedies of 1975

After the Supreme Court's Lau decision, DHEW officials launched a major Title VI enforcement program. Recognizing that few schools districts were providing any type of special instruction to LEP students, the federal government began the effort by developing remedial rather than compliance guidelines for districts not in compliance with Title VI under the Lau guidelines. These guidelines (informally called the Lau Remedies) specified proper approaches, methods, and procedures for: (a) identifying and evaluating national-origin minority students' English language skills, (b) determining appropriate instructional treatments, (c) deciding when LEP students were ready for mainstreaming classes, and (d) naming the professional standards to be met by teachers of language minority children. Under the Lau Remedies elementary schools were generally required to provide LEP students with special ESL instruction as well as academic subject-matter instruction through the students' strongest language until the students achieved proficiency in English sufficiently to learn effectively in a monolingual English classroom.

Enforcement by the Office of Civil Rights to insure districts meet their obligations under Lau has been drastically curtailed. From 1981 through 1985, school districts were nine times less likely to undergo a Lau compliance review than in the period from 1976 through 1980 (Crawford, 1986).

The Bilingual Education Act

Title VII originated in 1968 as a demonstration program to promote innovative ways of teaching LEP students. The Bilingual Education Act Title VII of the Elementary and Secondary Education Act (ESEA) of 1965, as amended, is the key federal legislation directed to language minority students. The stated policy of the act is to support educational programs that help to ensure both English-language proficiency and academic achievement for students served. On January 17, 1967, Texas Senator Ralph Yarborough and six co-sponsors introduced The American Bilingual Education Act, an amendment to the Elementary and Secondary Education Act of 1965. The legislation was designed to address "the special educational needs of the large numbers of students in the United States whose mother tongue was Spanish and to whom English was a foreign language." The focus of the law changed from "Spanish-speaking children" to "children of limited English-speaking ability." The original law focused on a remedial or compensatory program to serve children who were deficient in English language skills, and schools who were eligible needed to have a high concentration of students from low-income families.

Six years after its enactment, Congress reauthorized and substantially revised the Bilingual Education Act. The 1974 amendments expanded the programs by authorizing new grants for state and educational technical assistance, teacher training, and a national clearinghouse. The law authorized the voluntary enrollment of a limited number of English-speaking children in bilingual education programs.

In 1978, Congress again reauthorized and revised the Bilingual Education Act. The amendments clarified the definition of eligible children. The term *limited English proficient* (LEP) supplanted *limited English speaking* in recognition of the importance of reading, writing, understanding, and cognitive skills in addition to speaking (Lyons, 1994). Lyons (1995) stated that the "new definition, while arguably clearer and more comprehensive, reinforced the deficit approach to educating language minority students" (p. 3). Further amendments of the Bilingual Education Act (United States Public Law 100-927, 1988) put priority on establishing and operating bilingual projects, but also allowed for projects using nonbilingual approaches—called Special Alternative Instructional Programs—when bilingual instruction is not practical.

The Educate America Act of 1993

Although this bill is not legislation targeting minority school children, it is mentioned in this chapter because there are a significant number of bilingual and ESL learners in U.S. schools. The Educate America Act includes provisions for an equal education for all students. This bill was enacted on March 26, 1994 to further the development of voluntary national curriculum and performance standards and to provide funding to state education agencies to develop educational reform plans that help local school districts implement high educational standards for all students. This legislation is based on two fundamental concepts: (a) every child in school in the nation can work toward and achieve high standards, and (b) schools and communities have the obligation to provide every child with the opportunity to achieve at high levels. During 1995, this legislation was not fully implemented due to federal legislation movements to cut its funding.

All of these legislations are based on the premise of helping all children and working on their strengths.

CULTURALLY AND LINGUISTICALLY DIVERSE STUDENTS' STRENGTHS

All bilingual/ESL learners bring a lifetime of language strengths to the learning situation (Carrasquillo, 1994; Garcia, 1993). Among the most significant ones are:

1. *Skills in their first (native) language, which includes listening, speaking, reading, and writing.* Concepts already learned by the bilingual/ESL learners in the native language can be transferred into English and developed as students apply them to many second-language activities (Cummins, 1991).
2. *Broad, bicultural, cognitive, and affective experiences that enable them to survive successfully in "two worlds."* They bring to the learning experience different experiences (information concerning their customs, languages, and perceptions of the world) and background knowledge, which in turn will affect their conceptualization of the world and their personal psychological insights. They possess a broad cultural background as well as a global conceptual view that aids them in comprehending the semantics of English (Carrasquillo, 1994, 1995; Garcia, 1993).
3. *Social intelligence—personal psychological insights and the capacity for empathy.* Students have acquired valuable conceptualizations of the world around them in their native language. All these ideas and concepts that have been developed in the native language present a powerful language strength during the second-language acquisition process (Bialystok, 1991; Cummins, 1991).

Bilingualism, cognitive flexibility, and multiculturalism are some of the strengths of culturally and linguistically diverse students. These characteristics are briefly described next.

Bilingualism

Bilingualism is defined as demonstrating high levels of proficiency in two or more languages. Bilingualism is a complex linguistic development that may be measured along a continuum ranging from limited proficiency in two languages, to high levels of proficiency on both languages. Research on bilingual education indicates that balanced bilinguals, those who meet high levels of proficiency in two languages, enjoy certain cognitive benefits over their monolingual counterparts (Cummins, 1976, 1978, 1991; Diaz, 1983, 1985; Peal & Lambert, 1962). Bilinguals may have a wider and more varied range of experiences than monolinguals due to their operating in two languages and probably two or more cultures. Researchers have found that bilinguals perform better than their monolingual counterparts on a variety of visual-spatial and linguistic tasks, especially those in which the number of productions and complexity are considered (Galambos & Hakuta, 1988; Hakuta & Diaz, 1985; Lemmon & Goggin, 1989).

A number of linguistically and culturally diverse students in the United States are proficient bilinguals (Cummins, 1991). Proficient bilingualism refers to high levels of functioning in both the cognitive and social aspects of language (i.e., the ability to use both languages in academic settings), as well as the ability to become a full participant in the communities that use the languages. As stated by the Stanford Working Group (1994), "proficiency in two or more languages should be promoted for all American students. Bilingualism enhances cognitive and social growth, competitiveness in a global marketplace, national security, and understanding of diverse peoples and cultures" (p. 1). Therefore, it is advantageous to provide language minority students with more opportunities to develop their bilingualism.

Cognitive Strategies

There is a cognitive theory that states that because bilinguals switch between their two languages they may be more flexible in thinking. The underlying hypothesis is that because bilingual/ESL learners live and learn in two cultures and two languages and can speak (to some extent) two languages, the use of these two languages contributes to their increase in fluency, flexibility, originality, and elaboration in thinking (Cummins, 1978; Hakuta & Diaz, 1985; Lemmon & Goggin, 1989). In other words, bilingual learners may have two or more words for a single object or idea, and may enjoy more advanced processing of verbal material, more discriminating perceptual distinctions, more propensity to search for structure in perceptual situations, and more capacity to reorganize their perceptions to feed them back than monolingual counterparts (Ben-Zeev, 1977; Diaz, 1983, 1985; Holtzman, 1980). For example, bilingual children in Ben-Zeev's (1977) study were able to switch quickly to alternative interpretations or to search for new interpretations in cognitive tasks. These children corrected their errors faster compared with monolinguals. Ben-Zeev gave the first clue that bilinguals may have cognitive advantages regarding "communicative sensitivity."

Flexibility in problem-solving situations seems to be one of the ways in which bilinguals are more cognitively advantaged than monolinguals. Studies have shown that bilinguals tend to be more creative and score higher on measures of divergent thinking. This had been demonstrated by higher scores of fluency and flexibility that bilinguals have shown on measures of creativity (Holtzman, 1980). Bilinguals have shown greater awareness of the arbitrary nature of word-referent relationships and have been shown to better evaluate nonempirical statements. This may be due to the fact that bilingual children experience more varied possibilities for language processing and that, under some conditions, this may result in cognitive and academic advantages.

Fluent bilinguals have increased metalinguistic abilities that may facilitate earlier reading acquisition, in turn can lead to higher levels of academic achievement (Bialystok, 1988). This metalinguistic awareness is most developed when a child's two languages are developed to their highest level. The development of two languages to the fullest, particularly in the language minority/second language, encourages metalinguistic awareness. Galambos and Hakuta (1988) agree with Cummins (1976, 1978, 1991) that a certain level of proficiency must be obtained before the positive effects of bilingualism or metalinguistic awareness can occur. Bilingual children whose initial level of language proficiency in a single language is highly developed may be in a position to benefit from enrichment bilingual programs.

Biculturalism/Multiculturalism

The relationships among individuals and groups are essential to living, understanding, and working effectively with different cultural groups and individuals. A hypotheses exists that says that individuals who are proficient in two or more cultures are capable of functioning in multiple systems for perceiving, evaluating, believing, and acting according to the patterns of the various microcultures in which they participate. Individuals who have competencies in and can operate in two or more different and multiple cultures are not threatened by a rejection of the primary cultural identification. According to Burbules and Rice (1991), "one's identity will be more flexible, autonomous, and stable to the degree that one recognize one's self as a member of various different communities simultaneously" (p. 404). Biculturalism does allow a broad range of abilities on which one can draw on any given occasion as determined by the particular situation. As Baker (1993) said:

> Two cultures and two languages enable a person to have dual or multiple perspectives on society. Those who speak more than one language and own more than one culture are more sensitive and sympathetic, more likely to build bridges than barricades and boundaries. Rather than being subtractive as in assimilation, multiculturalism bequeaths an additive person and process. (p. 267)

It has also been said that one person who is multicultural has more respect for other people and other cultures than one who is monocultural. Individuals with competencies in several microcultures develop a fuller appreciation of the range of cultural competencies available to all individuals (Gollnick & Chin, 1990).

SOCIAL AND EDUCATIONAL CHALLENGES

There are many factors that negatively affect the academic performance of language-minority students. These factors are interactive and overlap, making it difficult to discuss them separately.

Social Challenges

Educators face other challenges beyond the obvious one of simple communication with these students. For example, concentrations of LEP students are often accompanied by concentrations of immigrant students. Census data show that in 1990, about 43% of all LEP students were immigrants. Both LEP students and immigrant students are almost twice as likely as other students to be poor.

About 30% of immigrant students and about 37% of LEP students were poor, compared with about 17% of all students (United States General Accounting Office, 1994). In addition, these students often have significant health and emotional needs, especially those immigrants who have experienced trauma of war and life in refugee camps in their native countries. Research data suggest that students from socioeconomically advantaged households tend to be more successful in school than are their less advantaged classmates, and that much of this success can be credited to supportive aspects of the family process rather than to more material advantages (Carrasquillo, 1991; Salerno, 1991).

Children are particularly vulnerable to poverty (National Center for Education Statistics, 1993). Poverty may affect students' social and mental development due to the deprivations often associated with such poverty, including lack of physical facilities, health insurance, proper nutrition, and parental involvement. Many immigrant and refugee children live a life of poverty and rural isolation in crowded dwellings where they lack privacy, toilets, shower facilities, comfort and basic medical attention (Trueba, 1989). In some cases the life of immigrant children and youth means abuse, malnutrition, poor health, ignorance, and neglect. Uprooting a child from his or her land can lead to a life of stigma and low status. Children and youth are vulnerable to becoming disoriented and discontent with society in general, which serves to decrease their interest in school matters and promote their engagement in risky behaviors (Miranda, 1990).

A valid point of discussion is home culture and language and the prevailing school culture and language. There are cultural and linguistic variations that need to be considered, especially those related to discourse patterns, nonverbal communication, socialization, and learning styles. According to Garcia (1993) and Sue and Padilla (1986), there exists a home-to-school mismatch. This mismatch is apparent not just in language differences but in dissimilarities in culture, values, and beliefs. The family and the child are expected to adjust to the system rather than the system adapting to new students. These authors agreed that the challenge is to identify these differences between and within ethnic minority groups and to incorporate this information into classroom practice.

In addition, because of the family's poverty, some of these students live in crowded apartments with other families. These factors contribute to school overcrowding by increasing the number of students living in individual school attendance areas (United States General Accounting Office, 1994).

Educational Challenges

Culturally diverse students confront many educational challenges that negatively affect their academic achievement and success in school. For purposes of this chapter, only six of these challenges are briefly described: the quality of schooling, students' mastery of the school language, the integrity of the academic assessment of the school, the transient nature of a significant number of these students, prior students' school experiences, and the quality of parental involvement.

One of the most important functions of schooling is to broaden the range of individuals' experiences and to help them develop sustained and deliberate attention to a topic or activity that makes more systematic learning possible. It is important that the experiences of the school environment, the curriculum, and the delivery of instruction are exciting and challenging, and that when the students' endeavors are successful they are given individual recognition for what they do and what they can do (Tattum & Tattum, 1992). Wells (1986) advises educators to insure these types of experiences because:

> Children who feel, or who are made to feel, unaccepted and incompetent may be slow to recover their self-confidence and, as a result, their ability to benefit from enlarged opportunities for learning that school provides may be diminished or even, in extreme cases, irrevocably damaged. (p. 68)

Students develop expectations for their own performance based on how others react to them and take this information into account when they evaluate their own performance (Tattum & Tattum, 1992). Students must be provided with an equal opportunity to learn the same challenging content and high-level skills that school reform movements advocate for all students (Stanford Working Group, 1994).

Students' language may influence their chances for success in the classroom. Native-language proficiency as well as English-language proficiency may affect students' ability to learn, especially the academic subjects' content and skills. It is a fact that most children have acquired a mastery of their mother tongue long before they start school. But for some children this mother tongue may be English, another language, or a combination of both, in many instances with limitations. Assessment of English-language proficiency is important for determining the appropriate level of English-language assistance. It is necessary to assess students frequently so that activities involving the appropriate degree of language difficulty are included in the planning and delivery of instruction. It has been said that current assessment instruments in English are inappropriate because they actually assess both content and language ability, particularly reading comprehension and writing. As a result, it is difficult to know whether a student is unable to demonstrate knowledge because of a language barrier or whether the student does not know the content material being tested. Often these assessments become measures of students' language proficiency rather than measures of content knowledge, as they are intended to be.

Schools conduct widespread assessments of students for entrance into programs and to identify their level of academic development to place them in appropriate grade-level instruction. The development of appropriate mechanisms to assess whether schools are meeting state performance and opportunity-to-learn policies is especially critical for linguistically and culturally diverse students. The literature on the assessment of language-minority students has identified some of the problems in using current standardized measurements to identify the linguistic, cognitive, and academic abilities of students (Canales, 1990; DeGeorge, 1988). It has been said that these standardized tests have limited the access of language minority students to more rigorous study at all educational levels and have prevented students from entering professional schools. They are also used to assign disproportionately large numbers of minority students to special education programs for the mentally retarded, learning disabled, and emotionally disturbed. Mercer (1979) said that these tests are based on an Anglo-conformity model of appraisal. In making inferences about children's "intelligence" or "aptitudes," present procedures presume that the United States is a culturally homogeneous society in which all children are being socialized into essentially the same Anglo tradition. Anyone who cannot pass the appropriate test certainly cannot be qualified to move onto further study. In fact, this type of testing limits the access of many culturally and linguistically diverse students to study the career of their choice. Therefore, it is necessary to conduct assessment measures for instructional purposes (selecting and using linguistically and culturally appropriate measures) so as to provide information and guidance to teachers, parents, and students on the progress being made by individual students in meeting the school instructional objectives. Educators must be careful not to label students intellectually inferior because they score poorly on standardized tests. These scores too often influence the teacher's expectations for the academic performance of students in the classroom (Canales, 1990; DeGeorge, 1988). Proper assessment must include the use of multiple forms of assessment (portfolio, journals, teacher evaluations, self-evaluations, criterion-referenced tests, and standardized tests). Such assessments should be in the language and form most likely to yield accurate and reliable information on what language-minority students know and can do. This assessment also determines when students are considered sufficiently fluent to succeed in all-English classrooms.

Often minority and culturally diverse students are highly transient, making continuity of instruction and planning difficult. They often continue to arrive through the school year, contributing in many cases to school overcrowding and putting them at a disadvantage in terms of the instructional program. In evaluating effective schools the length of time students are enrolled in a particular program is an important factor. The author's personal observations in evaluating programs in New York City are that, in general, Latino students, for example, move from one school neighborhood to another, and some relocate back and forth from the United States to their native countries, thus making it difficult to maintain a constant and developmental instructional plan. This is even more difficult when curriculum varies from district to district or from city to city.

Another particularly difficult challenge is the recent arrival of many immigrant students, including those of high school age, who have had little or no schooling and are illiterate even in their native language (Prewit Diaz, 1991; Salerno, 1991). Students represent many levels of academic preparedness and proficiency in both their native languages and in English. Schools are challenged to provide literacy development, especially written language development, to these students. In many school districts students are enrolled in the grade level corresponding to their age and are included in the regular curriculum in which they have to "swim or sink." Many of these students do not perform well in school. Although they may be passed to the next grade level, they have not mastered the necessary skills and knowledge to succeed in more advanced grade levels.

Parental involvement is an important factor in students' educational achievement. It is critical that parents of culturally and linguistically diverse students become involved in their children's education. This involvement goes beyond attending school meetings regularly. It involves parents as daily participants in their children's educational experiences. It is a challenge to get parents involved in their children's education. One major difficulty is that many parents are illiterate in their native language as well as in English. Strategies used to involve the parents vary. They include using interpreters, translating notices into a variety of languages, and providing parenting classes in a variety of subjects such as literacy in the parents' native language and English communication skills. Again, readers are reminded that many immigrant students arrive with limited schooling and are often illiterate in their native languages.

CONCLUSION

Demographic changes in the United States have brought about educational and social issues relating to language and academic learning. Educators across the nation are facing the challenge of educating students with whom they cannot easily communicate because of language and cultural differences. Culturally and linguistically diverse students bring cultural, cognitive, and linguistic characteristics to school that require educators' immediate attention. Cultural, linguistic, cognitive, and socialization factors influence cognitive and affective preferences and are manifested in incentives and motivation, interpersonal relationships, and patterns of intellectual abilities. Students' cultural identity as well as their knowledge of their first language are part of the academic foundation of their learning process. Because these students represent many diverse ethnic groups and bring to school the richness of many languages, educators need to assess their strengths and weaknesses in a variety of ways.

All learners deserve the most effective educational experiences possible. Educators expect all students to learn by using similar cognitive processes, to feel or perceive events similarly, to demonstrate similar patterns of behavior, and to demonstrate achievement. However, diversity (whether it be cultural, racial, ethnic, or linguistic) among learners means that educators cannot consider an entire class as a homogeneous group of learners who need the same educational experiences. Just as Anglo-American students differ significantly according to social class and geographic location, students of other cultures and languages also differ according to languages, values, traditions, customs, and educational experiences. Knowledge of culturally diverse students will generate appropriate attitudes that show concern for and caring, which in and of itself is the foundation for the development of the skills to plan and implement instruction that addresses the culturally diverse students' developmental needs and learning styles. Educators need to build on students' strengths—particularly creativity, special talents and gifts.

REFERENCES

Baker, C. (1993). *Foundations of bilingual education and bilingualism*. Clevedon, England: Multilingual Matters.

Baruth, L. G., & Manning, M. L. (1992). *Multicultural education of children and adolescents*. Needham Heights, MA: Allyn & Bacon.

Ben-Zeev, S. (1977). The influence of bilingualism on cognitive strategy and cognitive development. *Child Development, 48,* 1009-1008.

Burbules, N. C., & Rice, S. (1991). Dialogue across differences: Continuing the conversation. *Harvard Educational Review, 61,* 393-416.

Bialystok, E. (1988). Words as things: Development of word concept by bilingual children. *Studies in Second Language Learning, 9,* 133-140.

Bialystok, E. (1991). (Ed.). *Language processing in bilingual children*. Boston: Cambridge University Press.

Canales, J. (1990). *Assessment of language proficiency: Informing policy and practices*. Unpublished manuscript.

Carrasquillo, A. (1991). *Hispanic children and youth in the United States: A resource book*. New York: Garland.

Carrasquillo, A. (1994). *Teaching English as a second language: A resource guide*. New York: Garland.

Carrasquillo, A. (1995). *Language minority students in the mainstream classroom*. Clevedon, England: Multilingual Matters.

Council of Chief State School Officers. (1990). *School success for limited English proficient students: The challenge and state response*. Washington, DC: Author

Crawford, J. (1986, June). U.S. enforcement of bilingual plans declines sharply. *Education Week,* pp. 14-15.

Cummins, J. (1991). Interdependence of first- and second language proficiency in bilingual children. In E. Bialystok (Ed.), *Language processing in bilingual children* (pp. 70-89). Boston: Cambridge University Press.

Cummins, J. (1976). The influence of bilingualism on cognitive growth: A synthesis of research findings and explanatory hypotheses. *Working Papers on Bilingualism, 9,* 1-42.

Cummins, J. (1978). Bilingualism and the development of metalinguistic awareness. *Journal of Cross-Cultural Psychology, 9,* 131-149.

DeGeorge, G. P. (1988). Assessment and placement of language minority students: Procedures for mainstreaming. *Equity and Excellence, 23*(4), 44-56.

Diaz, R. M. (1983). Thought and two languages: The impact of bilingualism on cognitive development. *Review of Research in Education, 10,* 23-54.

Diaz, R. M. (1985). The intellectual power of bilingualism on cognitive development. *The Quarterly Newsletter of the Laboratory of Comparative Human Cognition, 7,* 16-22.

Fleischman, H. L., & Hopstock, P. J. (1993). *Descriptive study of services to limited English proficient students.* Arlington, VA: Development Associates.

Galambos, S. J., & Hakuta, K. (1988). Subject-specific and task-specific characteristics of metalinguistic awareness in bilingual children. *Applied Psycholinguistics, 9,* 141-162.

Garcia, E. E. (1993). Language, culture, and education. In L. Darling-Hammond (Ed.), *Review of research in education* (pp. 51-98). Washington, DC: American Educational Research Association.

Gollnick, P. C., & Chin, D. M. (1990). *Multicultural education in a pluralistic society.* New York: Macmillan.

Hakuta, K., & Diaz, R. M. (1985). The relationship between degree of bilingualism and cognitive ability: A critical discussion and some new longitudinal data. *Children Language, 5,* 319-344.

Holtzman, W. H. (1980). Divergent thinking as a function of the degree of bilingualism of Mexican-American and Anglo fourth-grade students. *Dissertation Abstracts International, 41,* 1490-A. (University Microfilms No. 80-21, 448).

Hopstock, P., & Bucaro, B. (1993). *A review and analysis of estimates of LEP student population.* Arlington, VA: Development Associates.

Lemmon, C. R., & Goggin, J. P. (1989). The measurement of bilingualism and its relationship to cognitive ability. *Applied Psycholinguistics, 10,* 133-155.

Lyons, J. (1995). The past and future directions of federal bilingual education policy. In O. Garcia & C. Baker (Eds.), *Policy and practice in bilingual education: Extending the foundations* (pp. 1-14). Clevedon, England: Multilingual Matters.

Miranda, L. (1990). *Latino child poverty in the United States.* Washington, DC: Children's Defense Fund.

Mercer, J. R. (1979). *System of multicultural pluralistic assessment.* New York: Psychological Corporation.

National Center for Education Statistics. (1993). *The condition of education.* Washington, DC: Government Printing Office.

New York State Education Department. (1987). *Learning about Haitians in New York State.* Albany: Author.

Peal, E., & Lambert, W. E. (1962). The relation of bilingualism to intelligence. *Psychological Monographs, 776*(27, Whole No. 546).

Peterson, M. (1983). The Indo-Chinese refugee child in Iowa: Talking with teachers. *Contemporary Education, 54,* 126-129.

Prewit Diaz, J. O. (1991). The factors that affect the educational performance of migrant children. *Education, 111,* 483-486.

Salerno, A. (1991). Migrant students who leave school early: Strategies for retrieval. *ERIC Digest.* Charleston, WV: Eric Clearinghouse on Rural Education and Small Schools.

Sue, S., & Padilla, A. (1986). Ethnic minority issues in the United States: Challenges for the educational system. In Los Angeles Evaluation, Dissemination and Assessment Center (Ed.), *Beyond language: Social and cultural factors in schooling language minority students* (pp. 35-72). Los Angeles: California State University.

Stanford Working Group. (1994). *Federal education programs for limited-English-proficient students: A blueprint for the second generation.* Stanford, CA: Stanford University.

Tattum, D., & Tattum, E. (1992). *Social education and personal development.* London: David Fulton Publishers.

Trueba, H. T. (1989). *Raising silent voices: Educating linguistically minorities for the 21st century.* New York: Newbury House.

United States Bureau of the Census (1992). *Current population reports (P25-1092). Population projections of the United States, by age, sex, race and Hispanic origin: 1992-205.* Washington, DC: Government Printing Office.

United States Bureau of the Census. (1993). *Population profile of the United States.* Washington, DC: Government Printing Office.

United States Department of Education. (1993). *Descriptive study of services to limited English proficient students.* Washington, DC: Planning and Evaluation Services.

United States General Accounting Office. (1994). *Limited English proficiency: A growing and costly educational challenge facing many school districts.* Washington, DC: Government Printing Office.

United States Public Law 100-297. (1988, April 28). *Bilingual education act. Title VII Bilingual Education Program.* Washington, DC: Government Printing Office.

Wells, G. (1986). *The meaning makers: Children learning language and using languages to learn.* Portsmouth, NH: Heinemann.

Yao, E. L. (1985). Adjustment needs of Asian immigrant children. *Elementary School Guidance and Counseling, 19,* 222-227.

Chapter 2

Culturally Diverse Gifted Students: A Historical Perspective

Giselle B. Esquivel
Fordham University

Sara G. Nahari
Queens College

Interest in the study of culturally diverse children is based on an expanded concept of giftedness. A historical overview is provided as to how this concept emerged from past developments to more recent perspectives.

Culturally diverse gifted students comprise children who are immigrant or of minority background and/or those whose language and culture continue to exert an influence in the way in which they demonstrate giftedness. Quite often these children have unrecognized gifted and creative potential or show exceptional abilities that are not easily identified. Historically, there has been an underrepresentation of culturally diverse children in gifted programs.

The National Longitudinal Study (NELS) of 1988, which looked at eighth graders throughout the nation, found that economically disadvantaged students were significantly underserved.

This study indicated that only 9% of students in the gifted and talented education programs were in the bottom quartile of family income, whereas 47% of program participants were from the top quartile in family income. Although the number of students served in the programs for the gifted and talented has increased in the past 20 years, it is clear that students from economically disadvantaged groups (which include a large number of culturally and linguistically diverse [CLD] students) are not being identified (U.S. Department of Education, 1991, 1993, 1994).

Several studies have been conducted to examine the reasons for the lack of recognition of these segments of the population in gifted and talented programs. Researchers (Barkan & Bernal, 1991; Harklau, 1994; Leung, 1994; Perrone & Aleman, 1983) have identified cultural, linguistic, and social influences surrounding the academic achievement of students as contributing factors to this underrepresentation. These factors may be summarized as follows:

First, there is insufficient knowledge and training of educators on cultural and linguistic issues (Bermudez & Rakow, 1990; Perrone & Aleman, 1983; Tharp, 1989). The cultural and linguistic diversity of this country is represented in the classroom by the many different set of values and beliefs that guide the members of different cultures. These values and beliefs impact their social interaction as well as their academic achievement, especially if these children grow up in minority subcultures whose achievement orientation is different from that of children of dominant groups (Perrone & Aleman, 1983). Some of these students differ from their peers not only in cultural background but also in language. Tharp (1989) suggested that differences in courtesies and conventions of conversation often result in children's brief, simple, and infrequent responses, which can be interpreted by schools as "low verbal ability," even for children who in other settings are highly verbal. This overlap between language and culture can also produce distinct behaviors in social skills and communication patterns that may be incongruent with mainstream values.

Second, researchers suggest that constriction in academic ability resulting from lack of experiential background within the host culture, social economic status, and a lack of English proficiency is often construed as poor academic performance by educators. This misinterpretation contributes to insufficient recognition of this group among the talented and gifted (Harklau, 1994).

Third, a lack of representation of these groups within the category of gifted and talented can partially be linked to the historical and traditional use of IQ scores as the primary criteria for placement of students in gifted and talented programs (Maker, 1987;

Marquez & Sawyer, 1993). The Gifted Education Policy Studies Program (Coleman, Gallagher, & Foster, 1994), in its analysis of state and local policies regarding eligibility for gifted programs for special populations of gifted students, found that despite recommendations and changes made in the criteria for identification of gifted students, primary areas for gifted identification across the United States still remain intelligence (IQ) and achievement tests (49 states still include these types of tests to identify gifted and talented students for their programs).

Fourth, researchers found that in addition to the use of standardized IQ tests, selection of the G/T is based on the presence or absence of particular abilities inherent to different cultural groups. Among many of the CLD students, cultural differences may produce manifestations of giftedness that differ from the traditional manifestations of giftedness in the majority culture. These environmental and culturally distinct demonstrations of giftedness are often not recognized by measurement instruments used for identification of the G/T as they represent norms based solely in the Anglo western culture. In addition, these measurements do not consider differences in learning styles and values of CLD students (Shade, cited in Leung, 1994).

In short, the main obstacle to the achievement of more representative percentages from the CLD population in G/T programs continues to lie in the identification process, as well as in the traditional definition of giftedness.

PAST HISTORICAL DEVELOPMENTS

Galton (1869) studied the nature of giftedness and of individual differences among men of genius. Galton defined *giftedness* as high intellectual ability possessed by a few individuals who were genetically endowed. Thus, he set a precedent for defining giftedness in terms of intelligence and heredity. Terman, the leader of the gifted child movement, was very much influenced by Galton's thinking in his interests and approach concerning the gifted. He viewed giftedness as being determined by high general intellectual ability and considered the possibility of its being measured through normative means. Although he recognized the effects of the environment on the development of talent, Terman was convinced by the prevailing notion of his time that intelligence, and thus giftedness, was largely hereditary. In 1925, he described his study of approximately 1,000 children identified as gifted through the use of the Stanford-Binet Intelligence Scale. The children were selected on the basis of an IQ score of 140 points or above. As a result of this study, which eventually became a longitudinal research project, a unidimensional definition of giftedness was established that ruled out a significant number of children with other outstanding abilities or unrecognized potential. In subsequent studies a child who failed to obtain a high IQ score was not considered gifted. This criteria excluded culturally or linguistically diverse children who may not do as well on a standardized intelligence or achievement test.

This traditional view was challenged by broader concepts of intelligence. Thurstone (1938) was able to discover about 20 specific talents, which he initially called primary abilities, and he questioned the premise that a child's mental endowment could be summarized by a single index such as the intelligence quotient. Guilford (1956) provided a turning point in the definition of giftedness by stressing the multidimensionality of human intelligence in his Structure of Intellect Model. He organized 120 possible specific high-level talents or abilities according to the types of mental operation utilized, the content involved in the thinking process, and the type of product resulting from such process. This multifactor approach to intelligence contributed to broadening the concept of what it means to be gifted.

Another critical growth point in the concept of giftedness is associated with greater interest in the area of creativity emerging during the 1950s. Thurstone (1952) observed that university students with high intelligence were not necessarily the most original in producing ideas. Guilford (1962) expanded on his concept of the divergent thinking process, which he defined in terms of flexibility, fluency, originality, and elaboration. Getzels and Jackson (1962) pointed to the fact that creativity is related to, yet distant from, intelligence. Torrance (1960, 1961, 1965) was another prominent investigator of creativity. He studied creativity within the context of culture and postulated that sociocultural factors influence the way in which creativity is defined and rewarded and the way in which it is expressed.

Along with creativity, other talents and abilities came to be recognized. For example, Strang (1958) referred to high social competence as an aspect of giftedness, and Taylor (1968) emphasized the role of nonintellective factors such as motivation and persistence. Based on the previously described historical developments, the concept of giftedness came to include the disadvantaged and the culturally diverse gifted child. In a U.S. Office of Education report, Marland (1972) defined giftedness as exceptional ability in one or more of the following areas:

1. High general intellectual ability
2. Specific academic aptitude
3. Creative or productive thinking
4. Leadership ability
5. Talents
6. Kinesthetic or psychomotor ability
7. Disadvantaged potential

Those with disadvantaged potential included women and individuals of low socioeconomic status, living in rural areas, or of culturally diverse background.

A recognition of diversity in gifted children led several researchers to study the gifted characteristics of children from various cultural groups. Bernal (1975) described his attempts to investigate what the construct of giftedness means in terms of the real world and outside of the academic community. His study, conducted in the "barrios" of three Texas metropolitan areas, involved as informants, adult members of the Mexican-American community with socioeconomic status ranging from lower class to upper middle class professionals. Based on information provided by these community members, Bernal found that Mexican-Americans perceive the gifted as being mature for their age; great imitators of adult behavior, regarded as leaders in both dynamic-expressive and quiet but influential ways, able to make suggestions valued by peers; able to grasp and pursue new ideas with persistence, able to maintain meaningful interactions with adults, able to acquire a deep structural understanding of the English language; and talented in musical arts and rhythm.

Chen and Goon (1976) described gifted disadvantaged Asian children as working diligently, being able to get along well with adults; and having particular strength in math.

Torrance (1969) provided a list of creative positives derived mostly from his studies of disadvantaged Black children, yet characteristic also of most culturally diverse gifted children. These creative positives include the ability to express feelings and emotions; the ability to improvise with commonplace materials; articulateness in role playing, creative movement, and dance; richness of imagery in language; figural fluency and flexibility; enjoyment and skill in group problem solving; responsiveness to the concrete; responsiveness to kinesthetic; humor; originality; emotional responsiveness; and quickness during warm-ups.

More recently, research has emphasized the study of gifted characteristics among balanced bilingual children or those who have comparable proficiency in at least two different languages. Some of the characteristics exhibited are flexibility in processing language, superior performance in verbal and nonverbal tasks involving concept formation, symbolic flexibility, creativity, analytic thinking and internal locus of control (e.g., Ben-Zeev, 1977; Cummins, 1978; Hakuta, 1985; Martorell, Esquivel, & Houtz, 1992).

CURRENT PSYCHOLOGICAL PERSPECTIVES OF GIFTEDNESS

Several theoretical approaches based on three major contemporary views in psychology—cognitive, developmental, and domain-specific—have further expanded the understanding of giftedness within a sociocultural context.

Representative of the concept of intellectual giftedness based on a cognitive approach is Sternberg's triarchic theory, which views intelligence through the study of mental processes. Sternberg (1986), suggested a framework for understanding intelligence that considers the individual's interactions with different environments within the social structure. Sternberg's triarchic theory contains three subtheories. The first subtheory relates to the mechanisms that lead to more or less intelligent behavior and links intelligence to the internal world of the individual. This componential subtheory specifies the potential set of mental mechanisms that underline exceptionally intelligent behavior regardless of the particular behavioral contents.

Sternberg's second subtheory, or "experiential subtheory," addresses the relationship between the components and the various levels of experience on the task for a given individual. This subtheory incorporates the ability of the individual to deal with novelty and the ability to automatize information processing.

The third subtheory, called "contextual subtheory," addresses the question of which behaviors are intelligent, for whom, and where those behaviors are intelligent, in other words, how the individual selects, shapes, and adapts to the real-world environment.

This triarchic theory of information processing provides a different way of defining intellectual giftedness as superior access to implementation of information. Thus, Sternberg (1993) suggested that people may differ widely in how they are intelligent and in ways in which they excel and make the most of their intellect as perceived by their society. Therefore, giftedness could take many forms as a result of different combinations distinctive of each of the elements of his theory.

Most recently, Sternberg (1993) proposed what he calls the "Pentagonal Implicit Theory of Giftedness," which includes the following five criteria for the identification of giftedness.

1. The excellence criterion, which states the individual is superior in some dimension or set of dimensions relative to peers.
2. The rarity criterion, which states that a gifted individual must possess a high level of an attribute that is rare relative to peers.
3. The productivity criterion, which states that the dimension(s) along which the individual is evaluated as superior must lead to, or potentially lead to, productivity.
4. The demonstrability criterion, which states that the superiority of the individual on the dimension(s) that determines giftedness must be demonstrable through one or more tests that are valid measurements.
5. The value criterion, which states that for a person to be labeled as gifted, he or she must show superior performance that is valued for that person by his or her society.

According to Sternberg (1993), what is relevant in this theory is not the value of one ability or another, but how the abilities work together. Furthermore, this theory is not just interested in the potential of the individual, but is concerned with productivity in everyday life and the demonstration of ability to produce significant products.

Representing the developmental approaches to giftedness, Gardner (1993) maintained that our culture has defined intelligence too narrowly, and challenged the validity of determining an individual's intelligence by administering a series of isolated tasks to be completed outside the natural learning environment of the individual. His theory of "multiple intelligences" embodies an expanded view of intelligence that comprises the capacity to solve problems and fashion things in a context-rich naturalistic environment rather than a more traditional view of intelligence as an unitary concept and defined operationally as the ability to answer items on a test of intelligence. Gardner (1993) defined intelligence as: "the ability to solve problems or fashion products that are valued in one or more cultural settings" (p. 7):

Human cognitive competence is best described in terms of a set of abilities, talents, or mental skills which we call intelligences. All normal individuals possess each of these skills to some extent; individuals differ in degree of skills and in the nature of their combination. (p. 15)

Gardner (1983) labeled these forms of intellectual accomplishment "multiple intelligences" (MI) and suggested that there are several main intelligences or talents. The criteria used to select these intelligences was based on two facts: first, that each one represented a cultural variable and a relatively autonomous set of skills for problem solving, and second, that each of these intelligences had an identifiable base in the human nervous system. Using these criteria Gardner identified seven distinct intelligences, with each one corresponding to a particular type of giftedness:

1. Linguistic intelligence, which reflects the capacity to think in words and use them effectively, whether orally or in writing. This intelligence involves the ability to use language to express and appreciate complex meanings. High degrees of linguistic intelligence are represented in writers, journalists, poets, and newscasters.

2. Logical and mathematical intelligence, or the intelligence of numbers and reasoning. It represents the ability to use numbers effectively and includes the processes of categorization, classification, inference, generalization, calculation, and hypothesis testing. Scientists, mathematicians, and computer programmers represent the presence of strong logical-mathematical intelligence.

3. Visual and spatial conceptualization, which includes the ability to perceive pictorial objects, depth of spatial ideas, and to orient oneself appropriately in a spatial matrix. This intelligence is portrayed by interior decorators, architects, scouts, or guides.

4. Musical intelligence includes the capability to discriminate, transform, compose, and express music. This intelligence includes sensitivity to music pitches, tone, and rhythms. Composers, music critics, musicians, and instrument makers exhibit this type of intelligence.

5. Bodily kinesthetic intelligence, which is the ability to use one's body to express ideas and feelings or the aptitute to create or transform things with one's hands. This type of intelligence is exhibited by actors, dancers, craftsmen, and sculptors.

6. Interpersonal intelligence, which is the talent to understand and demonstrate sensitivity to other peoples moods, feelings, and motivations and the

ability to respond in a pragmatic way to the cues of others. It permits a skilled adult to read the intentions and desires of others. This skill appears in therapists, political leaders, and teachers.

7. Intrapersonal intelligence, which can best be described as the knowledge of the internal aspects of a person, access to one's feelings and range of emotions. It is the ability to guide one's own behavior. Individuals who exhibit this intelligence have a strong sense of self, are confident, and work independently.

Gardner (1993) viewed these intelligences as independent of each other but at the same time as working together in complex ways. However, high levels of development in each one of these intelligences does not necessarily take place simultaneously. Each one of these intelligences is stimulated into action by activities that are valued within the culture of the individual, and their development is influenced by differential environmental conditions and demands. In other words, according to Gardner, intelligence is biological and psychological potential that varies among individuals and will reveal unique profiles of relative strengths. This potential can be realized to a lesser or greater extent depending on cultural and motivational factors that combine to determine the areas in which a given individual can succeed (Gardner, 1995). Gardner's theory presents the view of the gifted person not only as a result of high levels of development in one or more abilities, but also as dependent on the way these abilities interact as a system.

A psychosocial approach to the conceptualization of giftedness was proposed by Tannenbaum (1986), who defined talent as one of the aspects of giftedness, which he referred to as highly developed proficiency in highly demanding tasks. He further suggests that giftedness is not one thing but four talents, which he classified into four categories: (a) scarcity talents, which are forever in short supply and enable individuals to achieve major breakthroughs in their own particular fields (e.g., science, political leadership, social science, etc.); (b) surplus talents, which include those talents that contribute to the production of great art, literature, music, and therefore enable individuals to beautify the world; (c) quota talents, which embody those high-level skills needed to provide goods and services; and (d) anomalous talents, which are expressed in many prodigious feats and practical domains of excellence. This category would be the only one to include talents that demonstrate socially disapproved skills as they may be detrimental rather than beneficial to humanity (Tannenbaum, 1993). In general, Tannenbaum defined giftedness within a social context.

Representing the domain-specific approach, Feldhusen and Jarwan (1993) sustained that the definition of giftedness can be classified into six categories: psychometric trait, social needs oriented, educationally oriented, special talent, and multidimensional. In a multidimensional definition, general intellectual ability, positive self-concept, achievement motivation, and special talent are essential components in gifted individuals (Feldhusen, 1986a). The two concepts, talent and multidimensionality of giftedness, constitute the framework for studying or developing human abilities. For Feldhusen and Jarwan (1993) the term *talent* denotes outstanding skills in a specific domain, within an aesthetic or academic category. Talents emerge from general ability and develop through a combination of genetic dispositions, home and school experiences, and the student's unique interests and learning styles (Feldhusen, 1993-1994). Feldhusen (1995) and Gardner (1995), concur that the concept of "potential talents" or special intelligences encompasses a more diverse view of abilities and of the gifted and talented inasmuch as G/T represent a very heterogeneous population. Feldhusen (1993) stated that this view may serve as a better procedure in defining and nurturing high-level abilities in both underserved and favored populations.

Feldhusen (1993-1994) outlined four general domains for talent development in schools: academic-intellectual, artistic, vocational-technical, and interpersonal-social. In addition, he argued that a comprehensive approach to the development of any of these general domains requires the presence of both enriched instructional settings and enhanced environmental influences. Feldhusen (1993-1994) contended that this approach supports and encourages achievement at high levels of proficiency and the opportunity for actualization of their talents.

In addition, as a result of findings of studies on creativity and creativity tests, increased attention has been generated on the role of creativity in giftedness. These findings have led many educators to include creativity as another type of giftedness (Renzulli & Reis, 1986). Other researchers have examined the role of teachers, curricula, and instruction on development of creativity in students (Esquivel, 1995; Lopez, Esquivel, & Houtz, 1993; Treffinger & Isaksen, 1992).

Creativity has come to be viewed by many researchers as a basic component of giftedness, and some writers use the term as synonymous of giftedness or of productive, divergent, and critical thinking (Treffinger, Feldhusen, & Isaksen, 1994).

For Treffinger (1994), creative talent represents a complex synthesis of cognitive and affective processes, and its expression is influenced by environmental and situational factors. According to Torrance (Torrance & Goff, 1989) creativity is the process of sensing problems. This process involves several abilities: evaluating problems by detecting inconsistencies and missing elements; divergent thinking, which incorporates flexibility, fluency and originality; elaboration of ideas; and finally redefinition by modifying ideas.

Tannenbaum (1986) also equated giftedness with creativity. Creativity is integrated in each one of the five factors that must blend to produce a gifted individual:

> (a) Superior general intellect; (b) distinctive special attitudes, in a particular area of productivity or performance, which are reinforced by general intelligence; (c) the right blending of nonintellectual abilities which refers to the social, emotional, and behavioral characteristics that can release or inhibit the person's abilities (included in these non-intellectual abilities are self-concept, motivation, "metalearning" habits and adaptive postures that are necessary to achieve excellence); (d) a challenging environment which includes the opportunities offered by parents for children to engage in learning experiences outside of the school, family influences, and finally the influences of peers and school curriculum; and (e) chance, these are the opportunities that can originate anywhere, in the economy, the social milieu, the work place, the family, even within the body itself, that can affect a career. (p. 48)

CONCLUSIONS

Several important implications relevant to the definition, identification, and education of the CLDG/T students can be derived from these models and theories on giftedness and creativity. First, they offer a more comprehensive and diverse view of the abilities of the gifted and talented by defining giftedness as the presence of "potential talents" or special intelligences (Feldhusen, 1993; Gardner, 1993, 1995; Sternberg, 1993; Tannenbaum, 1986). Second, these models support the use of multiple criteria to identify student's strengths. Finally, they suggest that children can be thought to think, learn, and become more creative and recommend creation of curricula to develop these abilities (Feldhusen, 1986b; Maker, 1989; Renzulli & Reis, 1985; Treffinger, 1991).

REFERENCES

Barkan, J. H., & Bernal, E. (1991). Gifted education for bilingual and limited English proficient students. *Gifted Quarterly, 35*(3), 144-147.

Ben Zeev, S. (1977). The influence of bilingualism on cognitive strategy and cognitive development. *Child Development, 48*, 1009-1018.

Bermudez, A. B., & Rakow, S. J. (1990). Analyzing teacher's perceptions of identification for gifted and talented Hispanic limited English proficient (LEP) students at-risk. *The Journal of Educational Issues of Language Minority Students, 7*, 21-33

Bernal, E. M. (1974). Gifted Mexican American children: An ethnoscientific perspective. *California Journal of Educational Research, 25*, 261-273.

Chen, J., & Goon, S. (1976). Recognition of the gifted from among the disadvantaged Asian children. *Gifted Child Quarterly, 20*(2), 157-164.

Coleman, M. R., Gallagher, J., & Foster, A. (1994). *Gifted education policy studies program* (Updated report on state policies related to the gifted and talented students). Chapel Hill: The University of North Carolina at Chapel Hill.

Cummins, J. (1978). Bilingualism and the development of metalinguistic awareness. *Journal of Cross-Cultural Psychology, 9*(2), 131-149.

Esquivel, G. B. (1995). Teacher behaviors that foster creativity. *Educational Psychology Review, 2*(2), 185-202.

Feldhusen, J. F. (1986a). A conception of giftedness. In R. J. Sternberg & J. E. Davidson (Eds.), *Conceptions of giftedness* (pp. 112-127). New York: Cambridge University Press.

Feldhusen, J. F. (1986b). Policies and procedures for the development of defensible programs for the gifted. In C. J. Maker (Ed.), *Critical issues in gifted education: Defensible programs for the gifted* (pp. 235-244). Austin, TX: Pro-Ed.

Feldhusen, J. F. (1993-1994, Winter). Talent development as an alternative to gifted education. *The Journal of Secondary Gifted Education*, pp. 5-9.

Feldhusen, J. F. (1993, August). *Talent identification and development in education (TIDE)*. A paper delivered to a symposium of the World Conference on Gifted and Talented Children. Toronto, Canada.

Feldhusen, J. F. (1995, March). Talent identification and development in education (TIDE). *Understanding our Gifted*, pp. 10-14.

Feldhusen, J. F., & Jarwan F. A. (1993). Identification of gifted and talented youth for educational programs. In K. Heller, F. J. Mönks, & A. H. Passow (Eds.), *International handbook of research and development of giftedness and talent* (pp. 233-251). Oxford: Pergamon.

Galton, F. (1869). *Hereditary genius.* London: Macmillan.

Gardner, H. (1983). *Frames of mind: The theory of multiple intelligences.* New York: Basic Books.

Gardner, H. (1993). *Multiple intelligences: The theory in practice.* New York: Basic Books.

Gardner, H. (1995, November). Reflections on multiple intelligences: Myths and messages. *Phi Delta Kappa,* pp. 200-209.

Getzels, J. W., & Jackson, P. W. (1962). *Creativity and intelligence: Exploration with gifted students.* New York: Wiley.

Guilford, J. P. (1956). The structure of intellect. *Psychological Bulletin, 53,* 267-293.

Guilford, J. P. (1962). Potentiality of creativity. *Gifted Child Quarterly, 6,* 87-90.

Hakuta, K. (1985). Bilingualism and cognitive skills. *Journal of Mental Retardation, 23,* 302-307.

Harklau, L. (1994). "Jumping traks": How language-minority students negotiate evaluations of ability. *Anthropology and Education Quarterly, 25,* 347-363.

Leung, B. (1994). Culture as a contextual variable in the study of differential minority student achievement. *The Journal of Educational Issues of Language Minority Students, 13,* 95-105.

Lopez, E. C., Esquivel, G. B., & Houtz, J. C. (1993). Exploring the creativity skills of culturally and linguistically diverse students. *Creativity Research Journal, 6,* 401-412

Maker, C. J. (1989). Programs for gifted and minority students: A synthesis of perspectives. In C. J. Maker & S. W. Schiever (Eds.), *Critical issues in gifted education: Defensible programs for cultural and ethnic minorities* (pp. 1-4). Austin, TX: Pro-Ed.

Marland, S. (1972). *Education of the gifted and talented. Report to Congress.* Washington, DC: U.S. Government Printing Office.

Marquez, J. A., & Sawyer, C. B. (1993). Discrimination against LEP students in gifted and talented classes. *The Journal of Educational Issues for Language Minority Students, 12,* 117-127.

Martorell, M. F., Esquivel, G. B., & Houtz, J. C. (1992, March). *Bilingualism and creativity.* Paper presented at the meeting of the National Association of School Psychologists. Nashville, TN.

Perrone, P., & Aleman, N. (1983). Educating the talented child in a pluralistic society. In D. Omark & J. G. Erickson (Eds.), *The bilingual exceptional child* (pp. 269-283). San Diego, CA: College-Hill Press.

Renzulli, J. S., & Reiss, S. M. (1985). *The school wide enrichment model: A comprehensive plan for educational excellence.* Mansfield Center, CT: Creative Learning Press.

Renzulli, J. S., & Reiss, S. M. (1986). The enrichment triad/revolving door model: A school wide plan for the development of creative productivity. In J. S. Renzulli (Ed.), *Systems and models for developing programs for the gifted and talented* (pp. 216-266). Mansfield Center, CT: Creative Learning Press.

Sternberg, R. J. (1986). A triarchic theory of intelligence. In R. J. Sternberg & J. E. Davidson (Eds.), *Conceptions of giftedness* (pp. 223-243). New York: Cambridge University Press.

Sternberg, R. J. (1993). Procedures for identifying intellectual potential in the gifted: A perspective on alternative "Metaphors of Mind." In K. Heller, F. J. Mönks, & A. H. Passow (Eds.), *International handbook of research and development of giftedness and talent* (pp. 187-207). Oxford: Pergamon.

Strang, R. (1958). The nature of giftedness. In N. D. Henry (Ed.), Education for the gifted. *Yearbook of the National Society for the Study of Education, 57*(Part II), 64-86.

Tannenbaum, A. J. (1986). Giftedness a psychosocial approach. In R. J. Sternberg, & J. E. Davidson (Eds.), *Conceptions of giftedness* (pp. 21-52). New York: Cambridge University Press.

Tannenbaum, A. J. (1993). History of giftedness and "gifted education" in world perspective. In K. Heller, F. J. Mönks, & A. H. Passow (Eds.), *International handbook of research and development of giftedness and talent* (pp. 3-28). Oxford: Pergamon.

Taylor, C. W. (1968). Cultivating new talents: A way to reach the educationally deprived. *Journal of Creative Behavior, 2*, 83-90.

Terman, L. M. (Ed.). (1925). Mental and physical traits of a thousand gifted children. In *Genetic studies of genius* (Vol. I). Stanford, CA: Stanford University Press.

Tharp, R. G. (1989). Psychocultural variables and constants: Effects on teaching and learning in schools. *American Psychologist, 44,* 349-359.

Thurstone, L. L. (1938). *Primary mental abilities.* Chicago: University of Chicago Press.

Thurstone, L. L. (Ed.). (1952). Creative talent. In *Applications of psychology* (pp. 18-37). New York: Harper.

Torrance, E. P. (1960). Explorations in creative thinking. *Education, 81,* 216-220

Torrance, E. P. (1965). *Rewarding creative behavior: Experiments in classroom creativity.* Englewood Cliffs, NJ: Prentice-Hall.

Torrance, E. P. (1969). Creative positives of disadvantaged children and youth. *Gifted Child Quarterly, 13,* 71-81.

Torrance, E. P., & Goff, K. (1989). A quiet revolution. *Journal of Creative Behavior, 23,* 136-145.

Treffinger, D. J. (1991). Future goals and directions. In N. Colangelo & G.A. Davis (Eds.), *Handbook of gifted education* (pp. 441-449). Boston: Allyn & Bacon.

Treffinger, D. J. (1994). Productive thinking: Toward authentic instruction and assessment. *Journal of Secondary Gifted Education, 6,* 30-37.

Treffinger, D. J., Feldhusen, J., & Isaksen, S. G. (1994). Organization and structure of productive thinking. *Creative Learning Today, 4*(2), 4-10.

Treffinger, D. J., & Isaksen, S. G. (1992). *Creative problem solving: An introduction.* Sarasota, FL: Creative Learning Center.

U.S. Department of Education. (1991). *National education longitudinal study (NELS: 88) on gifted and talented education.* Unpublished study, Office of Educational Research and Improvement.

U.S. Department of Education. (1993). *National excellence: The case for developing America's talent.* Washington, DC: U.S. Government Printing Office.

U.S. Department of Education. (1994). *The 1992 elementary and secondary school civil rights compliance report and projected data for the nation.* Washington, DC: U.S. Government Printing Office.

Part 2

Gifted and Creative Characteristics in Culturally Diverse Children

Chapter 3

Learning Styles and Creativity in Culturally Diverse Children

Fern Sandler
Giselle B. Esquivel
Fordham University

Cultural diversity in U.S. classrooms today is a demographic reality. Changes in the population demographics over the last decade indicate clearly that teachers can expect to serve children from backgrounds that are increasingly diverse with regard to culture, language, and economic levels. The role of cultural diversity in the school reform process is reviewed by Jones and Winborne (1992) and highlighted is the belief that "the vision for the future" suggests that reform-minded educators as well as legislators must incorporate a broad range of cultural perspectives into school curricula, classroom instruction, student assessment, and other important areas of the educational process.

Diversity as defined by race, culture, language, and socialization poses serious challenges to our changing schools. The costs and consequences of the high number of at-risk and dropout minority students have been major concerns of educators and parents in recent years. Dropouts are more likely to be Blacks, Hispanics, and Native Americans rather than Whites or Asian Americans, and they are overrepresented in vocational and general tracks and in special education (cited in Dunn & Griggs, 1990).

The high rate of underachievement among minorities in the United States has led to the assumption that minorities may learn differently from Whites. Dunn and colleagues, in an analysis of learning styles of at-risk and dropout students in selected high schools, found that these students do learn in a processing style and with instructional strategies that significantly differ from those who perform well in comprehensive high schools (cited in Dunn & Griggs, 1990).

Although learning-style differences do appear to exist between and among various ethnic and cultural groups within the United States, research findings further suggest that there are apparently as many within group differences as between-group differences. In light of the latter finding, it is imperative that educators identify children at risk for failure or dropout, assess their individual learning styles, and begin enhancing each child's motivation to learn. As educators understand and accept that all children have the potential to learn, then teachers can teach to each individual student's learning style strengths (Dunn & Griggs, 1990).

COGNITIVE AND LEARNING STYLES

The cognitive-developmental approach to understanding how children learn and understand information has sprung in a very general way from the theory of cognitive developmentalist Jean Piaget, who emphasizes that changes in cognition occur with age. The concept of "cognitive style" can be described as a sort of personality trait of one's mental functioning. Cognitive styles pertain not to how well an individual thinks, but rather focus on the particular ways in which he or she may go about acquiring information (Dacey, 1989).

A primary aspect of cognitive-style research has become known as field independence/dependence. Witkin and his colleagues (Witkin & Goodenough, 1981), as well as many other researchers, have studied this phenomenon for several decades. Field independence refers to the ability to look at a whole picture or presented problem, break it up into parts, and then attend to the more relevant parts while blocking out the less relevant ones (cited in Dacey, 1989). Field dependence, therefore, refers to the tendency to use the external visual field or the body itself as a primary referent for perception (Witkin & Goodenough, 1981). Through the continuous interplay of theory and empirical research in the 1960s, the conceptualization of "cognitive style" emerged.

Witkin and Goodenough (1981) characterized cognitive styles as individual differences in process, rather than content; as pervasive and stable dimensions of individual functioning, showing itself in the perceptual, intellectual, and social domains. Their model further proposed that individual cognitive styles affect the development of ability patterns.

Simultaneous and sequential processing are two equally important dimensions of cognitive-processing-styles research. According to Luria's (1973) model, information is coded and processed either simultaneously or successively. Both processings are available to individuals. If simultaneous processing is utilized by an individual, then stimuli are arranged in a simultaneous manner, and all separate elements are synthesized together. When the serial order of incoming information is considered, then successive processing is used. Das and Molly (1975) describe these two processes further and state that simultaneous and successive processes are cognitive styles employed across age and cultural groups, intellectual levels, and socioeconomic backgrounds. The selection of either or both modes of processing is dependent on the nature of the task, an individual's habitual mode of processing information, and past experiences.

The variables investigated in much of the early work on cognitive style were single elements on a bipolar continuum. For example, children were either field dependent or they were field independent. Similarly, individuals either processed information simultaneously or successively. Cognitive styles that are seen on a bipolar dimension do not have clear high and low ends. This two-dimensional, either/or concept of cognitive styles was found to be quite limiting by many researchers. The process of acquiring and selecting information was perceived as value-laden and more complex than simply stating that all people either learned one way or the other. During the past two decades a multidimensional concept of explaining how children absorb and retain information has emerged (Dunn, Gemake, Jalali, & Zenhausern, 1990).

To date, one of the more comprehensive models explaining cognitive style is the Dunn and Dunn (1993) learning-style model. According to this model, *learning style* is defined as the conditions under which a person begins to concentrate on, process, internalize, and retain new and difficult information. This model has evolved over the past quarter-century and states that an individual's learning style comprises a unique combination of elements that permit receiving, storing, and then retrieving information and skills to which he or she has been exposed to and that they find relevant or interesting (Dunn & Milgram, 1993).

The Dunn and Dunn (1993) learning styles model traces its roots to two distinct learning theories: cognitive-style theory and brain lateralization theory. Cognitive-style theory suggests that individuals process information differently based on either inherent or learned traits. The brain lateralization theory states that the human brain's two hemispheres have different functions, and that the left hemisphere appears to be associated with emotions and spatial, holistic processing. Learning style was, therefore, defined by the Dunn and Dunn model as more than the environment in which learning occurs; it includes each human's emotional, sociological, physiological, and psychological characteristics as well (Dunn & Milgram, 1993).

As the Dunns and their associates conducted research to determine whether relationships existed among these cognitive dimensions and students' environmental, emotional, sociological, and physiological characteristics, they found that certain learning related variables often clustered together. Dunn and her associates have defined learning style in terms of an individual's unique reaction to 23 elements of instruction when learning new and difficult material. These elements include: immediate environment (noise level, temperature, light, and seating design), emotionality (motivation, persistence, responsibility, and need for external versus internal structure), sociological preferences (learning alone, with peers, or being with an adult), physiological traits (auditory, visual, tactile, or kinesthetic memory preferences), and cognitive and psychological inclinations (global vs. analytic processing styles, and impulsivity vs. reflectivity). Most individuals are believed to have between 6 and 14 elements that make up their strong learning style preference (cited in Dunn & Griggs, 1990).

The Learning Style Inventory (LSI) is a comprehensive approach to the identification of an individual's learning style. This inventory was first developed by Dunn, Dunn, and Price in 1975, and more recently revised in 1989. The instrument allows for an analysis of the condition under which students in grades 3-12 prefer to learn through an assessment of the 23 elements described earlier. In a comparative analysis of the style conceptualizations and psychometric standards of different instruments that measure learning style instructional preference, the Dunn, Dunn, and Price LSI was the only measure rated as having good or very good reliability and validity (cited in Dunn & Griggs, 1990).

The Learning Style Inventory has been used in research studies at more than 60 institutions of higher education across the nation demonstrating the unique learning-style characteristics of gifted, average, underachieving, at-risk, dropout, and special education populations. Experimental research findings document that when students are taught in environments and with approaches that complemented their learning styles, they achieve statistically higher test and attitude scores than when their styles were mismatched with environment or approach (Dunn, Beaudry, & Klavas, 1989).

Learning styles research is believed to offer a value-neutral approach to understanding individual differences, meaning that all qualities can be adaptive in particular circumstances (Witkin & Goodenough, 1981). When individual students' learning styles are detected and utilized to enhance their learning, students are given the opportunity to become involved in their learning. A flexible and responsive education should allow students to become aware of their individual styles, encourage students to follow their own interests, and facilitate the development of skills to support their individual creative efforts. Growing sensitivity and increased research on learning styles would enable many students to learn according to their strengths, increase their academic successes, enhance their personal productivity, and build confidence and positive attitudes (Jonassen & Grabowski, 1993).

LEARNING STYLES AND CULTURALLY DIVERSE CHILDREN

Many scholars who have been involved in the study of cognition and culture since the 1970s have moved their research from looking at culture as an independent variable affecting cognition to developing both theory and practice that build on the premise that cognitive development is intrinsically a cultural-historical process. Largely stemming from recent scholarly work on culture and cognition in the 1990s emerged a sociocultural perspective about the relationship between behaviors and activities to learning and development. This sociocultural perspective appears to hold promising insights into broad questions of how learning involves transformations not only of skills but also of identity (Rogoff & Chavajay, 1995).

Barrera (1993) stated that one of the primary functions of culture is to transmit essential knowledge from generation to generation. Embedded in every culture are behaviors associated with learning and teaching, and often a culture's values, beliefs, and traditions will influence behavioral preferences. The recognition of diverse sociocultural contexts on learning behaviors extends to include the following variables: a child's level of acculturation, characteristics of home and community environments, a child's preferred learning and interactive behaviors, a child's linguistic and sociocultural experiences and resources, a child's language history and usage patterns, and a child's linguistic and metalinguistic proficiency.

Research focusing on the extent to which ethnic and cultural differences influence learning and achievement can be traced to the 1960s and 1970s. Seminal findings of pioneer studies were reviewed by Dunn et al. (1990). Educators and social scientists found both cognitive and social variables influencing learning in various populations: Eskimos, Afro-Americans, Trinidadians, and Puerto Ricans. In addition, different sensory modality strengths were found among Chinese, Jewish, Black, Native American, and Puerto Rican students. Finally, the interaction contexts in which students preferred to learn were revealed for Mexican, Mexican-American, Hawaiian, Native American, and Caucasian students.

Hale-Benson (1986) has written extensively on Black childrens' distinct learning styles. She reviews the literature and defines this distinct learning style as culturally and biologically based. Her hypothesis was that because Black children grow up in a very distinct culture, they need an educational environment that recognizes their culture, strengths, and abilities and incorporates them into the learning process. Black children must receive from the educational system the skills they need to survive in society and to contribute to its creative development. Hale-Benson has advocated that teachers teach to the distinct learning styles of Black children and not continue the misperception in American education that White children are the norm.

Cohen (1969, cited in Hale-Benson, 1986) has identified two different styles of learning: the analytical style and the relational style. These two styles refer to differences in the methods of selecting and classifying information. Two processes that are measured by schools are the methods of selecting and organizing information and the growth of information. Cohen believes that the educational system, however, requires only one approach to cognitive organization, that of an analytic style. Not only does the school reward the development of the analytic style of processing, but the ideology and environment reinforces behaviors associated with that style. Cohen further states that students who do not develop these cognitive styles will be poor achievers in school. She believes that it is the relational style of learning that permeates the Black community. It is suggested that children develop their cognitive styles through the socialization they receive in their families and friendship groups. She concludes that children who participate in structured families in "formal" styles of group organization function with analytical cognitive style, whereas children who live in more fluid families with shared functions are more likely to utilize relational learning styles.

During the 1980s, eight major research studies were conducted to determine whether differences in learning style existed between and among various cultural groups as measured by the LSI. Dunn and Griggs (1990) reported an integrated review of these studies in which they compare, contrast, and synthesize findings with respect to the elements of instruction that comprise the identified domains on the LSI. The cultural groups represented within the United States were Black, White, Greek, Chinese, and Mexican. Other groups studied outside of the United States included Cree Indians from Manitoba, Puerto Ricans, Jamaicans, Bahamians, and Asians from Singapore. Although the findings were not always compatible, clear differences were found among the groups with respect to the patterns of strategies used and preferred by students (Dunn & Griggs, 1990).

Sternberg (1988a) defined an individual's style as his or her preferred way of utilizing abilities, rather than the cognitive abilities themselves. His theory of mental self-government states that there are three main thinking and learning styles: a legislative style, in which a person prefers to come up with his or her own working ideas; an executive style, in which a person prefers to be given guidelines to work within; and a judicial style, in which a person prefers to analyze the work of others. Sternberg believes that different cultural groups are likely to have different learning styles as a result of differential socialization experiences. Cultures, according to Sternberg, can foster and encourage any of these three styles. For example, a culture that appears to encourage the exploration of ideas is more likely to foster legislative styles among its members.

Although learning style differences are repeatedly reported as existing between and among various ethnic and cultural groups, the research on learning styles suggests that there are apparently as many within group differences as between-group differences. Accordingly, it seems that educators should place less emphasis on teaching to groups and more on teaching to individual learning style strengths (Dunn & Milgram, 1993).

LEARNING STYLES AND CREATIVITY

There are many existing definitions and theories of creativity. Creativity has often been discussed in terms of either the creative person, the creative product, or the creative process. The commonality among the definitions and theories is perhaps the intent to simplify and explain a very complex phenomenon. For purposes of our discussion, we sought to define creativity in terms of understanding the role of cognition and, more specifically, the role of individual learning styles in the creative person.

Although the early works on cognitive styles and field independence/dependence were not linked to the study of creativity, many creativity researchers have turned to this aspect of cognitive style. Researchers in creativity have begun to suspect that field-independent individuals were slightly more creative than their counterparts. In pursuit of a comprehensive theory on creative ability, creativity researchers felt that a creative person is someone who not only has achieved a high degree of field independence, but also can flexibly operate on a field dependent level when the problem calls for it. This cognitive flexibility to move from one mental process to another is called cognitive mobility (Dacey, 1989).

Sternberg's (1988b) Three Facet Model of Creativity posits that creativity is a peculiar intersection between three psychological attributes: intelligence, cognitive style, and personality/motivation. Taken together, these three facets of the mind help us understand the creative person. Sternberg describes the cognitive style or mental self-government of a person as a preference for creating one's own rules and doing things one's own way. Included in his creative intellectual styles is an anarchic form of mental self-government. Sternberg believes that anarchics have the ability to remove themselves from existing constraints, ways of seeing things, and ways of doing things. Anarchics are not to the tastes of either teachers, or parents, because the anarchics go against the *existing grain* (cited in Davis, 1992).

There is a diversity of definitions, theories, constructs and instrumentation of cognitive styles. Messick reviewed the variety of definitions and proposed that all the alternative conceptions imply that cognitive styles "are consistent individual differences in ways of organizing and processing information and experience . . . [and] tend to be pervasive and to cut across cognitive, intellectual, personality, and interpersonal domains" (1984, cited in Isaksen & Dorval, 1993). Despite the lack of clarity, a few trends are discernible. For example, nearly all the constructs of style seem to differentiate style from general ability. The level of performance is distinguishable from the manner in which individuals learn and process information.

This level-style distinction has also been useful by some researchers in reexamining previous creativity literature and helping to clarify the theoretical confusion often caused by clustering level and style. Creativity characteristics can become more meaningful and productive when put into categories that more accurately describe the qualitative differences in how people use their creative ability. In fact, in order to better develop people's creativity for future applications, a better understanding of both level and style needs to be accomplished (cited in Isaksen & Dorval, 1993).

Sternberg and Lubart (1995) believe it is important to distinguish creative style from creative ability. Style is not ability, but rather it is whether and how individuals use an ability. Thinking style is a key ingredient in creativity as it is needed to help complete the circuit, to switch on abilities that otherwise may lie dormant. The authors state that creative styles are to a large extent socialized. By this they mean that although heredity may play some role in the styles people possess, to a large extent we have certain styles because they are rewarded by factors in our environment. Because styles are socialized, they can therefore be taught. With proper instruction and reward, Sternberg and Lubart believe that children's creativity can be fostered and nurtured.

Just as teaching through learning styles has been demonstrated to be effective in significantly improving the performance and achievement of students with learning difficulties, it is believed that such instruction can also be effective in enhancing student growth in complex processes (Treffinger & Selby, 1993). Creativity is not a fixed trait that is present or absent in individuals, and it is believed that talents and creative potentials can be recognized and developed in many people. Isaksen and Treffinger (1985) proposed that Creative Problem Solving (CPS) involves three broad components of creative effort: understanding the problem, generating ideas, and planning for action. In each of these areas, learning styles can be useful in understanding possible strengths and limitations that individuals may experience when working on problems. Improved instruction in thinking skills and problem solving should be developed to respond to individual students' learning styles (cited in Treffinger & Selby, 1993).

In a pair of studies (Clark, 1964; Hamburg, 1964; cited in Toth & Baker, 1990) designed to examine the relationship among creative ability, intelligence, and learning styles, it was found that students who had high creative ability preferred open-ended methods of instruction over closed-structure learning experiences. The open-structure learning experiences were characterized by a process orientation, emphasis on the individual child, a democratic and flexible teaching style, and independent learning activities. The closed-structure learning experiences, in contrast, emphasized products, teacher-oriented assignments, and a fairly rigid teaching style.

Toth and Baker (1990) cite Torrance, who stated that the insensitivity of educators to the individual learning styles of creative students may reinforce patterns of underachievement. Torrance indicated that the inevitable pressures exerted against creative children in the traditional classroom can also foster social isolation. If the goal in education is to generate academically motivated, creative, and successful students, then educators must be equipped with skills on how to adjust their teaching to each students' individual learning styles.

CREATIVITY, LEARNING STYLES, AND CULTURE

On the surface, the dynamics of conformity pressures are not extraordinarily mysterious. We learn very early on as children that it is good to fit in and be correct, and bad to different and make mistakes. Social or cultural rewards normally follow correctness, but being different can elicit disapproval, criticism, or even create outcasts.

In better understanding what Sternberg (1988b) meant by the "existing grain," as mentioned earlier, we include in our discussion the roles of culture and of societal conformity pressures. Davis (1992) describes several blocks to address why we are all not more creative people. Cultural blocks include more than traditional learning characteristics; they include habits, rules, and traditions. Cultural blocks are based on cultural, social, or institutional norms and amount to social influences, expectations, and conformity pressures. These blocks can often inhibit the creative abilities and potential of an individual.

Davis (1992) reviewed the research conducted by Torrance (1977) and other investigators studying cultural blocks (Kang, 1989; Simberg, 1978; Van Gundy, 1987). Davis concluded that conformity pressures, regardless of age of onset, appear to be a societal or cultural phenomenon, rather than a biological or natural one. Furthermore, these pressures are very fundamental and are indeed inconsistent with an individual's innovative and creative thinking. As a general guideline, researchers state that we should not underestimate the influence of culture and societal conformity pressures when studying creativity.

Although no definition of creativity, to date, clearly exists for all culturally diverse people, Torrance's theory takes into account the importance of culture to its manifestation. Torrance's (1971, cited in Ford & Harris, 1992) definition states that creativity is a combination of ability, skills, and motivation. In Torrance's research on creativity in children, he was sensitive to the influences of life experiences of culturally diverse groups. He found that life experiences can influence children in both a positive and/or a negative way in preparation for creative ability. Torrance found significant correlations between the cultural value placed on creativity and the creative performance of children. He also stated that creativity appears to suffer in cultures and societies that do not appreciate creative people.

Torrance also found that in certain circumstances the family structure and life styles of potentially creative students from culturally diverse backgrounds can help foster creative potential as well. Several such contexts may include: (a) a lack of expensive toys and play materials can contribute to skill building by improvising with common materials; (b) large families of at-risk children can help develop skills in both group activities and problem solving; and (c) positive values placed by families on music, dance, and humor can keep alive abilities and sensibilities that tend to decline more in advantaged families (cited in Ford & Harris, 1992).

Raina (1993) wrote critically of the ethnocentric confines present in creativity research. It is Raina's belief that the vast literature on creativity to date has most often been pursued within ethnocentric boundaries, and that most theories and concepts lack universal validity. How various civilizations and philosophies have defined and approached creativity is not explored by researchers, and a genuinely compelling effort toward universalization of research validity is missing. Raina adds that few researchers have felt compelled to test their hypotheses in cultures other than Western ones. Torrance (1973) has investigated creativity in children from seven different cultural groups, five of which were outside the United States. Similar attempts, however, seem to be relatively rare. Much of the Western research on creativity is marked by radical exclusion of the study of creativity in other cultures, especially the diverse cultures of developing societies.

MacKinnon addressed this concern and wrote: "There is still need for plenty of research before we will have adequate . . . understanding of the role of education, social, and political factors in facilitating or inhibiting creative potential. The study of creativity will have to be cross-cultural in order to achieve the fullest possible answer to this question" (1987, cited in Raina, 1993).

CONCLUSION

Today, cultural diversity in U.S. classrooms is a demographic reality. Changes in the population demographics over the last decade indicate clearly that teachers can expect to serve children from backgrounds that are increasingly diverse with regard to culture, language, and economic levels.

Efforts to reform schools in the United States has gained considerable momentum since the 1980s. The focus on school reform is to increase school effectiveness, improve the educational process, and advance educational outcomes. The high rate of underachievement among minorities in the United States has led to the assumption that minorities may learn differently from whites. Dunn and colleagues, in an analysis of learning styles of at-risk and dropout students in selected high schools, found that these students do learn in a processing style and with instructional strategies that significantly differ from those who perform well in comprehensive high schools (cited in Dunn & Griggs, 1990).

To date, the literature suggest that learning-style differences do exist between and among various ethnic and cultural groups within the United States. Research findings further suggest that there are apparently as many within group-differences as between group differences. It is, therefore, imperative that educators identify children at risk for failure or drop out, assess their individual learning styles, and begin enhancing each child's motivation to learn. As educators begin to understand and affirm that *all* children have the potential to learn, then teacher's can teach to each individual student's learning style strengths (Dunn & Griggs, 1990).

Educators also have the opportunity to cultivate creativity, especially in the early years. Schools should respect and build on the creative and positive characteristics of various cultural groups. Schooling provides children the environment to develop the intellectual and interpersonal skills necessary to enhance their sense of independence, self-efficacy, and accomplishment. An instructional environment that is responsive to individual learning styles is more appropriate for creativity than an open classroom in which teachers assume students to be totally independent. Flexible and responsive education should allow students to follow their own interests and facilitate the development of skills to support their creative efforts. With growing sensitivity and increased research on culturally diverse children, many culturally diverse students will be able to learn to their learning-style strengths, nurture their creative potential, and grow to be contributing members of society.

REFERENCES

Barrera, I. (1993). Effective and appropriate instruction for all children: The challenge of cultural/linguistic diversity and young children with special needs. *Topics in Early Childhood Special Education, 13,* 461-487.

Dacey, J. S. (1989). *Fundamentals of creative thinking.* New York: Lexington Books.

Das, J. P., & Molly, G. N. (1975). Varieties of simultaneous and successive processing in children. *Journal of Educational Psychology, 67,* 213-220.

Davis, G. (1992). *Creativity is forever.* Dubuque, IA: Kendall/Hunt.

Dunn, R., Beaudry, J., & Klavas, A. (1989). Survey of research on learning styles. *Educational Leadership, 46,* 7.

Dunn, R., & Dunn, K. (1993). *Teaching secondary students through their individual learning styles.* Boston: Allyn & Bacon.

Dunn, R., Dunn, K., & Price, G. E. (1975). *Learning style inventory.* Lawrence, KS: Price Systems.

Dunn, R., Gemake, J., Jalali, F., & Zenhausern, R. (1990). Cross-cultural differences in learning styles of elementary-age students from four ethnic backgrounds. *Journal of Multicultural Counseling and Development, 18,* 68-93.

Dunn, R., & Griggs, S. A. (1990). Research on the learning style characteristics of selected racial and ethnic groups. *Reading, Writing, and Learning Disabilities, 6,* 261-280.

Dunn, R., & Milgram, R. M. (1993). Learning styles of gifted students in diverse cultures. In R. M. Milgram, R. Dunn, & G. E. Price (Eds.), *Teaching and counseling gifted and talented adolescents* (pp. 3-23). Westport, CT: Praeger.

Ford, D. Y., & Harris, J. J. (1992). The elusive definition of creativity. *Journal of Creative Behavior, 26,* 186-198.

Hale-Benson, J. E. (1986). *Black children: Their roots, culture, and learning styles.* Baltimore: Johns Hopkins University Press.

Isaksen, S. G., & Dorval, K. B. (1993). Toward an improved understanding of creativity within people: The level-style distinction. In S. G. Isaksen, M. C. Murdock, R. L., Firestien, & D. J. Treffinger (Eds.), *Understanding and recognizing creativity: The emergence of a discipline* (pp. 299-330). Norwood, NJ: Ablex.

Isaksen, S. G., & Treffinger, D. (1985). *Creative problem solving: The basic course.* Buffalo, NY: Bearly Ltd.

Jonassen, D. H., & Grabowski, B. L. (1993). *Handbook of individual differences: Learning and instruction.* Hillsdale, NJ: Erlbaum.

Jones, D., & Winborne, D. (1992). Consideration for cultural diversity in education reform: Elements of positive change. *New Directions for Educational Reform, 1,* 5-12.

Kang, C. (1989). *Gender differences in Korean children's responses to the Torrance Test of Creative Thinking from first to sixth grade.* Unpublished masters thesis, University of Wisconsin, Madison, WI.

Luria, A. R. (1973). *The working brain: An introduction to neuropsychology* (B. Haigh, Trans.). New York: Basic Books.

Raina, M. K. (1993). Ethnocentric confines in creativity research. In S. G. Isaksen, M. C. Murdock, R. L. Firestien, & D. J. Treffinger (Eds.), *Understanding and recognizing creativity: The emergence of a discipline* (pp. 435-453). Norwood, NJ: Ablex.

Rogoff, B., & Chavajay, P. (1995). What's become of research on the cultural basis of cognitive development? *American Psychologist, 50,* 859-877.

Simberg, A. S. (1978). Blocks to creative thinking. In G. A. Davis & J. A. Scott (Eds.), *Training creative thinking* (pp. 119-135). Melbourne, FL: Krieger.

Sternberg, R. J., & Lubart, T. I. (1995). *Defying the crowd: Cultivating creativity in a culture of conformity.* New York: Free Press.

Sternberg, R. J. (1988a). Mental self-government: A theory of intellectual styles and their development. *Human Development, 31,* 197-224.

Sternberg, R. S. (1988b). A three-facet model of creativity. In R. J. Sternberg (Ed.), *The nature of creativity.* New York: Cambridge University Press.

Torrance, E. P. (1973). Cross-cultural studies of creative development in seven selected societies. *The Educational Trends, 8,* 28-38.

Torrance, E. P. (1977). *Creativity in the classroom.* Washington, DC: National Education Association.

Toth, L. S., & Baker, S. A. (1990). The relationship of creativity and instructional style preferences to overachievement and underachievement in a sample of public school children. *Journal of Creative Behavior, 24,* 190-198.

Treffinger, D. J., & Selby, E. C. (1993). Giftedness, creativity, and learning style: Exploring the connections. In R. M. Milgram, R. Dunn, & G. E. Price (Eds.), *Teaching and counseling gifted and talented adolescents* (pp. 87-102). Westport, CT: Praeger.

Van Gundy, A. B. (1987). Organizational creativity and innovation. In S. G. Isaksen (Ed.), *Frontiers of creativity research* (pp. 358-379). Buffalo, NY: Bearly Ltd.

Witkin, H. A., & Goodenough, D. R. (1981). *Cognitive styles: Essence and origins.* New York: International Universities Press.

Chapter 4

Social and Emotional Characteristics of Gifted Culturally Diverse Children

Mary Kopala

Hunter College, City University of New York

The number of children who are members of diverse groups in the U.S. schools continues to grow. It has been estimated that such students are in the majority in 15 of the nation's largest school districts (Kellogg, 1988), and by the year 2000, one third of all elementary schoolchildren will be members of diverse groups.

Although many of the individuals who make up these groups were born in the United States, others have recently arrived in this country. Members of immigrant groups, in addition to having different cultural values than members of the dominant U.S. culture, also have recent experiences that may be different from those of individuals who have resided in the United States over time. For example, they may have lived in climates that are quite different from their current residence. Their diets and living conditions may have been different. Some may have experienced violence, war, and political upheaval. Many may have left loved ones behind.

In order to service gifted children who are members of these and other diverse groups, it is imperative that counselors, teachers, and school administrators recognize the necessity to learn about the history, culture, values, and experiences of these groups. They must understand (a) the affective issues that are relevant to gifted children, (b) the issues that are unique to gifted children who are members of diverse groups, and (c) how differences between and within diverse groups impact gifted children and may determine how one intervenes.

DEFINITION

Who is gifted? Terman (1926) defined *gifted individuals* as those who make up the "top 1% level in general intellectual ability, as measured by the Stanford-Binet intelligence scale or a comparable instrument" (p. 27, cited in Colangelo & Lafrenz, 1981). Other individuals identify gifted children as those who display high intelligence, that is, score over 130 on intelligence tests. Still other individuals define gifted to include those who exhibit extraordinary ability in music, the visual arts, verbal expression, movement, the acquisition and use of foreign language, and leadership (Kerr, 1991). Others insist that the "attainment of eminence . . . [is] the only way giftedness can be demonstrated" (Silverman, 1995, p. 11). Baldwin (1985) broadened these definitions and explained that giftedness:

> involves the presence of or the capacity for high ability, task commitment, and creative problem-finding ability in the cognitive, psychosocial, psychomotor, or creative areas either singularly or in combination. . . . Task commitment means that an individual commits energy and time to an area of interest. Above average ability refers to evidence of ability in any of the areas, which ranks above the average according to accepted local, national, or international norms. Creativity involves the ability to sense, to be intuitive, to feel, and to use these abilities in problem finding and problem solving. (p. 228)

In 1991, the Columbus Group began to focus on "the inner experience of the gifted person throughout the lifespan" (Silverman, 1995, p. 11). Their definition "recognizes the emotional component of giftedness: Cognitive complexity gives rise to emotional complexity" (p. 11).

These definitions are radically different from each other in that the earlier definitions are exclusionary, whereas the later definitions are inclusionary. This is critical when discussing females and culturally and linguistically diverse gifted individuals. A narrow definition would necessarily prohibit many individuals (primarily those from diverse groups) from being identified as gifted. The addition made by the Columbus Group extends definitions to allow for the inclusion of the female experience and the experiences of other members of diverse groups in the definition of giftedness.

AFFECTIVE AND SOCIAL ISSUES OF GIFTED CHILDREN

Although some authors suggested that gifted individuals were likely to be social misfits, research findings have mostly refuted their views. Recent findings suggest that gifted children are at least as well adjusted socially and psychologically and perhaps better adjusted than their nongifted peers (Janos & Robinson, 1985; Kelly & Colangelo, 1990; Olszewski-Kubilius, Kulieke, & Krasney, 1988; Richardson & Benbow, 1990; Sternberg & Davidson, 1986).

Some investigators (Hollingworth, 1942; Torrance, 1961; Webb, Meckstroth, & Tolan, 1982) have found that social adjustment is positively related to IQ. However, those children with IQs above 180 are less accepted by their peers who are gifted but have lower IQs (Hollingworth, 1942). Although exceptionally high-IQ children tend to be solitary, it may be because of a lack of companions with similar abilities. When these children find companions who are similar to themselves, they tend to be socially well adjusted (Robinson & Noble, 1991).

Generally, research suggests that gifted children and adolescents tend to be well adjusted, but not all gifted children behave the same. Differences in behavior result from differences among individuals. These differences may include differences in IQ (e.g., 130 vs. 180), gender differences, differences in socio-economic status, ethnic and racial group differences, cultural differences, and differences in life and academic experiences. For example, some studies suggest that adolescent girls tend to be less popular with boys than nongifted adolescent girls (Coleman, 1961; Keisler, 1955), and that they are concerned about the social stigma associated with being bright (Kerr, Colangelo, & Gaeth, 1988). Some adolescent girls express lowered self-confidence about their abilities (Bell, 1989; Buescher & Higham, 1989; Kelly & Colangelo, 1984; Reis & Callahan, 1989).

It has been suggested that some gifted students set unrealistically high standards for themselves, are inflexible in their routines, and accept feedback indiscriminantly. In addition, some gifted children may have temperaments that demand that they perform perfectly (Kerr, 1991). Although some individuals have suggested that a tendency toward perfectionism may lead to higher levels of stress and anxiety, the research does not suggest that gifted children experience more anxiety and stress than do nongifted children, and, in fact, some studies suggest that gifted children have lower levels of anxiety than nongifted children (Davis & Connell, 1985; Milgram & Milgram, 1976; Scholwinski & Reynolds, 1985).

Research studies have reached various conclusions regarding the social and emotional adjustment of gifted children, yet it remains true that gifted children pose unique issues regarding their social and emotional adjustment and at times do indeed experience psychological difficulties. Due to their superior intellectual ability, such children may be able to understand information before they have acquired adequate coping skills, or they may be given extraordinary responsibility, or parents may inappropriately share personal or family problems with them. Such dependence on them may lead these children to feel overwhelmed (Kerr, 1991).

Gifted individuals may face career issues that are not common among their nongifted peers. Some authors have suggested that gifted individuals often are interested in and capable of succeeding at many different careers and occupations. As a result they feel conflicted and, at times, immobilized because of this "multipotentiality." However, recently Achter, Lubinski, and Benbow (1996) examined the pervasiveness of multipotentiality among gifted students. They concluded that "an overabundance of high-flat ability and preference profiles among gifted students stems from the use of age-calibrated and, hence, developmentally inappropriate assessment tools having insufficient ceilings" (p. 65). Nevertheless, it is not appropriate to conclude that no students are interested in and capable of succeeding at a number of different careers.

If some gifted individuals are immobilized by numerous possibilities, others may foreclose early on an occupation, that is, gifted children may identify an early career interest and, consequently, not consider possible alternatives. If they are not encouraged to explore other options, they may make career choices based on a limited understanding of their interests.

Unfortunately, gifted children are frequently at risk for underachievement or dropping out of school. It is possible that neither the home nor the community provide the encouragement and resources children need to develop their ability or to take full advantage of school programs and resources. Family members may not know how to respond to the gifted child and may promote sibling rivalry or jealousy (Colangelo & Brower, 1987). Parents may feel inadequate and unable to provide the necessary resources for the gifted child to develop her or his potential. Parents may be reluctant to acknowledge their child's abilities in an effort to reduce their own feelings of inadequacy (McMann & Oliver, 1988).

Career issues, social and emotional problems, and the risk of underachievement are some of the challenges that gifted children and their parents must face. Clearly, the adjustment of gifted individuals can be complex.

GIFTEDNESS AND CREATIVITY IN CULTURALLY DIVERSE CHILDREN

When considering gifted children who are culturally or linguistically diverse, issues related to psycho-social adjustment may become even more complex than those issues faced by gifted children in general. Gifted children who are members of minority or immigrant groups face the same issues regarding emotional adjustment that all gifted children face; however, cultural and racial differences and varied experiences may create different problems or exacerbate feelings and difficulties that some of these children experience.

Identification of Culturally Diverse Gifted Children

A great deal of the research and literature about gifted culturally diverse children focuses on problems with identification of these individuals (e.g., Plucker, 1994; Swanson, 1995). The use of intelligence tests may be inappropriate for the identification of gifted children who are culturally or linguistically diverse because many tests are culturally or linguistically biased (Esquivel, Suzuki, & Kopala, 1993). Consequently, emphasis has been placed on research that attempts to discover which tests are appropriate for the identification of the gifted individual, who is also a member of a diverse group.

Despite attempts to select appropriate tests for use with members of diverse groups, and although some research (e.g., Chen & Goon, 1976, cited in Mistry & Rogoff, 1985; Davidson, Greenberg, & Gerver, 1962, cited in Mistry & Rogoff, 1985) suggests that gifted minority children and gifted mainstream children are similar in terms of personality characteristics, members of culturally diverse groups are less likely to be identified as gifted than are members of the majority culture (VanTassel-Baska, Patton, & Prillaman, 1989) and less likely to be involved in gifted classes (Ford, 1994). Consequently, these children and adolescents do not receive the services they need to develop their talents.

How cultural beliefs impact identification. There are various reasons why some children of diverse groups who are gifted may not be identified as gifted. Mistry and Rogoff (1985) discuss the relationship between cultural beliefs and views of intelligence. Examples of how various cultures define intelligence illustrate that culture and values play an important piece in identifying who is gifted and who is not:

> Goodnow (1984) advocates a shift from regarding intelligence as a quality people possess in varying degrees to regarding it as a judgment made by others when observing people's display of intelligent behaviors. Such a shift highlights the role of value judgments by individuals and by cultural groups in defining intelligence and focuses attention on the specific skills (signs of intelligence) on which these judgments are based. (cited in Mistry & Rogoff, 1985, p. 133)

In order to understand who is talented or creative, one must understand the culture from which the individual comes. For example, art ability could be an indication of one's giftedness. Yet a lack of knowledge about various cultures and the place of the creative arts in those cultures may further exclude some individuals from being identified as gifted. When the art work of children from various countries has been compared, notable differences have been found in the style, subject matter, and media used. Differences in emphasis also varies among countries, that is, some countries emphasize the process, whereas others emphasize the finished product. Japanese teachers focus on the process of creating art as opposed to the quality of the finished product:

> Displays of children's art work and other visual arrangements are not afforded priority because of a non-Western belief in the child's innate motivation to learn; and the high value attached to character development through self-discipline and hardship. . . . Competition is avoided because the Japanese Confucian educational tradition emphasizes making a child "human like" in the sense of being able to have harmonious relationships with others. (Mason, 1994, p. 16)

Cultural perspective of talent affects psychological adjustment. Although various disciplines and literature have examined the cultural perspective of talent, creativity, and intelligence, little attempt has been made to link this information to the affective and social development and adjustment of those students who are members of diverse groups and who are identified as gifted.

Creative achievement has traditionally been based on Western ideals of art, music, and so on (see, e.g., Delacruz, 1995; Hollingsworth, 1994; P. Smith, 1994; R. A. Smith, 1993, for discussion regarding the controversy surrounding the teaching of multicultural art). Often a culture's art or music has been less valued than Western ideals, and many countries have attempted to copy Western ideals of art rather than promoting the art of their own culture. Soyinka (1993) harshly criticized those African universities that have chosen to attempt to recreate British theaters by replicating Western style buildings or presenting opera in an effort to promote an arts mentality. He found these attempts to be repressive and controlling of the creative intellect. Furthermore, he suggested that Europeans have been slow to acknowledge and "accept the validity of a creative imagination for the African outside folklore and ritual" (p. 7).

If people believe that their creative imagination and the creative products of their culture are not as valuable as the creative products of the dominant culture, they close off part of their ethnic identity, that is, the creative products of their ethnic group. Such individuals may feel isolated from their culture and without part of their identity, thus, impacting their self-esteem. Because children who are not identified as gifted may not get the kind of help they need to develop their abilities, they may feel frustrated, have low self-esteem, and may not develop the skills necessary to achieve a high quality of life as an adult.

Environment affects the development of the talented child. Just as one's psychological health may be impacted by a disconnection from the culture's creative products, many of the issues gifted children from diverse groups face are the result of environmental or institutional forces rather than personality traits. Children may face prejudice from teachers who express doubts about their ability to succeed, thus they may not receive the encouragement they need (Lindstrom & Van Sant, 1986). Kitano (1994/1995) found in a retrospective study of diverse gifted women that many of these women had experienced neglect or discouragement by teachers, professors, or counselors. Some individuals attempted to counsel the women to embark on other, less prestigious careers; for example, some were instructed to follow secretarial tracks in high school. Similarly, a Latina colleague of the author of this chapter related that her counselor told her not to worry about the types of classes necessary for a career in psychology because it was likely that she would be married by the time she reached college age.

Some gifted children who are members of the majority culture become isolated socially (Betts, 1986) because of their superior intellect, yet the minority (or immigrant) child may experience this isolation to a greater degree. One may be rejected by his or her peers because of appearance or language differences or erroneous beliefs about the child's ethnic or racial group. Or the gifted child who chooses to enhance his or her abilities may be perceived as no longer wanting to belong to one's ethnic, racial, or cultural group. Ford-Harris, Schuerger, and Harris (1991) suggested that gifted Black children may be seen as selling out if they attempt to develop their talents through schooling, in which schooling is seen as a symbol of the dominant culture. Such children may be seen as having rejected their Black culture in order to succeed. This sets up a double bind in that these gifted children may feel a need to fail to achieve in order to be accepted by the Black culture.

To decide to develop one's potential may mean one must leave the cultural community, thus, causing problems of identity as well as social isolation (Lindstrom & Van Sant, 1986). Ethnic identity formation is an ongoing process (Casas & Pytluk, 1995) and is affected by the amount of contact and nature of contact that one has with one's culture: "Ethnic identity is an important and intricate part of the self-concept, whose development is influenced by the normative socialization processes that affect all persons in general, and by the intergroup phenomena resulting from the minority status of the ethnic individual" (Knight, Bernal, Garza, & Cota, 1993, cited in Casas & Pytluk, 1995, p. 159). The child who is forced to choose between his or her own culture and the culture that promotes his or her giftedness, and/or the gifted culture, may have serious identity conflicts.

The orthogonal cultural identification model suggests that one can identify with various cultures without diminishing one's identification with any of those cultures. However, Casas and Pytluk (1995) suggests that this may not always be the case:

> Socioeconomic and political realities may require an immigrant Hispanic woman to abandon her traditional sex role by working outside the home while embracing this role when at home with her family. Given that she was enculturated into one culture first and then acculterated into another, she might be able to reconcile and/or integrate both cultural realities; however, her female child, being socialized by acculturating parents, might not be able to maintain such an orthogonal perspective. This child might develop a singular sex-role identity informed by each of the respective cultures without the degree of choice that her mother was able to exert. (p. 173)

Similarly, such an orthogonal cultural identification may not be possible for the gifted Latina child. The gifted Latina child may attempt to develop a single identity that incorporates the traditional sex role, a working role, and a gifted role. In her attempt to develop a single identity, the gifted Latina child may experience identity conflict. As she attempts to incorporate her traditional sex role with her role as a gifted child in the dominant society and her future role as a member of the working world, she may believe that she can develop one role only at the expense of others. As she comes in contact with the values of the dominant culture, she may experience further difficulty because her family's values are in opposition to those of the dominant culture. Without a supportive family, the gifted Latina child who wishes to develop her talent may believe that she has no choice other than to abandon the traditional values of her culture. For example, Diaz (1996), in a case study, illustrated how one gifted girl took advantage of opportunities that required her to go away for several weeks during the summer. Although her family did not favor this separation, they did allow her to participate because the experience was important to her future success. However, such decisions resulted in her family feeling isolated from other Latinos in the community whose values were more traditional.

Career choice and cultural values. Career choices made by members of diverse groups are apt to be influenced by their cultural values. Members of some ethnic groups do not value education in the same way as members of the dominant culture. For example, traditionally, Italian families tend not to value higher education and may view it as a threat to the family (McGoldrick, Pearce, & Giordano, 1982). Should gifted children or adolescents choose to develop their abilities, they may be choosing to contradict their parents' beliefs. This conflict in values may be the cause of emotional difficulty for some children and may result in conflicts with parents.

Conflicts may arise when the gifted child wishes to choose a career that is not compatible with his or her cultural values. Rosario (1982) and Comas-Diaz (1987) suggested that working-class and middle-class Puerto Rican women favor motherhood and traditional marital relationships over their professional lives. Such a view may limit the possible career options the gifted Puerto Rican child or adolescent may consider once she realizes the demands of the profession are incompatible with the role and beliefs, or if the child chooses such a profession, she may find it difficult to resolve the conflict between the two roles.

Similarly, the gifted Latino may have difficulty pursuing his education, for example, if it is at the expense of caring for his family (*familismo*). That is, family expectations and obligations may interfere with one's devoting money and time to school work and developing one's talent or skill. It may be virtually impossible for these conflicting roles to coexist, and the individual may either abandon one or the other, or attempt to resolve the conflict by combining the least objectionable aspects of all the roles.

Cultural beliefs may restrict or influence career choices, but even when individuals choose to pursue a career that may not be compatible with their cultural values, often these individuals have other obstacles to overcome. Gifted minority individuals frequently face external barriers that may sabotage the development of their talents or their ability to pursue a career. Kitano (1994/1995) discussed data that suggest that women of color may have difficulty achieving in their career despite high academic achievement. These pressures can lead to discouragement and resistance to making career decisions (Lindstrom & Van Sant, 1986) when coupled with the career issues that some gifted individuals encounter, such as multipotentiality or early foreclosure (Kerr, 1981, 1991; Perrone, Karshner, & Male, 1979; Sanborn, 1979). The underachievement of gifted women of color, "despite high academic achievement or educational attainment" (Kitano, 1994/1995, p. 172), may discourage young women of color, thus influencing their career decisions.

The special case of the immigrant child. Gifted members of diverse groups face a number of issues that may affect their social and emotional development. Immigrant children face many of these same issues, but at times these issues are further complicated by the special circumstances of some immigrant children. The circumstances that surround the emigration may impact how well children and their families adapt to their adopted country and may influence the social and psychological development of the gifted child. Research (Wong-Rieger & Quintana, 1987) suggests that families who choose to emigrate in order to better their lives have a more positive acculturation experience. Furthermore, it may be more likely that these families will remain intact through the emigration and immigration. On the contrary, families that leave their homeland due to political reasons or because of war and other violence are less likely to acculturate quickly and easily and are more apt to suffer from acculturative stress.

Language may pose a problem for some immigrant children as well as for minority children born in the United States. For example, those individuals who speak with an accent may elicit negative judgments regarding their abilities and intelligence from native English speakers. Or peers and teachers may be frustrated by interactions with these children and, consequently, the children may not receive the attention and instruction they need. A recent case of an immigrant from

Hong Kong and another of a native Spanish speaker illustrate this. Both individuals, one a high school student and the other a college student, spoke and wrote grammatically correct English, yet their counselors and teachers had difficulty understanding their accents and repeatedly communicated to the students that they had a "language problem." Careful examination of both written and spoken work revealed that both students had an excellent grasp of English and English grammar. In a similar situation, two graduate students who were native Chinese speakers experienced difficulty when working in an assigned group project. The native English speakers became impatient and angry when they were forced to work with these two individuals. Although at the end of the project the English-speaking students acknowledged that the input of both native Chinese speakers was the catalyst that moved the project to its successful completion, it was also acknowledged that English speaking group members frequently became impatient or ignored the nonnative speakers.

Some immigrant children must cope with the stress that results from the migration experience and acculturation. Emotional effort and energy required to cope with these stressors may leave little energy for school work and the development of academic skills. As a result, children may achieve to a lesser degree than they did prior to coming to the new country.

Many immigrant children are separated from their caregivers during and after the migration experience. Consequently, they may not get the kind of attention they need from significant others. Parents who accompany their children during migration may not have the emotional energy to devote extra attention to their children because of the energy needed to cope with the stress of migration and acculturation. For the gifted child, this lack of attention may have a detrimental effect on the development of their talents or abilities. Helson (1971, 1976, in press) found creative women believed that being singled out as special by their parents contributed to the development of their talent. Zohar (1995) found that about one fourth of the participants in her study of mathematically gifted individuals frequently reported that as children they had had an intensive dyadic relationship with their mothers. It seems that at least for some gifted individuals, these intensive relationships may be important to the development of their special ability. For immigrant children who are separated from their parents for long periods of time, they may not have an opportunity for such an experience. Furthermore, single parents and parents who are of low social economic status may not have the time to devote to developing the intensive relationship necessary to develop the gifted child's ability.

Because the child may lack facility with the language of the host country there may be few mentors for the gifted immigrant student. Just as individuals report that their relationship with their parents impacted the development of their special abilities, many gifted individuals report important mentoring relationships. Mentors provide validation of their skills and abilities, as well as important connections necessary to the development of skills, ability, and/or career. Although there is no empirical evidence that suggests that these relationships promote the development of the gifted child's ability, the anecdotal evidence suggests that this is an area for investigation in immigrant children and adolescents. It is likely that with few mentors for immigrant children, they will not be able to develop fully. As a result they may feel inadequate and frustrated in their academic attempts.

APPROACHES TO WORKING WITH GIFTED CHILDREN AND ADOLESCENTS OF DIVERSE GROUPS

Psychoeducation must be made a priority if gifted children who are members of diverse groups are to develop to their potential. Such approaches can take the form of both individual and group counseling, and counselors must target school personnel, parents of gifted children, and the gifted children themselves. This is not to say that counselors should not intervene to facilitate change or provide support once children and adolescents experience difficulties, but rather that counselors must emphasize a proactive approach rather than a crisis intervention approach if they are to effectively utilize limited resources. Counselors must take the lead in developing and implementing programs that sensitize school personnel to working with all individuals who are members of diverse groups, as well as promoting the needs of the gifted student.

Interventions with School Personnel

Counselors may conduct professional staff development programs and consult with school personnel in order to sensitize individuals to ways of working effectively with members of diverse populations. Furthermore, school personnel must be educated to deliver better services to gifted children who are also members of diverse groups. Teachers, school psychologists, counselors, and school administrators must be sensitized to the unique issues that affect these children. Specifically, they must be made aware: (a) that gifted children who are members of diverse groups may go unidentified due to the use of biased instruments and other assessment methods used to identify the talented individual, (b) that their own behaviors and biases can prevent gifted children who are members of diverse groups from developing their potential, and (c) of the special problems these children are likely to encounter from external sources.

Frequently, school personnel are unaware that assessment methods that are routinely used may be biased against minority group members and individuals for whom English is not their first language. Alternative methods for identifying these children are being piloted. For example, Swanson (1995) described a pilot program that utilizes the Raven's Colored Progressive Matrix, Torrance's Thinking Creatively in Action and Movement, a teacher rating scale, and a peer nomination procedure to identify young gifted children. Counselors must serve as advocates for gifted children and adolescents by encouraging the use of such programs in their schools.

School personnel may be completely unaware of behaviors that discourage children from doing well in school. Teachers may have lowered expectations for students who are members of diverse groups or may discourage them from pursuing prestigious or nontraditional careers. One college student related how a teacher unfairly accused her of cheating when she achieved a high test score rather than praising her for excellence. School personnel must be sensitized to their tendencies to stereotype students based on race, ethnicity, or English language proficiency. These are the types of issues that school personnel can be sensitized to during professional development programs and consultation sessions.

Interventions With Parents

Counselors can be important sources of information for parents and can function as advocates for gifted children through outreach, home visits, and by facilitating parent groups. Counselors can focus on topics such as developmental issues children and adolescents encounter, career planning, cultural conflicts that are likely to occur between parents and children as the result of differences in acculturation rate, or ways to help the gifted child study at home. If there is little acceptance of a child's superior abilities, or if little premium is placed on education by the child's family, or if gifted education is perceived as equal to assimilation, counselors can encourage parents to accept that their children are special and have special needs.

Counselors can also help parents by providing family counseling. Through family counseling, parents may learn to better understand their gifted child and the issues with which the child is struggling. Furthermore, it can be helpful in teaching parents and children new ways to communicate and interact.

Family members who are less acculturated may resist providing the gifted child with the special education/help he or she needs, or they may not have the parenting skills necessary to nurture and promote the child's ability. Diaz (1996) suggested that parenting style strongly affects the gifted child. Those individuals who are supportive and encouraging of their child's ability and are flexible tend to promote the child's ability, whereas those who are controlling and adhere strongly to traditional cultural values may deter the growth of the child's ability. Parenting groups conducted by counselors can provide a forum for parents to discuss ways to promote their children's growth without giving up the cultural values that are important to them.

Counselors can help parents become aware of potential career opportunities for their children. Early introduction to career literature can prevent early foreclosure or perhaps prevent a child from selecting a career that is not appropriate to his or her ability. Parents can be taught the importance of their influence in their children's career decisions.

Interventions With Gifted Children and Adolescents

Counselors can facilitate both academic and personal growth of gifted children and adolescents through psychoeducation aimed at prevention of psychological problems and through timely interventions. Counselors can work with individuals and can facilitate groups. Preventive strategies can take the form of both individual and group counseling. Topics on which counselors can focus may include career counseling and planning, study skills, feelings associated with being gifted, and ethnic identity development issues.

Career counseling. Ethnic minorities are underrepresented in science and mathematics related careers (Moore, 1993) and are likely to have less knowledge about the world of work (Moore, 1986). Furthermore, members of ethnic minority groups are likely to discount careers that they perceive as incompatible with their socioeconomic status (Miller & Kastberg, 1995) or inaccessible to them (Evans, 1993). Counselors can provide early career counseling for gifted children. Early introduction to various career options helps to prevent children from eliminating possible careers. During the elementary and secondary school years, children and adolescents must be encouraged to consider various careers if they are to develop their potential. Career mentoring programs, group career exploration projects, field trips, and career nights are all activities that can help to encourage children and adolescents to consider occupations commensurate with their ability (Herr & Niles, 1994).

Counselors should encourage the gifted adolescent to pursue higher education. Too often adolescents are left to fend for themselves when it comes to filling out college applications or identifying sources of financial aid. Often counselors do not inform students of resources designed to help them develop their skills. Counselors must be diligent in providing information about college admissions procedures (including financial aid and scholarship information) and the identification of summer programs and institutes designed to develop the skills and abilities of gifted children. They must encourage adolescents to apply to various programs, they must inform parents of procedures and be available to explain how to navigate the system of higher education.

Counselors can help students prepare to deal with racisim and sexism as they pursue their education and enter the working world. Interviews with gifted women indicate that racism and sexism frequently interfered with their attainment of their achievement.

Gifted and ethnic identity issues. Structured groups for gifted children and adolescents can provide a place for these children to discuss giftedness and their thoughts and feelings about being gifted and a member of a diverse group. Gifted minority children may be in contact with their own culture, the dominant culture, and the gifted culture, thus providing the child with the opportunity to develop a variety of values and behaviors. They may also encounter values that are in conflict with the values of their culture. Similarly, the child may receive conflicting messages from all three cultures. For example, the child's culture may not encourage girls to develop their academic ability; the dominant culture may not reinforce girls in the classroom, while telling them that they are not achieving up to their potential; and the gifted culture may tell the young girl that she is capable of achieving many things. Such mixed messages may lead to confusion regarding one's identity. By sharing their thoughts and feelings in a safe environment with others who are similar in ability, these children can learn that they are not isolated in their giftedness. They can learn how others cope with identity and cultural conflicts.

Ruiz (1990) assumed that marginality is positively related to maladjustment, and that marginality coupled with pressure to assimilate causes dysfunctional behavior. Furthermore, Ruiz suggests that pride in one's own ethnic identity promotes mental health and allows individuals to make choices during the acculturation process that one would not have without a developed ethnic identity. When individuals do not identify with their own group, are unfamiliar with their culture, are rejected by their ethnic group, or receive messages that denigrate the group, ethnic identity conflicts may develop. Gifted children who are members of diverse groups or have immigrant status may be especially at risk for feeling marginal and may feel as if they are forced to choose membership in various groups, for example, their ethnic group, their peer group, and their family group. Group counseling can provide a forum for these children to receive the positive messages they need to hear in order to develop both as a gifted person as well as a member of a diverse group. As a result of group membership, they can develop feelings of belonging. Counselors can help children, especially gifted children, to develop pride in their cultural and ethnic heritage. They can provide support to these children as they begin to encounter conflicts between their culture and the dominant culture and/or the gifted culture.

With few role models who are gifted, gifted children who are also members of a minority may be confused about how they feel about their ethnic background and may be unable to feel comfortable in any of these social groups. Counselors can design and implement mentoring projects. Such programs can provide children with role models and intense dyadic relationships with children. Counselors can help children think through their confusion and reaffirm their culture while supporting the children's needs to develop their potential.

SUMMARY

Children and adolescents who are gifted and ethnically or linguistically diverse, or who are members of other diverse groups, face issues that are similar to other gifted children as well as unique issues. These individuals encounter unique external barriers that are not experienced by other gifted children. Furthermore, they may experience identity confusion due to their membership in groups that often have conflicting value systems.

Counselors can help these individuals with academic and personal concerns by intervening with school personnel and parents and by providing direct services to the gifted children. Professional development programs sponsored by counselors can sensitize school personnel to the special issues that gifted children who are members of diverse groups present. Counselors can help teachers become aware of how their biases may prevent these children from developing their potential. Parent groups can help parents understand their children's special needs, and counselors can promote discussions about how cultural values may conflict with gifted education. Counselors can intervene with gifted children by providing structured groups that focus on topics such as career exploration and the college application process as well as personal issues such as cultural conflicts and identity issues. Family counseling can be helpful in promoting ways for children and parents to communicate and can aid parents in understanding the struggles that are unique to the gifted child. By intervening with school personnel, parents, and the gifted children themselves, counselors can promote the development of the gifted child who is a member of a diverse group.

REFERENCES

Achter, J.A., Lubinski, D., & Benbow, C. P. (1996). Multipotentiality among the intellectually gifted: "It was never there and already it's vanishing." *Journal of Counseling Psychology, 43*, 65-76.

Baldwin, A. Y. (1985). Programs for the gifted and talented: Issues concerning minority populations. In D. Horowitz & M. O'Brien (Eds.), *The gifted and talented: Developmental perspectives* (pp. 223-249). Washington, DC: American Psychological Association.

Bell, L. A. (1989). Something's wrong here and it's not me: Challenging the dilemmas that block girl's success. *Journal for the Education of the Gifted, 12*, 118-130.

Betts, G. T. (1986). Development of the emotional and social needs of gifted individuals. *Journal of Counseling and Development, 64*, 587-589.

Buescher, T. M., & Higham, S. J. (1989). A developmental study of adjustment among gifted adolescents. In J. VanTassel-Baska & P. Olszewski-Kubilius (Eds.), *Patterns of influence on gifted learners: The home, the self, and the school* (pp. 102-124). New York: Teacher's College Press.

Casas, J. M., & Pytluk, S. D. (1995). Hispanic identity development: Implications for research and practice. In J.G. Ponterotto, J.M. Casas, L.A. Suzuki, & C. M. Alexander (Eds.), *Handbook of multicultural counseling* (pp. 155-180). Thousand Oaks, CA: Sage.

Colangelo, N., & Brower, P. (1987). Labeling gifted youngsters: Long-term impact on families. *Gifted Child Quarterly, 31*, 75-78.

Colangelo, N., & Lafrenz, N. (1981). Counseling the culturally diverse gifted. *Gifted Child Quarterly, 25,* 27-30.

Coleman, (1961). *The adolescent society.* New York: Free Press.

Comas-Diaz, L. (1987). Feminist therapy with mainland Puerto Rican women. *Psychology of Women Quarterly, 11,* 461-474.

Davis, H.B., & Connell, J. P. (1985). The effect of aptitude and achievement status on the self-system. *Gifted Child Quarterly, 29,* 131-135.

Delacruz, E. M. (1995). Multiculturalism and art education: Myths, misconceptions, misdirections. *Art Education, 48*(3), 57-61.

Diaz, E. I. (1996). Portraits of Puerto Rican gifted females who achieve and underachieve. In K. D. Arnold, K. D. Noble, & R. F. Subotnik (Eds.), *Remarkable women: Perspectives on female talent development* (pp. 225-241). Cresskill, NJ: Hampton Press.

Esquivel, G., Suzuki, L. A., & Kopala, M. (1993, February). *Culturally diverse gifted students: Identification, educational intervention and guidance.* Workshop conducted at the Tenth Annual Winter Roundtable on Cross-Cultural Counseling and Psychotherapy, New York.

Evans, K. (1993). Multicultural counseling. In L. K. Silverman (Ed.), *Counseling the gifted and talented* (pp. 277-290). Denver: Love Publishing.

Ford, D. Y. (1994). Nurturing resilience in gifted Black youth. *Roeper Review, 17,* 80-84.

Ford-Harris, D.Y., Schuerger, J. M., & Harris, J. J. III. (1991). Meeting the psychological needs of gifted black students: A cultural perspective. *Journal of Counseling & Development, 69,* 577-580.

Helson, R. (1971). Women mathematicians and the creative personality. *Journal of Consulting and Clinical Psychology, 36*(2), 210-220.

Helson, R. (1976). The creative woman mathematician. In L. H. Fox, L. Brody, & D. Tobin (Eds.), *Women and the mathematical mystique* (pp. 23-54). Baltimore: The Johns Hopkins University Press.

Helson, R. (in press). Creativity in women: Outer and inner views over time. In M. A. Runco & R. S. Albert (Eds.), *Theories of creativity* (rev. ed.). Cresskill, NJ: Hampton Press.

Herr, E. L., & Niles, S. G. (1994). Multicultural career guidance in the schools. In P. Pedersen & J. C. Carey (Eds.), *Multicultural counseling in schools: A practical handbook* (pp. 177-194). Boston: Allyn & Bacon.

Hollingworth, L. (1942). *Children above 180 IQ: Origin and development.* Yonkers, NY: World Book Company.

Hollingsworth, C. H. (1994). Port of sanctuary: The aesthetic of the African/American and the Barnes Foundation. *Art Education, 47*(6), 41-43.

Janos, P. M., & Robinson, N. M. (1985). Psychosocial development in intellectually gifted children. In D. Horowitz & M. O'Brien (Eds.), *The gifted and talented: Developmental perspectives* (pp. 149-195). Washington, DC: American Psychological Association.

Keisler, E. R. (1955). Peer group ratings of high school pupils with high and low school marks. *Journal of Experimental Education, 23,* 375-378.

Kellogg, J.B. (1988). Forces of change. *Phi Delta Kappan, 70,* 199-204.

Kelly, K., & Colangelo, N. (1984). Academic and social self-concepts of gifted, general, and special students. *Exceptional Children, 50,* 551-553.

Kelly, K., & Colangelo, N. (1990). Effects of academic ability and gender on career development. *Journal of the Education of the Gifted, 13,* 168-175.

Kerr, B. (1981). Career education strategies for gifted and talented. *Journal of Career Education, 7,* 318-325. (Reprinted in *Chronical Guidance Professional Service,* 1982, p. 994).

Kerr, B. (1991). *A handbook for counseling the gifted and talented.* Alexandria, VA: American Association for Counseling and Development.

Kerr, B., Colangelo, N., & Gaeth, J. (1988). Gifted adolescents' attitudes toward their giftedness. *Gifted Child Quarterly, 32,* 245-247.

Kitano, M.K. (1994/1995, Winter). Lessons from gifted women of color. *The Journal of Secondary Gifted Education,* pp. 176-187.

Lindstrom, R. R., & Van Sant, S. (1986). Special issues in working with gifted minority adolescents. *Journal of Counseling and Development, 64,* 583-586.

Mason, R. (1994, January). Artistic achievement in Japanese junior high schools. *Art Education,* pp. 8-19.

McGoldrick, M., Pearce, J.K., & Giordano, J. (1982). *Ethnicity and family therapy.* New York: Guilford.

McMann, N., & Oliver, R. (1988). Problems in families with gifted children: Implications for counselors. *Journal of Counseling and Development, 66,* 275-278.

Milgram, R. M., & Milgram, N. A. (1976), Personality characteristics of gifted Israeli children. *The Journal of Genetic Psychology, 129,* 185-194.

Miller, D. G., & Kastberg, S. M. (1995). Of blue collars and ivory towers: Women from blue-collar backgrounds in higher education. *Roeper Review, 18,* 27-33.

Mistry, J., & Rogoff, B. (1985). A cultural perspective on the development of talent. In F.D. Horowitz & M. O'Brien (Eds.), *The gifted and talented: Developmental perspectives* (pp. 125-144). Washington, DC: American Psychological Association.

Moore, E. G. J. (1986, April). *The influence of knowledge of the world of work on ethnic group differences in career aspirations.* Paper presented at the Annual Meeting of the American Educational Research Association, San Francisco.

Moore, E.G.J. (1993). Enhancing the educational attainment of minority youth. In J. Carlson & J. Lewis (Eds.), *Counseling the adolescent: Individual, family, and school interventions* (pp. 237-247). Denver: Love Publishing.

Olszewski-Kubilius, P. M., Kulieke, M. J., & Krasney, N. (1988). Personality dimensions of gifted adolescents: A review of the empirical literature. *Gifted Child Quarterly, 32,* 347-352.

Perrone, P. A., Karshner, W. W., & Male, R. A. (1979). Career development needs of talented students: A perspective for counselors. *School Counselor, 27,* 16-23.

Plucker, J. A. (1994). Issues in the social and emotional adjustment and development of a gifted Chinese-American student. *Roeper Review, 17,* 89-94.

Reis, S. M., & Callahan, C. M. (1989). Gifted females: They've come a long way—or have they? *Journal for the Education of the Gifted, 12,* 99-117.

Richardson, T. M., & Benbow, C. P. (1990). Long-term effects of acceleration on the social-emotional adjustment of mathematically precocious youths. *Journal of Educational Psychology, 82,* 464-470.

Robinson, N. M., & Noble, K. D. (1991). Social-emotional development and adjustment of gifted children. In M. C. Wang, M. C. Reynolds, & H. J. Walberg (Eds.), *Handbook of special education. Research and practice: Vol. 4. Emerging programs* (pp. 57-76). New York: Pergamon Press.

Rosario, L. (1982). The self-perception of Puerto Rican women toward their societal roles. In R. E. Zambrana (Ed.), *Work, family and health: Latina women in transition* (pp. 11-16). New York: Hispanic Research Center, Fordham University.

Ruiz, A.S. (1990). Ethnic identity: Crisis and resolution. *Journal of Multicultural Counseling and Development, 18,* 29-40.

Sanborn, M. P. (1979). Career development: Problems of gifted and talented students. In N. Colangelo & R. T. Zaffrann (Eds.), *New voices in counseling the gifted* (pp. 284-301). Dubuque, IA: Kendall-Hunt.

Scholwinski, E., & Reynolds, C. R. (1985). Dimensions of anxiety among high IQ children. *Gifted Child Quarterly, 29,* 125-130.

Silverman, L. K. (1995). Why are there so few eminent women? *Roeper Review, 18,* 5-13.

Smith, P. (1994). Multicultural issues: Dilemmas and hopes. *Art Education 47*(4), 13-17.

Smith, R. A. (1993). The question of multiculturalism. *Arts Education Policy Review, 94*(4), 2-18.

Soyinka, W. (1993). *Art, dialogue, and outrage.* New York: Pantheon.

Sternberg, R. J., & Davidson, J. E. (1986). *Conceptions of giftedness.* New York: Cambridge University Press.

Swanson, J. D. (1995). Gifted African-American children in rural schools: Searching for answers. *Roeper Review, 17,* 261-266.

Terman, L. M. (1926). *Genetic studies of genius: Mental and physical traits of a thousand gifted children.* Stanford, CA: Stanford University Pres.

Torrance, E. P. (1961). Problems of highly creative children. *Gifted Child Quarterly, 5,* 31-34.

VanTassel-Baska, J., Patton, J. M., & Prillaman, D. (1989). *The nature of disadvantaged gifted programs: A study of the fifty states.* Williamsburg, VA: Center for Gifted Education, College of William and Mary.

Webb, J. T., Meckstroth, E., & Tolan, S. (1982). *Guiding the gifted child.* Columbus: Ohio Psychology Publishing.

Wong-Rieger, D., & Quintana, D. (1987). Comparative acculturation of Southeast Asian and Hispanic immigrants and sojourners. *Journal of Cross-Cultural Psychology, 18,* 455-462.

Zohar, A. H. (1995). Mathematically gifted individuals. In R. Josselson & A. Lieblich (Eds.), *Interpreting experience: The narrative study of lives* (pp. 100-115). Thousand Oaks, CA: Sage.

Chapter 5

Bilingualism and Creativity

Mario Martorell
New York City Schools

For many years, a major concern of U.S. educators has been to identify gifted students using a broad concept of giftedness that extends beyond high general intellectual ability to include, among other factors, creativity and specific academic aptitudes and talents (Marland, 1972). In studying these various aspects of giftedness, a number of theorists and investigators have emphasized divergent thinking abilities in the creative process (Coriat, 1990; Esquivel & Lopez, 1988; Feldhusen & Hoover, 1986; Frasier, 1988; Houtz, Denmark, Rosenfield, & Tetenbaum, 1980). Recently, there has been increased interest in identifying gifted students entering the schools from culturally and linguistically diverse backgrounds (Cohen, 1990; Esquivel, 1985; Horowitz & O'Brien, 1986; Newman, Secada, & Wehlage, 1995; O'Tuel, 1995; Swanson, 1995; Valencia, 1985); however, there is a need for more investigation into the meaning and implications of test results when working with language-minority students.

The interpretation of a language minority student's profile, unlike that of a monolingual speaker, must take into consideration a number of additional factors that are often not considered such as language proficiency, degree of bilingualism, culture-specific cognitive and creative abilities, academic achievement, and cultural and interactional differences (Kessler & Quinn, 1987). Bilingualism is a term used to describe the linguistic attributes of an individual as well as his or her experiences; the importance of language proficiency in helping us understand bilingualism is imperative.

A related body of psychological literature has studied the effects of bilingualism on cognitive and creative abilities. Substantial psycholinguistic research indicates that bilingual individuals surpass monolingual counterparts in a wide range of abilities. These abilities include visual-spatial skills, productive thinking, cognitive flexibility, and concept formation. Although studies have corroborated the reliable and positive effects of bilingualism on cognitive abilities (Coriat, 1990), the degrees of bilingualism have not been clearly defined, and numerous questions that go beyond identification of gifted language minority students continue to plague educators, school psychologists and policy makers.

The purpose of this chapter is to explore the relation among language proficiency, cognitive abilities, creativity, and academic achievement in culturally and linguistically diverse students. Additionally, theoretical aspects of bilingualism and its development, from a psychological and sociological perspective, focusing on a historical overview as well as linguistic and educational aspects of bilingualism are described. Theories of second-language acquisition and their impact on cognitive abilities, creativity, and academic achievement are also discussed.

As complex as any assessment process is, the complexity increases when cultural and linguistic diversity are taken into account. Because of the biases of many formal testing procedures against students of diverse backgrounds, the identification of giftedness among bilingual students requires a mixture of knowledge, skills, and creativity, which educators can develop in order to limit bias in the identification and instruction process.

BILINGUALISM, LANGUAGE PROFICIENCY, AND DEGREE OF BILINGUALISM: A HISTORICAL PERSPECTIVE

The effect of bilingualism on childhood development has been a topic of investigation for many years (Arsenian, 1937; Baker, 1993; Cummins, 1980; Hakuta, 1984, 1985). Jensen (1962) described this situation:

Is this phenomenon of bilingualism a curse or a blessing? Or, is it neither? The question has captured the attention of governmental officials, school administrators, teachers, educational psychologists,

psychologists, anthropologists, sociologists, politicians, scientists, linguistics, speech correctionists, and personnel studying child development. This interest clearly suggests that bilingualism is a highly complex subject and that the answer is not an easy one. Many observers assert that bilingualism is such a disruptive interloper; but others claim that is not, and that, on the contrary, bilingualism is an asset. (p. 133)

The controversy surrounding bilingualism is magnified by the rapid ethnic change taking place in the United States (Martorell, Esquivel, & Houtz, 1990; U.S. Dept. of Commerce, 1991). The National Clearinghouse has recently disseminated estimates of limited English proficient students enrolled in school districts throughout the country showing that there are over 30 million individuals in the United States for whom English is not the primary language of the home. This number is expected to double for the year 2000. In fact, there are urban school districts throughout the United States in which 50% of the students come from non-English-speaking homes (Hakuta & Garcia, 1989).

Using data collected from local and state education agencies for 1993-94, the Clearinghouse listed the 20 school districts with the largest numbers of enrolled limited English proficient (LEP) students. Los Angeles Unified School District and New York City Schools ranked as the two school districts with the largest LEP enrollments (Macias, 1995).

Several questions have been raised regarding bilingualism and cognitive abilities. Does the ownership of two languages impede effective thinking processes? Do monolinguals, operating through one solid underlying model of language, have more cognitive advantages or disadvantages? Is a bilingual individual less or more capable than a monolingual to receive, transfer, store, and reproduce thoughts?

Review of the literature from the 19th century through the 1930s suggests that bilingualism has been associated with more disadvantages than advantages in terms of cognitive processes. Most studies during this period concluded that bilinguals showed greater mental confusion, lower intelligence quotients, and more disadvantages in thinking than their monolingual counterparts (Darcy, 1953; Saer, 1923). Those decades were called the Period of Detrimental Effects (Baker, 1993) because of the emphasis on negative consequences attributed to bilingualism. Research studies in this area were characterized by inconsistencies in defining language proficiency, problems in measuring intelligence, and flaws in methodological and statistical approaches when comparing monolingual and bilingual groups.

However, after the early 1930s, a series of research studies found no significant cognitive deficiencies between bilingual and monolingual groups. This Period of Neutral Effects shed light on the inadequacy of the early research. Historically, it served as a transitional period to highlight that bilingualism does not produce mental incapability or confusion among children. In fact, during this period it was established that when a group of bilingual children is compared to monolinguals on IQ or any other measure of cognitive ability, the two groups must be equal in all other respects. Research factors including sociocultural class, gender, age, type of school attended such as urban versus rural, subtractive versus additive environment, in which the children have acquired the first and second language should be considered.

Contrary to findings prior to 1960, Peal and Lambert (1962) showed that bilinguals surpassed monolinguals in most of the cognitive test and subtests when group differences in sex, age, and socioeconomic status were appropriately controlled. Positive results were attributed to the identification of degrees of bilingualism through which researchers were able to differentiate "pseudo-bilinguals" from "truly bilingual children or balanced bilinguals." Although the first group is dominant in one language and does not use the second language in communication, the second group can speak both with equal ease. Peal and Lambert's (1962) distinction of balanced bilinguals and pseudo-bilinguals made a significant methodological contribution to the field and gave credence to the importance of the notion of degree of bilingualism, initiating the Period of Additive Effects. In fact, Peal and Lambert (1962) concluded that bilingualism provides greater mental flexibility, the ability to think more abstractly, and superior concept formation. According to these researchers, the bilingual and bicultural environment enhances a positive transfer between the two languages, facilitating the development of verbal abilities.

BILINGUALISM: A MODERN VIEW

What is bilingualism? Does bilingualism refer strictly to the ability to be conversant in two languages with equal proficiency as a result of a second language acquisition (Jensen, 1962), or does it refer to the ability to interact appropriately within the social and cultural dimension imposed by both languages? (Hakuta, 1987). Most of the studies carried out on this topic clearly have established that bilingualism "is not just a bivariate function of linguistic proficiency in two languages but the intricacies of the social setting and oscillations between these linguistic proficiencies and social and emotional perspectives" (Hakuta & Garcia, 1989, p. 374).

The importance of language proficiency as a rich and multifaceted concept (Cummins, 1984) in understanding bilingualism is obvious. Padilla et al. (1991) and Ramirez (1985) viewed language proficiency as the ability to use language for both academic purposes and basic communicative tasks. Cummins's (1981) linguistic model identifies at least two major dimensions of language proficiency: (a) communicative language skills, and (b) academic language achievement. However, it is very important to note that most of the research on bilingualism has shown that many apparently contradictory findings about the effects of bilingualism on mental development have stemmed from a failure to distinguish possible levels of language proficiency or degrees of bilingualism (Diaz, 1983). As early as 1937, Arsenian clearly manifested the need to expand, define, and integrate the factors related to bilingualism that had previously been studied as a unidimensional construct. Degree of bilingualism was the first dimension proposed by Arsenian (1937), who stated objectively:

> Not all bilinguists are proficient to the same degree in the 2 languages used. The bilingualism of the very same person will vary in different periods of his life: One of the 2 languages may gain in ascendance, while the other declines. In other words, the proficiency of a bilinguist in 2 languages admits a variation, and this variation should, and can be measured for scientific investigation. (p. 19)

In addition, Arsenian stated that the degree of difference between the two languages that the bilingual individual possesses is as relevant as the degree of bilingualism. In Arsenian's (1937) words:

> The degree of difference between the 2 languages of a bilinguist is important from the point of view not only of the learning mechanism, but also of the thinking process; because the difference between the two languages usually denotes a difference in the culture and civilization of the two people using then, and hence denotes also a difference in the connotation of words which will influence the direction and the content of thought in the two languages. (p. 20)

Although Arsenian highlighted the importance of considering degrees of bilingualism in studying the phenomenon, all studies prior to 1960 lacked adequate identification of the sample's degree of bilingualism.

Because language proficiency is not a unidimensional construct, but rather a diverse multifaceted category consisting of various levels of abilities and domains, it follows that bilingual students are not a linguistically homogeneous population. With reference to bilingualism and biculturalism, for example, Hamayan and Damico (1991) reported that one popular belief is that bilingual individuals have native like fluency and proficiency in both languages, and that a bicultural individual is fully familiar with, and can operate with equal efficiency within, two distinct cultures. However, a continuum of proficiency or degree of bilingualism can be determined according to students' language competence and language performance, acquired in both formal school and natural settings. As an illustration, Ortiz (1984) demonstrated how Hispanic bilingual students present as (a) Spanish superior, (b) English superior, (c) equally English and Spanish superior, and (d) equally limited in either languages. Along this continuum we find Hispanic bilingual individuals with varying degrees of proficiency in either language.

THEORETICAL MODELS OF SECOND LANGUAGE ACQUISITION

During the past decades researchers have tried to understand bilingualism in its social context. Bilingualism has been viewed not only as a static phenomenon or an endpoint, but as a process in development. This is particularly relevant to the school-age population whose bilingualism is in process. Spolsky (1989) raised a question surrounding theoretical issues of second-language acquisition: "Who learns how much of what language under what conditions?" Psycholinguists, sociolinguists, and educational researchers have attempted to answer those questions producing several theoretical models. Baker (1996), citing several studies done over the last decade, discussed the skills and competences being learned under specific situations and highlighted the most relevant theories of bilingualism.

Among these theories of bilingualism, Lambert (1979) pointed out that attitude and aptitude are the most influential components for learning. They are the factors that motivate a learner to be proficient in the second language. This proficiency, in turn, develops and increases the individual's self-esteem and self-confidence. Along the same line and considering the social interaction, Ellis (1985) developed a theoretical framework in which five intertwined elements led to the acquisition of a second language:

(a) environmental, (b) linguistic input, (c) individual differences, (d) learner processes, and (e) linguistic output.

Schumann's (1978) Acculturation theory was based on the idea that language is one aspect of culture. His model proposed that the degree to which an individual acculturates within the host community will control to what extent he or she acquires the second language. Exploring community values and beliefs, Giles and Byrne's (1982) Accommodation theory proposed that the language behavior of an individual is determined by his or her reactions in terms of the beliefs, expectations, and perceived evaluations by other members of the community (Gardner, 1983).

Not unexpectedly, personality and affective variables have been integrated in models of second language acquisition. Gardner's model, often used in the study of second-language acquisition among children (Hakuta, 1987), is one of the most widely accepted because of its strong foundation, empirical support, and validity of those theories such as accommodation, acculturation, and social learning. Social learning theory (Rotter, 1966) describes the way in which expectancies function as important determinants of behavior in learning and achievement situations. Under this empirical support, Cummins' (1979) contextual interaction theory described how students' input factors (home language and second-language acquisition) interact with instructional treatments to contribute to the desired goals of second-language competence, cognitive development, and psychosocial adjustment.

Even though prior models of second language acquisition accounted for sociopsychoeducational and linguistic theories, they did not explain the internal mechanism through which children acquire a second language. However, Krashen's (1985) theory has dominated the educational research in second-language development. The five main elements comprised in this theory are: (a) acquisition versus learning, (b) natural order, (c) monitor, (d) input, and (e) affective filter factors. In general, this theory provides an educational and theoretical foundation in second language development as well as guidelines for teachers when working with students proficient in a language other than English. Krashen's model has been used in promoting high levels of proficiency in both native language and second language among bilingual children resulting in high academic achievement and in adequate psychosocial adjustment. In addition, Krashen's model relies on consideration of the ways in which an individual's beliefs and confidence about causality and control exert direct influence on his or her academic achievement.

BILIGUALISM AND ACADEMIC ACHIEVEMENT

Within the past decades, scholars from a wide variety of disciplines have given considerable attention to three factors that influence students' academic achievement: (a) cultural background, (b) native language, and (c) second-language development. In particular, researchers and educators have been highly interested in investigating the influence of second language acquisition on children's academic development.

The impact of bilingualism on academic achievement in bilingual settings has been extensively examined among Hispanics in the United States. Arreaga-Mayer and Greenwood (1986) in reviewing Valencia, Henderson, and Rankin's study, in which emphasis was placed on variables affecting academic achievement, reported that language proficiency strongly correlated with children's academic achievement. Wang (1988) also examined different achievement models for language minority students and established that ethnic language dominance facilitated quantitative academic achievement for Hispanic students. It was also found that the culturally and linguistically different students excelled in the subject areas that require minimal English language skills (Cummins, 1981).

Corroborating previous findings, Mayer (1988) found that a substantial improvement of the students' academic gains made each semester in math, reading, and spelling closely correlated to a teaching program that incorporated the use of the students' home language (Spanish) and instruction in English as a second language. Mayer's analyses emphasized that even in one semester of bilingual instruction, the second-language gains made by the limited English proficient students were statistically significant when compared to the gains of a group receiving monolingual instruction.

An important perspective regarding second-language acquisition for newly arrived students has been emphasized by Cummins (1981). Cummins highlighted the need to make the distinction between basic interpersonal communicative skills (BICS) and cognitive/academic language proficiency (CALP). Although the former dimension refers to oral fluency, phonology, and sociolinguistic competence, the latter strongly correlates with academic achievement and school progress. It is estimated that the average period of acquisition for BICS requires approximately two years, whereas for CALP it takes about five to seven years to achieve (Cummins, 1981). The benefits of bilingualism on the school progress were further supported by Amaral's (1988) study, which showed that teaching Spanish as a second language to a group of mainstream students improved their academic achievement.

BILIGUALISM AND COGNITIVE ABILITIES

Although the term *bilingualism* has been associated with individuals' language proficiency, several questions have been raised by educators and researchers about the varying levels of bilingualism seen among individuals and among groups. What can account for differences in levels of bilingualism among individuals and among groups? To what causes can variations in performance be attributed? Do bilinguals and monolinguals differ in terms of their cognitive and thinking processes? Does owning two languages produce differences in processing information?

The effects of bilingualism on the measurement of cognitive abilities has been of interest to researchers for many decades. The bilingual individual's superiority in those tests in which mental manipulation and reorganization of visual stimuli were necessary was clearly established over that of their monolingual counterparts by Peal and Lambert (1962). The authors concluded that "the broader a child's experience, the higher the probability that he will have come into contact with the type of ideas and situations that will assist him in his performance" (p. 15).

Along the same line and based on Piaget's developmental model, Liedtke and Nelson (1968) studied the differences among bilingual (French and English) and monolingual (English) first graders on concept formation abilities. Findings suggested that bilingual individuals surpassed their monolingual counterparts in all aspects measured (linear measurement). This conclusion was corroborated six years later in a study done by Bain (1975). On tests requiring formal operations, the performance of a group of bilingual children at the concrete operational stage was superior to that of a group of monolingual children at the same stage.

In Ben-Zeev's (1976, 1977) studies, Hebrew/English bilingual children showed superiority when compared to monolingual counterparts in symbol substitutions and verbal transformation tasks (cognitive flexibility). In symbol substitution tasks involving children's ability to substitute words in a sentence according to the experimenter's instructions, the most salient strengths found among bilinguals were: (a) superiority on linguistic abilities, (b) higher level of attention to both the structure and details from the tasks and experimenter, and (c) more sensitivity to feedback from the tasks and from the experimenter (Diaz, 1983).

Transference from one language to another language and a sophisticated analytic strategy toward linguistic structure were the main interpretations for the superiority of bilinguals made by Ben-

Zeev. Corroborating these conclusions, Cummins's (1978) study suggested that Irish-English bilingual children develop an early capacity to focus and analyze the structural properties of language. This process is known as metalinguistic awareness.

In a second experiment, with Ukrainian-English bilingual students, Cummins (1978) also investigated children's metalinguistic awareness or "looking at language rather than through it to the intended meaning" (p. 132). Cummins consistently found that bilingualism fosters an analytic orientation to linguistic input.

Diaz and Hakuta (1981) investigated the awareness of grammatical errors in bilinguals' first language and the ability to perceive first and second languages as two independent systems. They found that balanced bilinguals demonstrated a greater ability to correct their own grammatical errors and to detect linguistic confusion between the first and second language than their monolingual counterparts. They also found that, contrary to popular belief, balanced bilingual individuals showed awareness of the language system and properly separated the use of their two languages. Moreover, longitudinal studies that examined the relationship between bilingualism and the ability to detect ambiguity in sentences and to paraphrase different meanings among Puerto Rican Spanish dominant and English-speaking children substantiated that native language proficiency and bilingualism consistently impact positively on metalinguistic awareness as well as on nonverbal measures (Galambos & Hakuta, 1988; Hakuta, 1987).

Hakuta (1987) posited a dilemma in interpreting these results: "Why should becoming bilingual, a primarily linguistic activity, have a strong impact on nonverbal cognitive abilities?" (p. 1386). Causal relationships have been difficult to establish; however, Hakuta and Diaz's (1985) analysis of this issue suggested that linguistic strategies might be used to process information. Additionally, in a well-designed study, Diaz (1985) examined the relationship among bilingualism, verbal, and nonverbal abilities in a school district. On repeated measures analyses, Diaz firmly substantiated that second-language acquisition fostered children's verbal and nonverbal abilities, even when proficiency in native language was controlled for. Thus, verbal strategies serve as a mediator in the visual, manual, problem-solving tasks. This verbal mediation could explain the bilinguals' superior performance on nonverbal tasks.

BILINGUALISM AND CREATIVITY

Central to Rotter's (1954) social learning theory, a series of theoretical and empirical models have served to establish the importance of an individual's beliefs and expectancies regarding creativity. Several studies have corroborated that creativity is a function not only of cognitive processes but of affective attributes. These interact to produce behavioral strategies that are qualitatively unique when compared with the more conventional modes of thought (Strickland, 1989). Hence, creativity is closely identified with divergent productions and transformations and with the ability to take different perspectives and different approaches to a given problem. Also, because creativity can be trained and/or enhanced in particular settings (Starko, 1995; Torrance, 1990), it can therefore be influenced by cultural, social, environmental, and linguistic factors (Diaz, 1983; Nelson, 1987; Sternberg & Lubart, 1993; Torrance, 1966).

Prior to the work of Guilford (1968), creativity was measured with conventional intelligence and aptitude tests that often failed to identify creative individuals because such tests had been specifically designed to predict academic success. Guilford, however, delineated specific abilities that could distinguish between creative and noncreative individuals, thus providing a basis for identifying and assessing creativity. In his view, among the most important factors exhibited by creative individuals are the ability to synthesize and analyze, the ability to redefine and to produce new meanings by combining dissimilar elements, the ability to evaluate one's own thought and performance, and the manifestation of ideational fluency and flexibility (Coriat, 1990; Feldhusen & Hoover, 1986; Sisk, 1987; Sternberg & Lubart, 1991; Wallach, 1985).

Torrance's research in the 1960s into the relationship between creative thinking and motivation favored Guilford's model. His work solidly established that the "asking and guessing process" forms part of the concept of creativity (Frasier, 1988; Khatena, 1982; Torrance, 1966). Presbury, Benson, Fitch, and Torrance (1988) stated that "the degree of creativity depends upon the extent to which the ideas or result of the process are novel, valuable, differ from previous ideas, or approaches, can be applied in other situations, and go beyond the common place" (p. 26). These features had been identified by Guilford (1959) in his theory on the structure of intellect and highlighted by Meeker (1978) and Torrance (1974) as divergent thinking abilities. Because Torrance's concept of creativity stresses the individual's ability to take a different perspective to a given problem, researchers in the field of creativity among culturally different and language-minority students generally choose Torrance's conceptualization as a framework (Carrasquillo, 1991; Esquivel & Lopez, 1988; Kitano, 1986; Robles-Torres, 1988).

Torrance, Wu, Gowan, and Aliotti (1970) investigated the effect of bilingualism on creativity among monolingual and bilingual Chinese and Malaysian third, fourth, and fifth graders in schools in Singapore. Scores for fluency, originality, flexibility, and elaboration were obtained on the Torrance Test of Creative Thinking (TTCT). The overall results showed that bilingual students surpassed their monolingual counterparts on elaboration and originality tasks. Similarly, Landry (1974) supported the fact that learning two languages in elementary school has significant positive effects on creativity as measured by divergent thinking tasks on the TTCT. The sample utilized in Landry's investigation included urban and rural Mexican Americans, Puerto Ricans, and Cuban Americans for whom degree of bilingualism was carefully determined according to their linguistic proficiency in English and in Spanish. Interpretations of Landry's analysis indicated that those students who acquired a second language at the elementary school level were better "divergent thinkers" than their monolingual counterparts. It was also found that the flexibility developed by acquiring a second language was conducive to increasing students' creative abilities.

Recently, the findings about connections between bilingualism and creativity explored in Martorell's (1991) study with gifted and nongifted Hispanic bilingual study have strong implications for research and application in the field of education. The finding, for example, that well-balanced bilingual students among the nongifted population demonstrated superior levels of creativity and higher indices of academic achievement lends support to the desirability of allowing students sufficient time to develop full proficiency in both languages. Although this may not be of cardinal importance to the bilingual gifted students in our schools, because these are the students likely to have a superior level of creativity, it is probably critical for our bilingual nongifted students, the ones most at risk for school failure (Carrasquillo, 1991; Ramirez, Yuen, & Ramey, 1991).

Numerous studies on bilingualism have posited a significant and positive relationship between second language acquisition and creativity: Bilingualism accelerates the development of certain mediating cognitive factors, which in turn enrich creativity and other cognitive areas (Hakuta & Garcia; 1989; Heath, 1988). There are many indications that second language learning promotes social skills, sensitivity, and moral development in childhood (Hakuta,

1985); increases levels of cognitive flexibility, metalinguistic awareness, and academic achievement (Bialystock, 1988; Cummins, 1984); fosters visual-spatial abilities (Hart, 1987); and develops cognitive skills and flexibility (Lemmon & Goggin, 1989), even among mentally retarded children (Witaker, 1985).

In sum, investigations of the impact of second language proficiency on cognitive processes point to bilingualism not as the sole factor, but as a powerful and beneficial one in the enhancement of creativity, verbal and nonverbal concept formation, thinking processes, and academic achievement among all children, including those identified as limited English proficient or at risk.

Additionally, the studies about bilingualism and creativity investigated in this chapter have strong implications for research and application in the field of education. Contrary to what parents and educators may believe that it is expedient and acceptable to use a "quick exit" policy from bilingual instruction once a student has performed at the minimum cutoff level on a sampling of language proficiency skills, the usefulness of such a practice appears contraindicated by the findings of the literature. First, it is a questionable assumption that students able to handle conversational English are also able to process language at the level required for success in the monolingual English classroom. Second, conversely, as the literature reviewed, once time and instruction have permitted the development of full bilingual proficiency, there is likely to be a positive effect of these language skills upon academic achievement and creative abilities.

Finally, because bilingualism was found to be highly significantly related to creativity, it would be recognized as a salient factor in instructional models of developing and identifying creative individuals as well as distinguishing gifted from nongifted individuals. Thus, the literature further highlights the need to broaden the repertoire of tools commonly used to discriminate giftedness so that a broad variety of attributes in addition to academic achievement may be considered. A measure of exceptionality that highly correlates with giftedness, such as level of creativity, should be more widely employed. As a result, identification procedures would be more likely to overcome biases in the classification of giftedness among various populations and, in particular, would broaden the concept of giftedness among bilingual and language-diverse students.

REFERENCES

Amaral, O. M. (1988). Spanish as a second language instruction at the elementary level within a two-way bilingual program (Doctoral dissertation, University of Massachusetts). *Dissertation Abstracts International, 49*, 3289A.

Arreaga-Mayer, C., & Greenwood, C.R. (1986). Environmental variables affecting the school achievement of culturally and linguistic different learners: An instructional perspective. *NABE Journal, 10*(2), 113-136.

Arsenian, S. (1937). *Bilingualism and mental development: A study of the intelligence and the social background of bilingual children in New York City* (Contributions to Education No. 712). New York: Columbia University Press.

Bain, B. (1975). Toward an integration of Piaget and Vygotsky: Bilingual consideration. *Linguistics, 16*, 5-20.

Baker, C. (1993). *Foundations of bilingual education and bilingualism.* Clevedon Hall, England. Multilingual Matters Ltd.

Baker, C. (1996). *Foundations of bilingual education and bilingualism.* Clevedon Hall, England: Multilingual Matters Ltd.

Ben-Zeev, S. (1976). The effects of bilingualism in children from Spanish-English low economic neighborhoods on cognitive development and cognitive strategy. *Working Papers on Bilingualism, 9*, 83-122.

Ben-Zeev, S. (1977). The influence of bilingualism on cognitive strategy and cognitive development. *Child Development, 9*, 83-122.

Bialystock, E. (1988). Levels of bilingualism and levels of linguistic awareness. *Developmental Psychology, 24*, 560-567.

Carrasquillo, A. L. (1991). *Hispanic children and youth in the United States: A resource guide.* New York: Garland.

Cohen, L. M. (1988). *Meeting the needs of gifted and talented minority language students: Issues and practices.* (ERIC Document Reproduction Service No. ED 309 592)

Coriat, A. R. (1990). *Los ninos superdotados: Enfoque psicodinamico y teorico* [Gifted children: A psychodynamic and theoretical emphasis]. Barcelona: Editorial Herder.

Cummins, J. (1978). Bilingualism and the development of metalinguistic awareness. *Journal of Cross-Cultural Psychology, 9*, 131-149.

Cummins, J. (1979). Linguistic interdependence and the educational development of bilingual children. *Review of Educational Research, 49*, 222-251.

Cummins, J. (1980). Psychological assessment of immigrant children: Logic or intuition? *Journal of Multilingual and Multicultural Development, 1,* 97-111.

Cummins, J. (1981). Four misconceptions about language proficiency in bilingual education. *NABE Journal, 5*(3), 31-45.

Cummins, J. (1984). *Bilingualism and special education.* San Diego: College Hill Press.

Darcy, N. T. (1953). A review of the literature on the effects of bilingualism upon the measurement of intelligence. *Journal of Genetic Psychology, 82,* 21-57.

Diaz, R. M. (1983). Thought and two languages: The impact of bilingualism on cognitive development. *Review of Research in Education, 10,* 23-54.

Diaz, R. M. (1985). The intellectual power of bilingualism. *Quarterly Newsletter of the Laboratory of Comparative Human Cognition, 7,* 16-22.

Diaz, R. M., & Hakuta, K. (1981, April). *Bilingualism and cognitive development: A comparison of balanced and non-balanced bilinguals.* Paper presented at the meeting of the Society for Research in Child Development, Boston.

Ellis, R. (1985). *Understanding second language acquisition.* Oxford: Oxford University Press.

Esquivel, G. B. (1985). The effects of special classroom placement on the creativity, self-concept, and academic achievement of culturally different gifted children. *SABE Journal, 1,* 18-25.

Esquivel, G. B., & Lopez, E. (1988). Correlations among measures of cognitive ability, creativity, and academic achievement for gifted minority children. *Perceptual and Motor Skills, 67,* 395-398.

Feldhusen, J. F., & Hoover, S. M. (1986). A conception of giftedness, intelligence, self-concept, and motivation. *Roeper Review, 8*(3), 140-143.

Frasier, M. M. (1988, August). *Torrance verbal and figural tests: Measuring general creative thinking processes.* Paper presented at the 96th Annual meeting of the American Psychological Association, Atlanta. (ERIC Document Reproduction Service No. 304 466)

Galambos, S. J., & Hakuta, K. (1988). Subject-specific and task specific characteristics of metalinguistic awareness in bilingual children. *Applied Psycholinguistics, 9,* 141-162.

Gardner, R. C. (1983). Learning another language: A true social psychological experiment. *Journal of Language and Social Psychology, 2,* 219-237.

Giles, H., & Byrne, J. L. (1982). An intergroup approach to second language acquisition. *Journal of Multilingual and Multicultural Development, 3*(1), 17-40.

Guilford, J. P. (1959). Three faces of intellect. *American Psychologist,* *14,* 469-479.

Guilford, J. P. (1968). *Intelligence, creativity, and their educational implications.* San Diego: Knapp.

Hakuta, K. (1984). *The causal relationship between the development of bilingualism, cognitive flexibility, and social-cognitive skills in Hispanic elementary school children* (Contract G-81-0123). Arlington, VA: National Clearinghouse for Bilingual Education. (ERIC Document Reproduction Service No. ED 264 314)

Hakuta, K. (1985). Bilingualism and cognitive skills. *Journal of Mental Retardation, 23,* 302-307.

Hakuta, K. (1987). Degree of bilingualism and cognitive ability in mainland Puerto Rican children. *Child Development, 58,* 1372-1388.

Hakuta, K., & Diaz, R. M. (1985). The relationship between degree of bilingualism and cognitive ability: A critical discussion and some new longitudinal data. *Children Language, 5,* 319-344.

Hakuta, K., & Garcia, E. (1989). Bilingualism and education. *American Psychologist, 44,* 374-379.

Hamayan, E. V., & Damico, J. S. (1991). *Limiting bias in the assessment of bilingual students.* Austin, TX: Pro-ed.

Hart, N. J. (1987, August). *Intellectual test patterns: Bilingual and monolingual gifted and nongifted children.* Paper presented at the 95th Annual Convention of the American Psychological Association, New York City, NY.

Heath, I. A. (1988). Investigating the relationship between creativity and communicative competence strategies among bilingual and bidialectal adolescents (Doctoral dissertation, Florida State University, 1987). *Dissertation Abstracts International, 48,* 3100A.

Horowitz, F. D., & O'Brien, M. (1986). Gifted and talented children: State of knowledge and directions for research. *American Psychologist, 41,* 1147-1152.

Houtz, J. C., Denmark, R., Rosenfield, S., & Tetenbaum, T. (1980). Problem solving and personality characteristics related to differing levels of intelligence and ideational fluency. *Contemporary Educational Psychology, 5,* 118-123.

Jensen, V. J. (1962). Effects of childhood bilingualism. *Elementary English, Part 1,* 132-143; *Part 2,* 366-385.

Kessler, C., & Quinn, M. E. (1987). Language minority children's linguistic and cognitive creativity. *Journal of Multilingual and Multicultural Development, 8,* 173-185.

Khatena, J. (1982). *Educational psychology of the gifted.* New York: Wiley.

Kitano, M. K. (1986). Gifted and talented Asian children. *Rural Special Education Quarterly, 8,* 9-13.

Krashen, S. (1985). *The input hypothesis: Issues and implications.* London: Longman.

Lambert, W. E. (1979). *Child rearing values: A cross national study.* New York: Praeger.

Landry, R. G. (1974). A comparison of second language learners and monolinguals on divergent thinking tasks at the elementary school level. *Modern Language Journal, 58,* 10-15.

Lemmon, C. R., & Goggin, J. P. (1989). The measurement of bilingualism and its relationship to cognitive ability. *Applied Psycholinguistics, 10,* 133-155.

Liedtke, W. W., & Nelson, L. D. (1968). Concept formation and bilingualism. *Alberta Journal of Educational Research, 14,* 225-232.

Macias, R. F. (1995, September). CA LEP enrollment continues slow growth in 1995. *University of California, Linguistic Minority Research Institute, 5*(1), 1-2.

Marland, S. P. (1972). *Education of the gifted and talented.* Report to the Congress of the United States by the U.S. Commissioner of Education. Washington, DC: U.S. Government Printing Office.

Martorell, M. F. (1991). Language proficiency, creativity, and locus of control among hispanic bilingual gifted children (Doctoral dissertation, Fordham University, New York). *Dissertation Abstracts International, 52-09 A.*

Martorell, M., Esquivel, G. B., & Houtz, J. C. (1990). Evaluation of bilingual school psychology program: An exploratory study. *Psychological Reports, 66,* 287-291.

Mayer, J. E. (1988). The empowerment of ethnolinguistic minority students through an interactive pedagogy within an additive bilingualenvironment (Doctoral dissertation, University of San Francisco). *Dissertation Abstracts International, 49,* 3642A.

Meeker, M. (1978). Nondiscriminatory testing procedures to assess giftedness in Blacks, Chicanos, Navajos, and Anglos. In A. Y. Baldwin, G. H. Gear, & L. J. Lucito (Eds.), *Educational planning for the gifted: Overcoming cultural, geographic, and socioeconomic barriers* (pp. 17-28). Reston, VA: Council for Exceptional Children. (ERIC Document Reproduction Service No. ED 161 173)

Nelson, S. B. (1987). Cooperative instructional settings: Effects on divergent production by Mexican-American pupils (Doctoral dissertation, Arizona State University). *Dissertation Abstracts International, 48,* 1712A.

Newman, F., Secada, W., & Wehlage, G. (1995). *A guide to authentic instruction and assessment: Vision, standards, scoring.* Madison: Wisconsin Center for Education Research.

Ortiz, A. (1984). Choosing the language of instruction for exceptional bilingual children. *Teaching Exceptional Children, 16,* 208-212.

O'Tuel, F. S. (1995). *Evaluation report: Javits gifted and talented students education program.* Unpublished report. Columbia, SC: Creative Learning Press.

Padilla, A. M., Lindholm, K. J., Chen, A., Duran, R., Hakuta, K., Lambert, W. E., & Tucker, G. R. (1991). The English only movement, myths, reality, and implications for psychology. *American Psychologist, 46,* 120-130.

Peal, E., & Lambert, W. E. (1962). The relation of bilingualism to intelligence. *Psychological Monographs, 76,* 1-23.

Presbury, J. H., Benson, A. J., Fitch, J., & Torrance, E. P. (1988, November). Children and creativity. *Communique,* p. 26.

Ramirez, A. G. (1985). *Bilingualism through schooling: Cross cultural education for minority and majority students.* Albany: State University of New York Press.

Ramirez, J. D., Yuen, S. D., & Ramey, D. R. (1991). *Final Report: Longitudinal study of structure English immersion strategy, early-exit and late-exit transitional bilingual education programs for language minority children* (Contract No. 300-87-0156). Washington, DC: U.S. Department of Education.

Robles-Torres, R. (1988). The relationship between creativity and self-esteem in Puerto Rican kindergarten children (Doctoral dissertation, The Pennsylvania State University). *Dissertation Abstracts International, 49,* 2595A.

Rotter, J. B. (1954). *Social learning and clinical psychology.* New York: Prentice-Hall.

Rotter, J. B. (1966). Generalized expectancies for internal versus external control of reinforcement. *Psychological Monographs, 80*(1 Whole No. 609).

Saer, D. J. (1923). The effects of bilingualism on intelligence. *British Journal of Psychology, 14,* 25-38.

Schumann, J. (1978). *The Pidginization process: A model for second language acquisition.* Rowley, MA: Newbury House.

Sisk, D. (1987). *Creative teaching of the gifted.* New York: McGraw-Hill.

Spolsky, B. (1989). Review of key issues in bilingualism and bilingual education. *Applied Linguistics, 10*(4), 449-451.

Starko, A. J. (1995). *Creativity in the classroom.* White Plains, NY: Longman.

Sternberg, R. J., & Lubart, T. I. (1991). An investment theory of creativity and its development. *Human Development, 34*, 1-31.

Sternberg, R. J., & Lubart, T. I. (1993). Creative giftedness: A multivariate approach. *Gifted Child Quarterly, 37*, 7-16.

Strickland, B. R. (1989). Internal-external control expectancies: From contingency to creativity. *American Psychologist, 44*, 1-12.

Swanson, J. D. (1995). Gifted African American children in rural schools: Searching for the answers. *Roeper Review, 17*(4), 261-266.

Torrance, E. P. (1966). *Torrance tests of creative thinking: Norms-technical manual.* Princeton, NJ: Personnel Press.

Torrance, E. P. (1974). *The Torrance tests of creative thinking: Norms-technical manual.* Bensenville, IL: Scholastic Testing Service.

Torrance, E. P. (1990). *The Torrance test of creative thinking: Norms-technical manual, figural (streamlined) forms A and B.* Bensenville, IL: Scholastic Testing Service.

Torrance, E. P., Wu, J. J., Gowan, J. C., & Aliotti, N. C. (1970). Creative functioning of monolingual and bilingual children in Singapore. *Journal of Educational Psychology, 61*, 72-75.

United States Department of Commerce, Bureau of the Census. (1991). *The Hispanic population in the United States: March 1990* (Current Population Reports, Series p-20, No. 449). Washington, DC: Author.

Valencia, A. A. (1985). Curricular perspectives for gifted limited English proficient students. *NABE Journal, 10*(5), 65-76.

Valencia, R. R., Henderson, R. W., & Rankin, R. (1981). Relationship of family constellation and schooling to intellectual performance of Mexican American children. *Journal of Educational Psychology, 73*(4), 524-532.

Wallach, M. A. (1985). Creativity testing and giftedness. In F. D. Horowitz & M. O'Brien (Eds.), *The gifted and talented: Developmental perspectives* (pp. 99-123). Washington, DC: American Psychological Association.

Wang, L. L. (1988). A causal analysis of achievement models for language minority students in the United States: A linear structural relations (LISREL) approach (Doctoral dissertation, University of Illinois at Urbana-Champaign). *Dissertation Abstracts International, 49*, 3210A.

Witaker, J. H. (1985). Cognitive performance as a function of bilingualism in students with mental retardation. *Journal of Mental Retardation, 23*, 302-307.

Part 3

Identification and Assessment of Gifted and Creative Abilities in Culturally Diverse Students

Chapter 6

Multicultural Issues in the Testing of Abilities and Achievement

Robert J. Sternberg[*]
Yale University

Imaginese ser alguien que no entienda bien el inglés, pero necesita tomar pruebas en este idioma. Sin duda, sería un gran reto sacar buenas calificaciones en dichas pruebas. Por ejemplo, su cociente intelectual parecería más bajo en estas circunstancias. Además, no se sentiría muy listo ahora mismo leyendo estas frases.

If you don't read Spanish, your comprehension of these lines was probably pretty minimal. The lines say:

Imagine yourself to be someone who does not understand English very well, but you have to take tests in this language. Undoubtedly, it would be quite a challenge to score well on these tests. For example, your IQ would appear to be lower under these

---

*The work reported herein was supported under the Javits Act program (Grant #R206R50001) as administered by the Office of Educational Research and Improvement, U.S. Department of Education. The findings and opinions expressed in this report do not reflect the positions or policies of the Office of Educational Research and Improvement or the U.S. Department of Education.

circumstances. Moreover, you would not be feeling very bright right now reading these sentences.

Fortunately, as a reader of English, you rarely or never encounter a situation in which you have to take tests in a language that is not your own. But many children face this kind of situation on a regular basis. The tests they take do not adequately reflect their abilities and achievements because they are forced to take tests in a language that is not fully their own. Some of them find the very act of taking such a test to be foreign to them. But their inability fully to compete on tests will not only hurt them on these tests, but also later on, when their test scores are likely to become self-fulfilling prophecies.

THE PRINCIPAL DILEMMA: SELF-FULFILLING PROPHECIES

In our society test scores are important gatekeepers because they measure, to a greater or lesser extent, attributes we value in children as well as adults. Suppose, though, that we decided that what we really value is physical attractiveness—that this attribute is the one on the basis of which we ought to decide who is to be given more opportunities and who fewer. Such a decision would not be a particularly hard one to make because to some extent we have already made this decision: Physically attractive people already are given far more opportunities in life, in almost every domain (Hatfield & Sprecher, 1986). So we would merely be institutionalizing what we already do.

Now, instead of being evaluated for scores on IQ tests, SATs, ACTs, GREs, and the like, people would be evaluated for their physical appearance. To get into Harvard as an undergraduate, for example, you would have to rate pretty close to Tom Cruise or Nicole Kidman in appearance, and to get into Harvard Law you perhaps would have to look even better! You could clean up on the Law Boards, but without a body to match, you could kiss law school goodbye.

Now, after, say, three decades of this new system, the grandchildren of Richard Herrnstein and Charles Murray come along and evaluate the physical appearance of lawyers, doctors, college professors, and of other people in high-prestige occupations; they also evaluate the physical appearance of people who clean houses, sweep streets, collect garbage, and the like—people in low-prestige occupations. They note that the people in the high-prestige occupations are substantially better looking than the people in the low-prestige occupations. And what do they conclude? That there is an invisible guiding hand at work—a natural force—in which people who are good looking are the cream of society who rise to the top, and people who are plain looking are the dregs who sink to the bottom.

The conclusion is silly, of course. In reaching it we are confusing an invention (a system of social stratification based on good looks) with a discovery. We are taking a cultural artifact and acting as though it were a law of nature. But is that not what Herrnstein and Murray (1994) and others are doing when they draw the same conclusion about IQ—confusing a system we have invented with an edict of nature? We might have created another system, and in most of history people have. For example, during the Middle Ages, if you were born a serf you died a serf, even if you had an IQ of 180.

When we create a system, the system will inevitably have effects that result from the system, but perhaps only from that system and no other. Whatever means we use to sort people is likely to create self-fulfilling prophecies as we advance the people who do well by those criteria and hold back people who do not do so well. Typically, we never give the ones who do not do well on the sorting devices a chance to show what they might really have been able to do.

Self-fulfilling prophecies have been shown to exist via experimental paradigms (Rosenthal & Jacobson, 1968) and in metaanalysis (Harris & Rosenthal, 1985), but many of us do not need the statistics to find examples of them. In my own case low scores on IQ tests as a young child resulted in my being treated as rather stupid by my teachers in the early grades. The teachers had low expectations, I met their low expectations, they were happy, and I was happy that they were happy. Everyone was happy, but my work was really quite mediocre.

When I was in the fourth grade, I had a teacher who, for whatever reason, had higher expectations. I really liked this teacher, and I wanted to meet her expectations too. For the first time I found myself to be an A student. I was amazed, even if my teacher was not. But I never even considered the possibility that my higher achievement was a result of ability—that the test scores might have been mistaken. Rather, I, like so many achievers with low test scores, thought that I had found some way around my lack of abilities.

Children with diverse cultural backgrounds are often penalized on tests of ability. They, like so many others, can quickly become victims of self-fulfilling prophecies.

What are some of the factors that lead students from diverse cultural backgrounds to be at a disadvantage on conventional tests of intelligence? Indeed, what effects does culture have on testing in general? I consider these questions next.

THE NATURE AND IMPORTANCE OF ABILITIES DIFFERS CROSS-CULTURALLY

Conventional intelligence tests were designed originally to predict academic performance, and academic prediction is what they have always done best, except for prediction of scores on other tests. But academic performance is not equally valued in every culture and indeed is not terribly highly valued even in our own culture as a mark of success in adulthood. As people advance through their lives, academic performance becomes less important, pretty much without regard to people's culture or job within that culture.

Gladwin (1970) has documented the case of the Puluwat, who are able to navigate ships from one island to another without any obvious cues. If most of us were to take a test relevant for performance in their society, chances are we would do quite poorly. Differences in cultural adaptation apply not only in exotic cultures. The skills required to survive in modern-day Liberia, Rwanda, or even Bosnia might leave many high-IQ people dead. Even in modern-day Russia, many of the high-IQ people who made it into once prestigious jobs such as that of college professor are now extremely poor and in some cases having trouble surviving, whereas people who have entrepreneurial skills but not necessarily the highest IQs have risen to the top.

Differences in what is valued are not limited to cross-national comparisons. Such differences can be found in the United States as well. Consider, for example, the results of a study we did in San Jose, CA (Okagaki & Sternberg, 1993). We studied members of several ethnic groups such as Caucasians, Mexicans, Mexican Americans (second-generation), Hmong, Cambodian Americans, and the like. We discovered that members of different ethnic groups had different conceptions of what they considered to be intelligent in their children. For example, some groups emphasized more cognitive-competence skills, and other groups emphasized more social-competence skills. We also investigated teachers' conceptions of intelligence; the teachers, like some of the parents, emphasized cognitive-competence skills. More critically, perhaps, we discovered that the overall school performance of children in each group was extremely well predicted by the match between the parents' conception of intelligence and the teachers' conception. The better was the match, the more intelligent the children were considered by their teachers. But arguably what was appreciated was the match in what the children had been taught to value and what their teachers valued. In other schools, different things might have been valued, with different results.

Shirley Heath (1983) did a study in North Carolina that revealed similar results. Looking at members of three communities she found that parents in two of the communities valued very much the development of verbal skills, whereas parents in one of the communities valued very much the development of nonverbal skills. These values reflected communication patterns in each of the communities. Thus, most of the communication in two of the communities occurred through verbal channels, whereas much and possibly most of the communication in the other community occurred through nonverbal channels. But schools, of course, value verbal more than nonverbal communication, with the result, again, that the children whose parents emphasized more certain aspects of intelligence did better in school than did the children of parents emphasizing other aspects.

Of course, one could argue in both the Okagaki-Sternberg and the Heath studies that the parents in some groups are just more intelligent, or have a better system of values, than do the parents in other groups. This case, however, would be hard to make persuasively. For one thing, the parents' views genuinely did reflect the skills that were valued in one or another community. For another thing, the skills emphasized in the communities that were at odds with the values of the school actually are important skills. Social competence, for example, is indeed important in life, and its importance probably increases with age. Whereas IQ points may get you through a school situation, they probably will not be sufficient to get most people through their job, or even through a job interview, but social skills might. Similarly, nonverbal communication is very important in many aspects of life. For example, during a job interview most of the information that matters to the candidate is nonverbal. Interviewers rarely provide verbal feedback, such as that the interview is going poorly. But they often provide this feedback nonverbally. If the candidate is sensitive to the nonverbal communication, he or she may be able to change his or her act before it is too late. Insensitivity to such communication is likely to result in a lost job opportunity. In sum, what the school values does not fully reflect the culture's values, especially as people move through their lives.

Such differences are not just hypothetical. For example, on a recent trip to Oxford University, I was told by a professor of psychology that a difficulty many students have on their final exams at the end of their academic career is that the professors who evaluate the essays value highly creativity. Many students are not used to going well beyond the given in writing essays. In contrast, I had an employee who did her undergraduate work at the University of Beijing. She told me precisely the opposite: Going beyond the given on a final exam would be, more or less, the kiss of death. What is valued as intelligent can differ quite widely across cultures.

THE NATURE AND IMPORTANCE OF ABILITIES VARIES OVER TIME

In a rapidly changing society, the abilities that lead to successful adaptation at one point in time are not necessarily the abilities that lead to successful adaptation at another point in time. For example, consider "mathematical ability." In the early tests of Louis Thurstone (Thurstone & Thurstone, 1941), this ability was measured by numerical computation. Although certainly numerical computation never measured the whole of mathematical ability, during the 1940s or 1950s, for example, numerical computation was in fact an important part of succeeding in many schools as well as real-world mathematical endeavors. By the 1960s, the updated version of the same test (Thurstone & Thurstone, 1962) required solution of fairly routine mathematical word problems. Computation was important, but much less so. Today, computational ability has come to be of rather limited importance. For example, children taking the mathematical section of the SAT are allowed to use a calculator. So much for computational ability. Over time, what has mattered has changed.

Similarly, literacy abilities are quite important for even modest success in today's society. Two hundred years ago much of the population could hardly read, and there are still nonliterate cultures today. Are literacy abilities important in these cultures? Probably not. But the cultures that are nonliterate today may be literate in some years, and literacy abilities may become much more important.

At one time, the ability to run fast was quite central to survival. If you could not outrun certain predators, you were dead. If the trend toward violence continues in our society, such abilities may become more important again. Right now, though, such abilities are not generally in high demand, except among some kinds of athletes. Creative abilities, on the contrary, have become extremely important—probably more so than in past generations. Why? Because the rate at which society is changing places creative abilities at a premium (Sternberg & Lubart, 1995). The business climate, for example, is changing extremely rapidly. What worked for Apple or IBM at one time may soon no longer work. The managers who run these companies and who are unable to keep up with the rapid changes in the world soon find their businesses failing.

WHAT CONSTITUTES "GOOD" PERFORMANCE VARIES CULTURALLY

Joe Glick (Cole, Gay, Glick, & Sharp, 1971) asked adult members of the Kpelle tribe to sort names of various kinds of objects such as names of fruits, names of vegetables, or names of vehicles of conveyance. Glick found that the adults sorted functionally rather than taxonomically. For example, they might sort "apple" with "eat" or "car" with "gas," rather than sorting various kinds of apples together, under the word "apple," and then "fruits," and perhaps then "foods." The Kpelle way of doing this task would be considered, in the West, cognitively immature. It is the way young children would complete the task. Indeed, virtually any theorist of cognitive development (e.g., Piaget, 1972) would view functional sorting as inferior. On the vocabulary section of an intelligence test such as the Wechsler or the Stanford-Binet, a functional definition of, for example, an automobile as using gas would receive less credit than a taxonomic definition of, for example, an automobile as a vehicle of conveyance. Glick tried without success to get the Kpelle to sort in an alternative way.

Finally, Glick gave up and started packing up. As an afterthought, he asked a member of the tribe how a stupid person would sort. The man had no trouble sorting the terms taxonomically. In other words, he considered stupid what a Western psychologist would consider smart. Why? Because in everyday life, for the most part, our thinking really is functional. For example, we think about eating an apple; we do not think about the apple as a fruit, which is a food, which is an organic substance.

Differences in what is considered intelligent occur not only on tests, but also in occupational situations. For example, in order to get promoted to full professor in the United States, the name of the game is typically scholarly publication. There is a considerable emphasis on making significant new contributions to knowledge. In Spain and in other European countries, publication is important too. But promotion is critically dependent on the individual's passing a "capacitation" examination, which requires the candidate to show both broad and deep knowledge of the work of many different theorists and researchers in a given field. Spanish scholars therefore must spend large amounts of time studying the work of scholars in their own and related fields. What in the United States might be viewed as a rather poor use of one's time, given the U.S. reward system emphasizing publication, would be viewed as an excellent use of time in Spain, because without the scholar's spending the time to learn about all the related work, the promotion simply never will come.

Such examples may seem exotic; they are not. They occur in everyday life as well. In Israel people have what might be called a "direct" style in their social interactions. They say things to each other, even to people in authority, that people would probably never say to each other in the United States, and that they would never even think of saying in the United Kingdom. The statement that would be perceived as insulting and demonstrating very low social intelligence in the United States might seem quite reasonable in Israel.

As another example, I discovered on an airplane that the polite behavior that leads people on one side of a jet airplane to defer to people on the other side in sharing use of limited bathrooms leads one on an Israeli plane to have a very full or possibly burst bladder. What a person from the United States might consider polite becomes actually rather stupid and definitely maladaptive.

WHAT CONSTITUTES "GOOD" PERFORMANCE VARIES EVEN WITHIN CULTURE

When I teach even low-level college courses, I tell my students that I expect their essays on tests to show at least some creativity. I want the students to show that they can come up with some ideas of their own. Students who merely spit back information cannot get an "A" on one of my exams. Not all professors think this way. When I was an undergraduate in the very same university and department in which I am teaching today, my very first test was an essay test. I thought that an essay test meant that the professor wanted us to be creative. I was wrong. On that first test I got a 3 out of 10. The professor explained that he had 10 points he wanted us to make, and that our score on the test was the number of points out of 10 that we had actually made. The very same creative thinking could lead either to an "A" or an "F" even in the same department; it all depended on who was doing the evaluation. The professor is still teaching and grading in the same way.

These differences apply not only to students. The managerial behavior that is likely to be valued in a small new startup company may not be valued much in a more mature company. Indeed, the founder of Apple Computers was eventually kicked out of his own company because of a feeling that a style that worked early on was no longer working later on, when the company had become more mature. Similarly, the same values that lead to a talk being valued at a psychology department such as Yale's might lead to the talk being looked at as quite weak at Carnegie-Mellon, and vice versa. From my experience, Yale expects much more a top-down explanation of why the underlying question is important and why the theory is compelling; Carnegie Mellon places more emphasis on a detailed computer simulation that shows that the model is sufficient to be enacted on the computer. What is seen as smart in one place may be seen as rather stupid in another, and vice versa.

The previous example shows the extent to which what is valued as intelligent, or creative, varies with time and place. Van Gogh's work is worth a fortune today; but Van Gogh died a pauper. Many of the most respected novels of today were thoroughly panned by critics when they first appeared. Some scientific work that was viewed as laughable when first presented is now often valued (e.g., Copernicus's heliocentric theory of the solar system), whereas other scientific work that got considerable attention when it was first published is now viewed as laughable (e.g., cold fusion). Often, what we value as "good" even within a society changes with time, place, and who is doing the valuing.

Our own theory of creativity (Sternberg & Lubart, 1995) suggests that often highly creative work is not particularly valued at the time that it is created. On the contrary, it is often viewed as silly and even as worthless. When we receive feedback on our work from the culture at large, we need not only to consider the feedback seriously, but also to evaluate what it is worth.

TESTS CAN BE UNBIASED IN A NARROW SENSE AND BIASED IN A BROAD SENSE

The psychometric definition of test bias is that a test is biased if it systematically underpredicts or overpredicts for a given group. In such a circumstance the predicted scores are either too high or too low for a particular group, given that group's range of test scores. From the point of view of this definition, analyses of test bias have shown ability tests to be more or less unbiased (Herrnstein & Murray, 1994; Jensen, 1980).

In this narrow sense of bias, the analyses that have been done are fair and accurate. The problem is that this sense of bias is, in fact, too narrow. The problem is that often the criterion can share the same bias or biases as the predictor. For example, conventional tests of intellectual abilities measure primarily memory and analytical abilities; they hardly measure two other domains of abilities—creative and practical abilities (Sternberg, 1985a, 1988b, 1996), nor, for the most part, were they intended to measure these other abilities.

One could argue, however, that creative and practical abilities are at least as important as, and possibly even more important than, analytical abilities in everyday life. For example, to be successful in writing, art, business, science, teaching, or pretty much any other occupation, one needs to have both creative and practical as well as analytical skills. An artist or writer could not succeed very well without at least some good ideas for writing and without some ideas as to how to reach the intended audience. In order to keep up with changing markets in business, a business executive needs to be creative and see things in new ways; he or she also needs to know how to get along with people. Many teachers find that the very same set of lectures that works so well with one group of students does not work well with another. The teachers need the creativity to change their lectures in order to reach a new group of students and the practical skills to know whether they are succeeding in reaching these new students.

We have done a five-year research study in order to demonstrate the kind of broad bias being discussed here (Sternberg, Ferrari, Clinkenbeard, & Grigorenko, 1996). We selected students to be high in analytical, creative, practical, or all three kinds of abilities; and we selected as well a group of students low in all three kinds of abilities. We then taught the students introductory psychology in a way that either matched or mismatched their patterns of abilities. Students could be taught in a way that emphasized analytical, creative, or practical thinking, or memory. Some students were matched: The way they were taught was compatible with their pattern of abilities. Other students were mismatched so that the way they were taught was not compatible with their pattern of abilities. All students were then assessed for achievement in terms of memory, as well as analytical, creative, and practical achievements.

We found that students who were taught in a way that matched their pattern of abilities achieved at a significantly and substantially higher level than did students who were mismatched. In other words, students who were mismatched suffered. I believe that such mismatching occurs extremely frequently. In my own case I was a creative learner in an introductory-psychology course emphasizing memorization, and I had a grade of C to show for it. The point is that most courses are designed for the very same kinds of learners (memory and analytical learners) who typically test well on conventional assessments of abilities. In other words, both the predictors and the criteria are biased in the same ways.

BOTH ABILITY AND ACHIEVEMENT TESTS CONFOUND STYLES WITH WHAT THEY ARE SUPPOSED TO MEASURE

Thinking and learning styles are preferred ways of using abilities, rather than abilities themselves (Sternberg, 1988a, 1997; Sternberg & Grigorenko, 1995). For example, in my own theory of mental self-government (Sternberg, 1997), a person with a legislative style likes to come up with his or her own ideas and ways of doing things; a person with an executive style likes to be given a structure or a framework within which to do things; and a person with a judicial style likes to judge, evaluate, and analyze people and their work.

Different cultural groups are likely to have different distributions of styles because of differential socialization experiences of their members (Sternberg, 1988a). For example, a culture that encourages questioning and exploration of cultural customs is more likely to foment a legislative style, whereas a culture that discourages or forbids such questioning and exploration is more likely to foment an executive style.

With regard to these and other styles, tests are not and cannot be neutral. They will inevitably favor some styles over others. For example, multiple-choice tests tend to structure the examination situation for the test taker, and those tests that emphasize recall of structure and content are probably going to be most comfortable for people with a predominantly executive style. Essay tests or projects that encourage people to be creative and explore near or even beyond the boundaries of what they have been taught are more likely to foster a legislative style, and multiple-choice or essay tests that encourage analysis and evaluation of ideas are going to be more comfortable for those with a judicial style. More importantly, abilities or achievements are likely to be confounded with styles because the person scoring the material will generally be unable to separate stylistic preference from the abilities or achievements supposedly being measured by the tests. An implication of this point of view is that one would wish to test using a variety of formats, to cancel out the benefits that will attend on any one stylistic group if a test has only one format for test items.

SUCCESS CAN BE ACHIEVED FAILURE

We almost always tend to think of higher test scores as synonymous with greater success. But it is simply not the case that better performance on something is always culturally valued. For example, many if not most men would have no hesitation in describing themselves as "terrible cooks" or "unable to sew." Indeed, some men who sew might prefer to keep it to themselves. Similarly, an intellectual might actually brag that he or she is a "terrible athlete." Those who have succeeded in the world may even have the luxury of confessing to how poorly they did on tests as a child, or how poorly they did in school; for them, their later success renders these earlier performances irrelevant.

In the same way poor scores on tests can end up being badges of honor rather than of shame. Among some youths—especially adolescents—good performance in school may be viewed as counternormative. For them, high scores on tests are nothing to brag about. Quite the contrary! Ray McDermott (1974) has used the term *achieved failure* to describe this kind of mental set. We need to realize that it may be quite common, despite our desire for test takers to share our own set of values, that high scores are synonymous with success.

Such achieved failure may seem to be limited to those who are of low socioeconomic class, or who are society's losers. But such an equation simply does not work. During the days of the draft, for example, many middle- and upper-middle class youths "faked bad" on physical and mental examinations in order to avoid the draft. Some youths of today may have the same fear of college that many youths had in the past of the draft. They may view college as a place where they can be labeled as failures. What better way to avoid this threat than to do poorly on tests—standardized or otherwise.

Many of us may remember how, when we were in high school, popularity, not intellectual power, was the coin of the realm. Little has changed. At the high school level (and at other levels as well), girls sometimes may avoid looking too smart so as not to appear unattractive to boys, and boys may do the same to fit into their social group. Excessively high grades or scores may label one as a misfit. In sum, then, we cannot merely assume that what we view as success will be viewed as success by those who actually take our tests.

HIGHLY CULTURE-BASED INFORMAL KNOWLEDGE OFTEN MATTERS MORE THAN LESS CULTURE-BASED FORMAL KNOWLEDGE

When we ask what kinds of knowledge we really need to succeed in life, we often realize that informal knowledge is at least as important as, and arguably more important than, formal knowledge (Sternberg, 1996; Sternberg, Wagner, & Okagaki, 1993; Sternberg, Wagner, Williams, & Horvath, 1995). Informal knowledge is the knowledge we need to succeed in a given endeavor that is not formally taught, that usually is not verbalized, and that often is deliberately hidden from those in a given environment. For example, it might pertain to how really to get a promotion versus how to get one in theory, or how really to get elected to political office versus how to get elected in theory.

Whereas the laws of physics, or the principles of biology, or the rules for recording history may be rather similar from one culture to another, informal knowledge is not. Informal knowledge in these instances would pertain, for example, to things such as how to get one's work recognized and rewarded in physics, how to get government grants in biology, or how to write an analysis of historical events that will be well received in a given cultural context (which, for example, might be different for the same events in, say, Libya and Israel).

Tests typically tend to measure formal rather than informal knowledge, with very few exceptions (see Sternberg et al., 1995). Although the formal knowledge tested in some areas may differ from one culture to another (e.g., the particular literature studied and evaluated may be somewhat different in France versus Great Britain), the school will be the primary place for teaching such knowledge in both cultures, and so the two cultures may be measuring roughly equivalent achievements, albeit with different content. On the contrary, the kinds of people who succeed in business may be more different from one culture to another, or even one subculture to another, depending on informal knowledge. The person who succeeds as an executive in a mature technology company may be different from the one who succeeds in the startup company because the informal knowledge required for success is so different, as may be the kind of person who will learn it. In sum, informal knowledge and even the acquisition routes for it may differ greatly from one culture to another, but such differences are typically not reflected in ability or achievement tests.

MOST CULTURES AROUND THE WORLD ARE COLLECTIVISTIC RATHER THAN INDIVIDUALISTIC

In a survey of cultures around the world (Triandis, 1972; see also Matsumoto, 1996), the United States was found to be the most individualistic of all of the cultures studied. In general, members of the United Kingdom also tended to be highly individualistic, whereas most hispanic cultures tended to be quite collectivistic, as did many Asian and African cultures. What is valued in terms of performance is quite likely to differ across cultures, depending on the cultures' relative levels of individualism versus collectivism.

For example, we in the United States tend more than most cultures to value people who stand out from the crowd, the Horatio Algers who work themselves up from rags to riches and dominate over others economically, or perhaps intellectually or otherwise. Not every culture has this same set of values. In Norway, for example, scarcely an exotic culture, people speak of the "Law of Jante," according to which the head that sticks out above the others is cut off. The value that is placed on individual excellence on tests, for example, may differ from one culture to another.

In describing a study she did among Maya people of Central America, Patricia Greenfield (1997) has reported that the idea of taking a test and not being able to consult others for help appeared to be quite strange. After all, if you individually do not know the answer, why not ask others who do? And from a certain point of view, such behavior makes perfect sense. Indeed, in our everyday lives, when we encounter problems we cannot solve, we often seek out others who can solve them. But our testing procedures generally forbid such a practice. Forbidding it is not even consistent anymore with the type of cooperative learning that is being encouraged in many schools today.

Who is viewed as excelling may differ in the two types of cultures. For example, Michael Cole, in observations of children working together in a cooking class (Laboratory of Comparative Human Cognition, 1982, 1983), found that children who could not cook on their own were actually quite successful when working together as a team. One might judge their abilities quite differently in the team versus an individual setting, just as those of us who do research often find that certain people who are quite effective individually (or in a group) are not nearly so successful in a group (or individually).

SPEED IS IMPORTANT—IN SOME PLACES

In the United States, we generally tend to value speed as an important aspect of intelligence (Sternberg, 1985b; Sternberg, Conway, Ketron, & Bernstein, 1981). But not all cultures of the world value speed equally, or even do all subcultures within the United States (Berry, 1984). Indeed, a more common cultural notion is that it is not speed but depth of thinking that is crucial to intelligence. The intelligent person is not the person who answers many multiple-choice items quickly, but rather the person who reflects deeply on problems and situations, seeing many points of view, and then carefully considers their value for solving the problem at hand.

Indeed, even we in northern North American and Western Europe who more value speed recognize the importance of depth, profundity, and careful reflection. For example, if someone needs to decide whether to get married, to take a particular job, to buy a particular house, or whatever, the person is unlikely to be complimented for making such a decision without carefully reflecting on it. Someone who bragged that he or she made such an important decision in the seconds that are usually allowed for answering multiple-choice questions would scarcely be viewed as particularly intelligent. In other words, even we who so much value speed recognize its limitations in real-world intelligent performance. That is not to say speed is never important. If you are driving, you may have to do some split-second thinking to avoid an accident. But such cases seem to be the exception rather than the rule in everyday intelligent thinking.

We now have in the United States the odd and perhaps dysfunctional situation in which some parents want their children labeled as learning-disabled or otherwise disabled so that their children will receive special services, and perhaps even more importantly, will be allowed to take tests such as the Scholastic Assessment Test (SAT) untimed. Such a situation makes no great sense in that it essentially rewards people for being labeled as deficient in some way. Certainly we need a better system!

LANGUAGE PROBLEMS ARE COMMON, NOT RARE

As more and more of our population in the United States speaks English only as a second language, we need to recognize that those for whom English is a second language scarcely can compete on an equal basis with those for whom English is a first language.

For example, a child who grows up speaking Spanish in the home will scarcely be in a position to do as well on the verbal section of the Scholastic Assessment Test, or any other similar test, as will a child who grows up speaking English.

Even everyday fluency in a language guarantees little by way of test scores. For example, I am a relatively fluent Spanish speaker and have no trouble reading ordinary texts. But the kinds of texts and vocabulary presented on conventional ability and achievement tests quite high level, often above the level that will be needed for many kinds of academic work. As a result, even people with facility may be penalized.

In some schools I have visited, an allowance is made for immigrants, but only up to a point. Thus, immigrant children may be viewed as a separate category, right up to the point that they have lived for a fixed number of years in this country, sometimes three. Thus, the child who has lived in the United States for two years and 364 days will be viewed as disadvantaged by the tests, whereas the child who has lived in the United States for three years and one day will not be. Such a system is obviously in need of fixing.

At the graduate level, many schools use the Test of English as a Foreign Language (TOEFL) in place of or in addition to tests such as the Graduate Record Examination (GRE) for applicants from other countries. But such a test is neither equivalent to the GRE in what it measures, nor is its use necessarily advisable. For example, one of the most successful students we have had in our own graduate program at Yale almost was not admitted because her TOEFL score was below the minimum considered "acceptable" by graduate-school officials. Indeed, when she arrived, her English was not particularly good, but within a few months she was speaking as well as most natives, and after a few years she was writing better than many natives as well. We need to consider not only how much English the individual has learned, but also the individual's ability to learn English further, or any other language.

We need also to recognize that language is a much more general concept than just the kind of language we speak or read in our everyday lives. Computer languages are languages, as can be other kinds of symbol systems such as the language of mathematics or the language of logic. Many children from other cultures may actually be quite superior in some of these languages; or they may not be. For example, the kinds of geometric symbols that are touted by some to be bases for the culture-fair measurement of intelligence (e.g., Cattell & Cattell, 1963) are really not culture-fair at all. Children who do not receive Western schooling are likely to be less familiar with such symbols than are children who do receive such schooling. As a result, they are likely to not compete well on such tests. Various studies have shown that when children or adults are tested in ways that suit their cultural patterns of adaptation, their scores are better and may even exceed those of Western individuals who would otherwise have looked "smarter" (Kearins, 1981; Wagner, 1978).

SIMILARITY AS THE MAIN BASIS OF INTERPERSONAL ATTRACTION

There is now a vast amount of literature suggesting that the single most powerful predictor of interpersonal attraction is similarity: We tend to be attracted to those who are similar to ourselves (e.g., Byrne, 1971; see Sternberg, 1988c). Few findings in psychology have been so well replicated.

This finding has implications for our understanding of the effects of culture on our interpretation of test scores. We tend to be attracted not just to those who are interpersonally like ourselves, but also to those who are intellectually like ourselves. Because we are a culture that values and advances people with high test scores, those in the power structure, who gained access to it in part by virtue of testing well, are likely to be attracted to others like themselves. However, as a result, those in power may not allow for abilities and achievements that differ in kind from their own. They may truly not recognize that the tests they use measure not some abstracted set of abilities or achievements, but rather what is valued in a culture.

Often, when we visit a foreign country where we do not speak the language, we feel stupid. Of course we do: We can hardly understand what is going on. That is the way many children and adults feel in our culture. We need to give them the chance to compete on an equal footing, just as we would wish such a chance in a foreign land.

There is a story that, in slightly modified form, goes like this: A teacher dies and ascends immediately to heaven. He is met by St. Peter, who shows him the grounds and introduces him to some of the other residents. Pointing to one resident, St. Peter says: "Here is a man you will want to get to know. This man is the greatest poetic talent who ever lived." "Wait a minute," replies the teacher. "Certainly you're mistaken. I know that guy. He was in one of the high school English classes I taught. He could hardly speak a word of English, and his SATs were terrible. I failed him, and he ended up being a shoemaker. Greatest poet—hah—he didn't have a chance." "Precisely," answered St. Peter.

REFERENCES

Berry, J. W. (1984). Towards a universal psychology of cognitive competence. In P. S. Fry (Ed.), *Changing conceptions of intelligence and intellectual functioning* (pp. 35-61). Amsterdam: North-Holland.

Byrne, D. (1971). *The attraction paradigm*. San Diego, CA: Academic Press.

Cattell, R. B., & Cattell, A. K. (1963). *Test of g: Culture fair, scale 3*. Champaign, IL: Institute for Personality and Ability Testing.

Cole, M., Gay, J., Glick, J., & Sharp D. W. (1971). *The cultural context of learning and thinking*. New York: Basic Books.

Gladwin, T. (1970). *East is a big bird*. Cambridge, MA: Harvard University Press.

Greenfield, P. (1997). You can't take it with you. Why ability assessments don't cross cultures. *American Psychologist, 52,* 1115-1124.

Harris, M. J., & Rosenthal, R. (1985). Mediation of interpersonal expectancy effects: 31 meta-analyses. *Psychological Bulletin, 97,* 363-386.

Hatfield, E., & Sprecher, S. (1986). *Mirror, mirror. . . The importance of looks in everyday life*. Albany: State University of New York Press.

Heath, S. B. (1983). *Ways with words*. New York: Cambridge University Press.

Herrnstein, R. J., & Murray, C. (1994). *The bell curve*. New York: Free Press.

Jensen, A. R. (1980). *Bias in mental testing*. New York: Free Press.

Kearins, J.M. (1981). Visual spatial memory in Australian aboriginal children of the desert regions. *Cognitive Psychology, 13,* 434-460.

Laboratory of Comparative Human Cognition. (1982). Culture and intelligence. In R. J. Sternberg (Ed.), *Handbook of human intelligence* (pp. 642-719). New York: Cambridge University Press.

Laboratory of Comparative Human Cognition. (1983). Culture and cognitive development. In P. Mussen (Series Ed.) & W. Kessen (Vol. Ed.), *Handbook of child psychology* (pp. 295-359). New York: Wiley.

Matsumoto, D. (1996). *Culture and psychology*. Belmont, CA: Brooks/Cole.

McDermott, R. P. (1974). Achieving school failure: An anthropological approach to illiteracy and social stratification. In G. Spindler (Ed.), *Education and the cultural process* (pp. 82-118). New York: Holt, Rinehart, and Winston.

Okagaki, L., & Sternberg, R. J. (1993). Parental beliefs and children's school performance. *Child Development, 64*(1), 36-56.

Piaget, J. (1972). *The psychology of intelligence*. Totowa, NJ: Littlefield Adams.

Rosenthal, R. R., & Jacobson, L. (1968). *Pygmalion in the classroom*. New York: Holt, Rinehart and Winston.

Sternberg, R. J. (1985a). Implicit theories of intelligence, creativity, and wisdom. *Journal of Personality and Social Psychology, 49,* 607-627.

Sternberg, R. J. (1985b). *Beyond IQ: A triarchic theory of human intelligence*. New York: Cambridge University Press.

Sternberg, R. J. (Ed.). (1988a). Mental self-government: A theory of intellectual styles and their development. *Human Development, 31,* 197-224.

Sternberg, R. J. (1988b). *The triarchic mind: A new theory of human intelligence*. New York: Viking.

Sternberg, R. J. (1988c). *The triangle of love*. New York: Basic.

Sternberg, R. J. (1996). *Successful intelligence*. New York: Simon & Schuster.

Sternberg, R. J. (1997). *Thinking styles*. New York: Cambridge University Press.

Sternberg, R. J., Conway, B. E., Ketron, J. L., & Bernstein, M. (1981). People's conception of intelligence. *Journal of Personality and Social Psychology, 41,* 37-55.

Sternberg, R. J., Ferrari, M., Clinkenbeard, P., & Grigorenko, E. L. (1996). Identification, instruction, and assessment of gifted children: A construct validation of a triarchic model. *Gifted Child Quarterly, 40,* 129-137.

Sternberg, R. J., & Grigorenko, E. L. (1995). Styles of thinking in school. *European Journal of High Ability, 6*(2), 1-18.

Sternberg, R. J., & Lubart, T. I. (1995). *Defying the crowd: Cultivating creativity in a culture of conformity*. New York: Free Press.

Sternberg, R. J., Wagner, R. K., & Okagaki, L. (1993). Practical intelligence: The nature and role of tacit knowledge in work and at school. In H. Reese & J. Puckett (Eds.), *Advances in lifespan development* (pp. 205-227). Hillsdale, NJ: Erlbaum.

Sternberg, R. J., Wagner, R. K., Williams, W. M., & Horvath, J. A. (1995). Testing common sense. *American Psychologist, 50*(11), 912-927.

Thurstone, L. L., & Thurstone, T. C. (1941). *Factorial studies of intelligence*. Chicago: University of Chicago Press.

Thurstone, L. L., & Thurstone, T. C. (1962). *Tests of primary mental abilities* (rev. ed.). Chicago: Science Research Associates.

Triandis, H. C. (1972). *The analysis of subjective culture*. New York: Wiley.

Chapter 7

Identifying Gifted and Creative Linguistically and Culturally Diverse Children

Emilia C. Lopez

Queens College of the City University of New York

> Yet I am almost afraid to hope, to
> dream again that something will be
> done to make better use of the
> creative potentials this country
> has in its minority/disadvantaged
> gifted and talented children.
>   (Torrance, 1978, p. 292)

During the 1970s, in an article entitled "Dare we hope again?," Torrance (1978) strongly argued for the need to cultivate and nurture the gifted and creative abilities of linguistically and culturally diverse (LCD) children. Today, educators and psychologists continue to stress the importance of identifying LCD children in order to provide them with the opportunities to develop their special skills. This chapter examines the factors that are contributing to the underrepresentation of LCD children in programs for the gifted and creative. In addition, promising procedures designed to improve identification practices are discussed.

DEFINING THE LCD GIFTED AND CREATIVE POPULATION

LCD children reside in homes in which a language other than English is used either exclusively or in conjunction with a second language. National statistics indicate that as of 1992-93, 7% of the public school enrollment in grades K through 12 is comprised of students with limited English proficiency (U.S. Dept. of Education, 1994). This increase is attributed to the large influx of immigrants from a wide variety of language and cultural backgrounds. Urban areas within the states of California, New York, Texas, and Florida include significant numbers of children from LCD backgrounds (Bureau of the Census, 1992). In New York City, for example, children from LCD backgrounds represent over 140 languages, and more than 15% of the student population is eligible for bilingual and English as a Second Language (ESL) programs (New York City Public Schools, 1993). As a group, LCD children demonstrate heterogeneous characteristics in terms of language abilities (i.e., spectrum ranges from children who speak little or no English to children who are bilingual) and cultural differences (i.e., differences in behaviors, beliefs, and values).

LCD *gifted* and *creative* children demonstrate extraordinary abilities in one or more areas of performance including general intelligence (Renzulli 1973; Sternberg, 1988), academic aptitude; productive thinking; leadership ability, visual and performing arts, and psychomotor ability (Marland, 1972). In the area of creativity, they demonstrate significant strengths in such areas as divergent thinking skills (Guilford, 1956), flexibility, fluency, originality (Guilford, 1967), and production of novel material (Torrance, 1984).

Because individual cultures stress specific intellectual abilities and talents, the ways in which LCD children express their gifted and creative abilities are directly influenced by their cultural backgrounds (Melesky, 1984; Torrance, 1963). Maker, Nielson, and Rogers (1994) elaborate as follows:

> For example, oral storytelling may be a common form of linguistic giftedness in some cultures, while writing novels may be more common in others. The form of a particular language may also influence the expression of giftedness. Navajo has many rich, descriptive words and few nouns, while English has many nouns

and categories. . . . Such differences may influence the expression of both linguistic and logical-mathematical giftedness. (p. 5)

THE STATUS OF LCD CHILDREN IN PROGRAMS FOR THE GIFTED AND CREATIVE

According to Smith and Luckasson (1995), although LCD children "comprise about 30 percent of the school-age population, less than 20 percent are included in gifted education programs" (p. 314). Children from Hispanic, Native American, and Pacific Islander backgrounds are typically reported as underrepresented in gifted and creative programs (Cheng, Ima, & Labovitz, 1994). Although some reports indicate that children from Asian-American backgrounds are overrepresented in programs for the gifted and creative (e.g., Chinn & Hughes, 1987), the numbers mask group differences within the Asian-American population. Cheng et al. (1994) examined the cultural backgrounds of students in the second largest school district in California. The investigators found that 28% of the population in the gifted programs they examined were from Chinese, Korean, and Japanese backgrounds (i.e., Asian), whereas 6% were from Vietnamese, Khmer, Laotian, and Hmong backgrounds (i.e., Southeast Asian). The investigators reported that Asian students were more likely to be identified "reflecting both their cultural emphasis on schooling and their home country schooling preparation for test taking" (p. 40).

Within the LCD population, limited English proficient (LEP) children are significantly underrepresented in gifted programs. LEP children are typically identified in school districts through language proficiency tests. These students are eligible for bilingual education and/or English as a Second Language (ESL) programs. However, their LEP status also means that they are usually not referred or even considered for gifted and creative programs. Barkaa and Bernal (1991) argue convincingly that one does not have to be fluent in English to be intelligent. Similarly, one does not have to be fluent in English to be creative.

Contributing Factors

The variables underlying the underrepresentation of LCD children in programs for the gifted and creative are numerous. Cheng et al. (1994) speculate that teachers may not refer children from LCD backgrounds if they exhibit behaviors very different from the mainstream. For example, many Asian and Pacific Islander students value collaboration and do not exhibit competitive behaviors that are often encouraged in our schools. Such cultural differences can deter school personnel from recommending students who are perceived as lacking the characteristics typical of gifted and creative students in the mainstream.

An emphasis on definitions of giftedness that stress cognitive and academic giftedness may also contribute to the underrepresentation of LCD children in programs for the gifted and creative (Adderholdt-Elliot, Algozzine, Algozzine, & Haney, 1991; Melesky, 1984; Richert, 1985). Adderholdt-Elliot et al. (1991) recently found that only 58% of the directors of programs for the gifted and talented they surveyed across the country indicated using a more expansive definition of giftedness and talented that included intellectual ability and academic aptitude as well as productive thinking, leadership ability, visual and performing arts, and psychomotor ability (Marland, 1972).

The implementation of definitions that emphasize academic and cognitive aspects implies that children with creative abilities are not being identified for gifted and creative programs (Renzulli, 1973; Torrance, 1984). Studies investigating the relationship between intelligence and creativity indicate that creativity is only moderately correlated with intelligence, and that highly creative children do not necessarily demonstrate high intelligence and/or achievement (Esquivel & Lopez, 1988; Guilford, 1967; Rampual, Singh, & Didyk, 1984; Toth & Baker, 1990). Consequently, programs searching for the brightest in cognitive and academic terms will not necessarily identify highly creative children.

Issues of definition are also of concern in the identification of creative LCD children. According to Taylor (1975), what is regarded as creative in one culture may not be creative in another. Because individuals develop behaviors and skills supported by their surrounding environment (Sternberg, 1988), their creative abilities are expressed within the context of what is valued within their own cultural group (Torrance, 1969). Thus, LCD children may express their creative abilities in ways that deviate from the traditional standards of creative behavior (Baldwin, 1985). Asians and Native Americans, for example, nurture values related to interdependence, collective decision making, and group cohesiveness (Florey & Tafoya, 1988). These are values that are not typically emphasized in traditional creativity measures.

A preference for normed measures of intelligence and achievement in the identification of gifted and creative LCD children is another factor contributing to underrepresentation (Mitchell,

1988). Adderholdt-Elliot et al. (1991) reported most programs tended to rely on the results of normed academic achievement and IQ tests when identifying gifted and talented children. On a more recent study, Hunsaker (1994) found that many districts do not use alternative strategies to identify LCD gifted populations.

Richert (1987) argues that the overemphasis on normed cognitive and academic tools places LCD children at a disadvantage because they tend to score poorly on academic and cognitive tests that are insensitive to their linguistic and cultural backgrounds (Armour-Thomas, 1992). Normed measures of cognition and achievement are criticized for a number of reasons that include (a) norming and standardization samples that are not representative of children from LCD backgrounds; (b) questionable validity for bilingual and LEP children, whose scores may reflect English-language knowledge instead of academic or cognitive functioning; and (c) test items that are unfamiliar to children from LCD backgrounds (Armour-Thomas, 1992).

Efforts to adopt normed cognitive and academic measures for bilingual and LEP children has led to the frequent use of translated tests. The process of test translation is questionable because of a number of difficulties encountered when translating test items from one language to another. Because the translations are often performed on the spot or while the children are being assessed, translation errors can significantly change the content of the items (Lopez, 1994). In addition, the developmental level of a word or concept may change from one language to the other, and some vocabulary concepts cannot be translated because there are no equivalent words in the second language. These translation problems can have a direct effect on the tests' validity and ultimately on students' scores.

Tests translated and published outside of the United States are also frequently used. These translated tests often include vocabulary that does not reflect the diverse linguistic and cultural backgrounds of LCD children in this country. In addition, tests translated in other countries include norms that are not representative of LCD children in the United States.

Measures of creativity validated with LCD students are also scarce, and there is much concern that this population is not being identified because the instruments and procedures used to measure their creativity skills have the same biases previously identified in the assessment of achievement and cognitive skills. Despite the fact that there are over 225 different creativity tests measuring such areas as divergent thinking, attitudes and interests, personality variables, verbal and figural skills, math/science, movement/dance, dramatics, artistic abilities, and musical strengths, only 16% of those 225 tests have been the subject of known research and validation studies with the general population, and even fewer have been validated with LCD populations (Haensly & Torrance, 1990).

The Torrance Test of Creative Thinking (TTCT; Torrance, 1974) appears to be the most frequently recommended creativity test with LCD children and the most widely validated with this population (Davis, 1989; Torrance, 1972). Translated versions of the TTCT are available; however, they also demonstrate limitations in their validity.

Finally, Richert (1987) voices the concern that many LCD children are not identified as gifted and creative because they do not exhibit well-developed skills in those areas. For example, LCD children from low socioeconomic environments or with few previous educational experiences may fail to meet eligibility criteria despite demonstrating their creative potential outside of school-related situations.

THE IDENTIFICATION OF GIFTED AND CREATIVE LCD CHILDREN

Renzulli (1973) frequently referred to the importance of developing the creative abilities of all individuals. He argued that unidentified and underdeveloped gifted and creative abilities in LCD populations implied unrealized potentials and wasted social resources.

Pearson and DeMers (1990) suggest that gifted and creative programs provide LCD children with opportunities to develop the special abilities and skills they possess. They also add that specially designed programs allow students to socialize with others who demonstrate similar abilities, concerns, and interests.

Several studies suggest that children identified and placed in gifted and creative programs benefit socially as well as academically. For example, Esquivel (1985) found that placement in a gifted program resulted in higher creativity skills and higher self-concept for economically disadvantaged culturally different children. In a recent study, Smith, LeRose, and Clasen (1991) followed a group of minority children from kindergarten to high school and found that placement in gifted programs resulted in zero dropout rates for gifted minority students. In contrast, the investigators found that 45% of the gifted minority children who did not participate in the program dropped out by high school.

Promising Procedures Designed to Improve Identification Practices

The factors that are contributing to the underrepresentation of LCD children in programs for the gifted and creative are numerous. Presently, there is a need to implement identification practices that will provide LCD children with opportunities to participate in such programs. The procedures discussed next are recommended to accomplish the goals of increasing referrals, enhancing assessment practices, and ultimately, increasing the number of LCD children in programs for the gifted and creative.

Use broader definitions of intelligence and giftedness. Broader definitions acknowledge that intelligence is a construct that includes a variety of traits, and that individuals demonstrate heterogeneous profiles that include cognitive strengths as well as weaknesses. Gardner's (1983) Theory of Multiple Intelligences, for example, proposes a definition of intelligence that identifies seven types of intelligences; linguistic, logic and mathematical, musical, visual and spatial conceptualization, bodily kinesthetic, interpersonal, and intrapersonal. His theory proposes that individuals can demonstrate strengths in one or several of these types of intelligences.

Definitions of giftedness that include a variety of strengths that go beyond intelligence and achievement also enhance the identification process. To illustrate, Renzulli's (1973) definition of giftedness includes children who demonstrate strengths in the areas of creativity and task commitment. Gardner's (1983) theory also acknowledges that most people are gifted or highly competent in at least one of the seven types of intelligences. Gardner's and Renzulli's concept of giftedness provides educators involved in the identification of gifted LCD children with opportunities to recognize individuals who demonstrate well-developed abilities in areas other than cognition and achievement. The identification of children with special talents in the areas of music, art, sports, and other performance areas is also recommended (Richert, 1985; Torrance, 1978).

Apply definitions of giftedness that acknowledge the influence of cultural factors. Because cultural factors influence the specific ways in which giftedness and creativity are expressed, gifted and creative abilities are best measured within the context of the cultural background of the student (Melesky, 1984; Torrance, 1963, 1984). Bernal and Reyna (1974) recommend using assessment tasks that examine the kinds of excellence that are valued by the particular culture or subculture of the child. For example, Bernal (1974) developed interviews that elicited the perceptions of parents and other community members about gifted Mexican American children. The study found that Mexican Americans tended to identify as gifted and talented those children who demonstrated curiosity, verve, and desire for self-improvement.

Encourage referrals of preschool LCD children. Haensly and Torrance (1990) stress the importance of recognizing gifted and creative children during the early years of schooling. Identification during the preschool years provides LCD children with early exposure to environments that nurture their gifted and creative abilities (Borland & Wright, 1994).

Encourage referrals from multiple sources. Parents are effective sources of referrals because they are able to identify strengths that LCD children exhibit in the home and the community. Their observations of gifted and creative abilities are also framed within the context of the cultural background of the family.

Nominations from teachers (e.g., ESL and bilingual teachers) and other school personnel (e.g., counselors, school psychologists) are useful. The research suggests that training targeted toward helping school personnel to identify characteristics of gifted and creative culturally different children results in referrals of students who demonstrate special talents and abilities (e.g., creativity; Richert, 1987). Referral sources who are familiar with the students' level of language proficiency and with their progress in acquiring English as a second language are often able to identify those children who demonstrate particular strengths in language related areas.

Peer nominations are also valuable as children are well able to identify peers who they perceive as specially talented in a variety of areas (Melesky, 1984; Richert, 1987). Richert (1987) cautions that self nominations may only attract students who are highly motivated or who have high self-esteem. Pearson and DeMers (1990) provide a number of recommendations as to how to use nominations with gifted culturally diverse children (e.g., nominations should reflect goals of program, use researched based scales).

Use identification procedures that tap LCD children's potentials. Cheng et al. (1994) recommend dynamic approaches that are process oriented and apply a test-teach-test strategy. Dynamic approaches provide LCD children with opportunities to demonstrate their cognitive potential with testing tasks that are more closely linked to their classroom experiences. Feuerstein (Feuerstein, Rand, & Hoffman, 1979) and Budoff (1975) developed dynamic approaches that are applicable with LCD populations of gifted and creative children.

Use a variety of assessment measures. Normed measures of intelligence and creativity are available. However, assessment personnel must evaluate their appropriateness for children from LCD backgrounds in terms of language, culture, socioeconomic status, and prior education. Among the factors that need to be taken into consideration are reliability, validity, norms, standards for administration, and sources of cultural bias (Figueroa, Sandoval, & Merino, 1984). Testing of the limits is recommended in the administration of formal measures (Sattler, 1992). Task demonstrations, time extensions, and changes in presentation modes are some of the strategies that are utilized when testing limits. Bensen (1992) also recommends adapting measures to the backgrounds, experiences, and culture of LCD children. Adaptations include substituting items for more culturally appropriate items and allowing children to respond in more than one language.

Alternative measures of assessment such as the Cartoon Conservation Scales (DeAvila, 1977) can also be utilized to identify children's cognitive strengths. Nonverbal measures of intelligence and creativity are recommended to provide a language-free measure of LCD children's abilities. The nonverbal tests of intelligence available to assess LCD children include the Standard Progressive Matrices (Raven, 1958), the Columbia Mental Maturity Scale (Burgemeister, Blum, & Lorge, 1972), the Leiter International Performance Scale (Leiter, 1979), the Test of Nonverbal Intelligence-2 (TONI-2) (Brown, Sherbenou, & Johnson, 1990), and the Universal Nonverbal Intelligence Test (UNIT) (McCallum & Bracken, 1997). Creativity measures such as Torrance's Tests of Creative Thinking also have nonverbal versions for children in the early elementary years. In addition, Torrance (1980) developed the Thinking Creatively in Action and Movement test for preschool students.

Among the informal cognitive and academic measures recommended to assess LCD gifted children are observation scales, checklists, inventories, product judgments, interviews, portfolios, biographical data, and case studies. Mistry and Rogoff (1985) recommends the use of informal creativity measures as an additional source of assessment data with LCD students. Informal methods of creativity include divergent-thinking tasks as well as inventories, biographical data, questionnaires, rating scales, and observations (Davis, 1989; Haensly & Torrance, 1990; Hocevar, 1981; Michael & Wright, 1989). The Alpha Biographical Inventory (Institute for Behavioral Research in Creativity, 1968) is an example of an informal tool that is designed to collect background data in a biographical format. Case studies, performance-based products (e.g., tape recording of a musical performance), and portfolio assessment are very useful in identifying students with special talents in such areas as music and sports.

In a recent study, Hunsaker (1994) found that the method most frequently used by the districts surveyed in his study to identify disadvantaged gifted children was expanding the assessment base with such measures as checklists, rating scales, portfolio assessment, and behavioral observations. Overall, most of the subjects who participated in the survey indicated that they were aware of the advantages of using such techniques. Hunsaker also reported that school district personnel were generally dissatisfied with these alternative measures because they were costly, time-consuming, and they required personnel trained in the characteristics of giftedness. Some districts, however, reported using informal measures very infrequently because they found them difficult to utilize (i.e., subjective, time-consuming) and unsuccessful in identifying disadvantaged children (i.e., children from low socioeconomic and minority backgrounds). Overall, these results suggest that training is necessary to assist school personnel to recognize the advantages of using informal methods of assessment.

Adderholdt-Elliot et al. (1991) note that using multiple sources of information (i.e., formal and informal measures) is problematic because of difficulties in deciding what data to rely on when children demonstrate high functioning in some measures and low or average functioning on others. The interpretation of qualitative data that do not yield scores is also problematic unless clear criteria are developed to judge outcomes (Davis, 1989; Patton, Prillaman, & Van Tassel-Baska, 1990). Reis and Renzulli (1991) recently developed the Student Product Assessment Form, an instrument designed to judge the creative products of children referred to gifted and talented programs. Products are judged and rated in terms of a number of factors that include diversity of resources used, appropriateness of resources, originality of ideas, and original contribution. Although the instrument has been field tested and includes validity and reliability data, its utility must be established with LCD gifted children.

Assess LCD children's language skills. The language skills of LCD children referred to gifted and creative programs should be assessed for three principal reasons. First, gifted and creative LCD children often demonstrate strengths in their language skills. For example, LEP children with special gifts in the areas of language demonstrate rapid and significant growth in the acquisition of their English skills. Empirical research also suggests that bilingual children demonstrate cognitive and creative strengths in concept formation, classification, and metalinguistic awareness (Diaz, 1990). Thus, special talents in language-related areas is a criteria that can be applied in identifying LCD gifted and talents children.

Second, the language proficiency of LEP and bilingual children should be established to determine the language(s) of assessment (Lopez, 1995). The assessment of language proficiency involves assessing students in both their first and second languages to evaluate their ability to communicate effectively. Language-proficiency data guide assessment personnel in determining if students need to be assessed in their first and/or second languages in the areas of cognition, academics, and creativity. Failure to assess LEP and bilingual gifted students in their most proficient language can result in misinterpretation of data and misclassifications.

Third, language-proficiency data aide school personnel in determining the appropriate language(s) for instruction. To illustrate, language-proficiency data are very helpful in determining bilingual children's ability to use and understand classroom language that is abstract and academic oriented (i.e., the level of language proficiency referred to as cognitive academic language proficiency [CALPS] by Cummins, 1984). Gifted and creative LEP and bilingual children who lack the appropriate language academic skills in English are best served in programs that offer support in the native language while also providing English as a second language (ESL) services.

Formal tools are available to assess bilingual children's language-proficiency skills; however, they demonstrate a number of limitations (e.g., most are not available in languages other than Spanish and English; they evaluate a limited range of domains; see Ramirez, 1990, for a discussion on language-proficiency assessment). Interviews, observations, language samples, and checklists are some of the informal tools recommended to establish proficiency levels with LEP and bilingual children (Lopez, 1997; Payan, 1989).

Assess LCD children in natural environments. Ecological assessment models place assessment within authentic domains and natural environments. As such, assessment is conducted in classroom settings and other milieus (e.g., play groups, home) that are part of students' daily experiences. The assessment tools used often involve behavioral observations and dynamic approaches.

Maker et al. (1994) designed an ecological assessment model based on Gardner's (1983) Theory of Multiple Intelligences. The model was designed to identify multicultural populations of children for enrichment programs. During assessment activities, the children engaged in problem-solving activities in their regular classroom settings. Tasks such as building constructions (e.g., rainbows, mountains), solving complex puzzles, telling stories, and completing math worksheets and writing tasks were presented while students interacted in small groups. Trained observers recorded children's problem-solving behaviors and described their products. Profiles of students' strengths across spatial, logical-mathematical, linguistic, interpersonal, and intrapersonal intelligences were obtained. The investigators reported that "students identified through this process make gains equal to or greater than students identified by traditional standardized tests when placed in special enrichment programs" (p. 8). They also found that the process resulted in identification of equitable percentages of students from various ethnic, cultural, linguistic, and economic groups.

Borland and Wright (1994) used a similar process to identify preschool gifted children from minority economically disadvantaged backgrounds. During screening activities, the children were observed in their classrooms while they engaged in free play and structured academic activities. Portfolios, dynamic assessment methods, and standardized tests were also used in the identification process.

Cheng et al. (1994) reported using ethnographic assessment methods that were based on an ecological model. For example, students were observed over time in multiple settings while interacting with school personnel as well as peers. Students' language skills were assessed in naturalistic environments.

Interpret testing results within the context of the children's specific linguistic and cultural backgrounds. Evaluators involved in the identification of gifted and creative LCD children must demonstrate knowledge in the areas of language development, second-language acquisition, acculturation, and the relationship between culture and the expression of intelligence, giftedness, and creativity. This knowledge base should be applied in interpreting all testing results in an unbiased manner.

Use flexible identification criteria. Programs utilizing flexible criteria are able to identify LCD students who demonstrate special talents in single as well as multiple areas. Lopez, Esquivel, and Houtz (1992) describe a gifted program designed to meet the needs of disadvantaged culturally different gifted and creative children. The program's identification process was flexible as it utilized formal as well as informal measures of intelligence, achievement, and behavior (e.g., task commitment, initiative). Nominations, observations, and permanent products were among some of the measures used to identify students. All the results were considered, and the students only needed to demonstrate exceptional ability or potential on any two of the three characteristics mentioned to qualify for the program.

Programs can also be flexible in terms of the assessment tools used and the data collected. To illustrate, the assessment tools and data can be tailored to highlight the specific strengths of individual children. Thus, a student who is gifted in academic areas may submit a written portfolio, whereas a musically talented student can perform a musical piece. LEP children can also be admitted based on their performance on measures administered in their native language. Although time-consuming, a more flexible process may result in the collection of data that highlights individuals' special talents.

The Schoolwide Enrichment Triad Model utilizes a flexible approach to identify children with high potential (Renzulli & Reis, 1994). The model uses both informal as well as formal assessment tools and combines them through the Total Talent Portfolio. The portfolio includes data about children's abilities, interests, and learning styles. The information compiled is used to determine which talent development opportunities to offer through regular classes, enrichment clusters, and special services (Renzulli, 1995).

Baldwin's Identification Matrix 2 (Baldwin, 1984) also examines data in the areas of intelligence, achievement, creativity, motivation, and leadership ability. The matrix assigns weighted scores to those areas of functioning, and cutoff scores are used to identify students eligible for gifted and creative programs. The advantages of using such a system is that a variety of information is considered while using local norms to determine program eligibility (Pearson & DeMers, 1990).

Use qualified assessment personnel. Personnel involved in the identification of gifted and creative LCD children should have the skills needed to work with this population. Knowledge of issues related to the assessment of LCD children is critical (e.g., administration of measures, limitations of assessment tools, interpretation of assessment data within the context of cultural and language issues). In addition, evaluators should demonstrate knowledge in the use of appropriate and effective procedures to identify gifted and creative LCD children (e.g., use of informal measures, adaptation of measures to children from LCD backgrounds).

Use screening and identification panels that reflect the cultural and linguistic backgrounds of the LCD children. Decisions related to the identification of children for gifted and creative programs are often made by committees that examine assessment data and make recommendations as to the children that should be accepted into the programs. Committees reflecting the cross-cultural experiences of children in the district are helpful in compiling information about how individuals from specific cultural groups may express their gifted or creative abilities (Reis & Renzulli, 1991). Committees with a cross-cultural membership also serve the purpose of enhancing the process by representing the diverse views of the student body and the community.

Implement programs that nurture LCD children's gifted and creative potential. Richert (1987) recommends the development of enrichment programs that provide the academic and social support needed for students to develop their special gifts and talents. Programs with a cross-cultural perspective provide LCD children with opportunities to cultivate the gifted and creative abilities valued within different cultures. Such programs utilize a multicultural curriculum while allowing students to participate in activities and tasks that match their learning styles as framed by their cultural experiences (Renzulli, 1973, 1995). Children from LEP and bilingual backgrounds also benefit from bilingual programs for the gifted and creative.

Train referral sources to recognize LCD children with gifted and creative potential. Torrance (1972) reported higher referral rates of economically disadvantaged children after training teachers to recognize the behavioral characteristics of giftedness in this student population. Woods and Achey (1990) also found that teacher training resulted in increases in the referrals of African American, Native American, Asian, and Hispanic children to gifted programs. Referral sources profit from training in areas such as understanding the effect of culture on behavior, gaining familiarity with the cultures of the students they work with, and learning about the tools and procedures used to identify LCD children.

Involve parents in the identification of LCD gifted and creative students. Parents make a number of significant contributions in the identification of LCD gifted and creative children. For example, parents contribute through nominations as they have critical insights into their children's behaviors in the home setting and other situations (e.g., playing with peers, afterschool activities). Parent interviews are helpful in collecting information relevant to the students' development of special talents and skills as well as the modes of expression nurtured by the families' cultural backgrounds (Melesky, 1984). Borland and Wright (1994) reported using Let-Me-

Tell-You-About-My-Child cards in English and Spanish. In these cards, classroom teachers asked parents to list anything their children did at home that reflected their special abilities or interests.

Involving parents in the identification process implies that school personnel must improve the communication channels between the home and the school settings (Melesky, 1984). Amodeo and Flores (1981) pointed out that the parents' cultural and linguistic backgrounds must be taken into consideration in terms of how parents are asked to contribute to the process. For example, many parents from Hispanic backgrounds view school personnel as experts and feel somewhat uncomfortable in making suggestions to the school staff. Parents who speak a language other than English often hesitate to participate in the identification process due to language barriers. School personnel who reflect the linguistic and cultural backgrounds of the community are instrumental in encouraging such parents to participate. Trained interpreters can also be used to communicate with parents who speak languages other than English. Melesky (1984) recommended improving the communication between school and community leaders (e.g., church groups) to encourage parent participation and to identify potential talents.

Encourage collaboration and consultation across programs. Bilingual and English as a Second Language (ESL) personnel working with staff from gifted and creative programs are able to identify students with potential or well developed gifted and creative abilities. Collaborative efforts between personnel from these programs are also important in developing curriculum activities and creative tasks that nurture LCD students' special talents in their own bilingual and ESL programs.

CONCLUSION

Children from LCD backgrounds are underrepresented in programs for the gifted and creative. In a recent study investigating identification practices for gifted programs, Hunsaker (1994) reported that many educators did not accept that the concept of giftedness is manifested in all populations. He concluded that there is a need to recognize that "traits, aptitudes, and behaviors associated with the giftedness construct are manifested differently in various cultural groups" (p. 76).

It seems clear that significant changes are needed to alter the status of LCD students in such programs. Efforts must be continued in the practical as well as the research arenas to understand how language and culture play a significant role in how children express their talents and gifts. These efforts seem critical in helping LCD children to achieve their full potential as well as their own hopes and dreams.

REFERENCES

Adderholdt-Elliot, M., Algozzine, K., Algozzine, B., & Haney, K. (1991). Current state practices in educating students who are gifted and talented. *Roeper Review, 14*, 20-23.

Amodeo, L., & Flores, L. J. (1981, November). *Early identification of minority gifted: The state of the art.* Paper presented at the annual conference of the Texas Association of Bilingual Educators, El Paso.

Armour-Thomas, E. (1992). Intellectual assessment of children from culturally diverse backgrounds. *School Psychology Review, 21,* 552-565.

Baldwin, A. Y. (1985). Programs for the gifted and talented: Issues concerning minority populations. In F. D. Horowitz & M. O'Brien (Eds.), *The gifted and talented: Developmental perspectives* (pp. 223-249). Washington, DC: American Psychological Association.

Baldwin, A. Y. (1984). *Baldwin Identification Matrix 2. Identification of gifted and talented students* (2nd ed.). New York: Trillium Press.

Barkan, J. H., & Bernal, E. M. (1991). Gifted education for bilingual and limited English proficient students. *Gifted Child Quarterly, 35*, 144-147.

Bensen, A. (1992). Serving the culturally diverse. *Communicator, 22*, 11-12.

Bernal, E. M. (1974). Gifted Mexican American children: An ethnoscientific perspective. *California Journal of Educational Research, 25*, 261-273.

Bernal, E., & Reyna, J. (1974). *Analysis of giftedness in Mexican-American children and design of a prototype identification instrument: Final report* (No. OEC-47-062-113-307). Austin, TX: Southwest Educational Development Laboratory.

Borland, J. H., & Wright, L. (1994). Identifying young, potentially gifted, economically disadvantaged students. *Gifted Child Quarterly, 38*, 164-171.

Brown, L., Sherbenou, R. J., & Johnson, S. K. (1990). *Test of Nonverbal Intelligence-2.* Austin, TX: Pro-Ed.

Budoff, M. (1975). Measuring learning potential: An alternative to the traditional intelligence test. In G. Gredler (Ed.), *Ethical and legal factors in the practice of school psychology: Proceedings of the First Annual Conference in School Psychology* (pp. 75-89). Philadelphia: Temple University Press.

Bureau of the Census. (1992). *Statistical abstracts of the United States, 1992.* Washington, DC: U.S. Government Printing Office.

Burgemeister, B. B., Blum, L. A., & Lorge, I. (1972). *Columbia Mental Maturity Scale* (3rd ed.). New York: Harcourt Brace Jovanovich.

Cheng, L. L., Ima, K., & Labovitz, G. (1994). Assessment of Asian and Pacific Islander students for gifted programs. In S. B. Garcia (Ed.)., *Addressing cultural and linguistic diversity in special education: Issues and trends* (pp. 30-45). Reston, VA: Council for Exceptional Children.

Chinn, P. C., & Hughes, S. (1987). Representation of minority students in special education classes. *Remedial and Special Education, 8*(4), 41-46.

Cummins, J. (1984). *Bilingualism and special education: Issues in assessment and pedagogy.* San Diego: College-Hill.

Davis, G. A. (1989). Testing for creative potential. *Contemporary Educational Psychology, 14,* 257-274.

DeAvila, E. A. (1977). *Cartoon Conservation Scales: Examiner's handbook.* Larkspur, CA: Linguametrics.

Diaz, R. M. (1990). Bilingualism and cognitive ability: Theory, research, and controversy. In A. Barona & E. E. Garcia (Eds.), *Children at risk: Poverty, minority status, and other issues in educational equity* (pp. 91-99). Washington, DC: National Association of School Psychologists.

Esquivel, G. B. (1985). The effects of special classroom placement on the creativity, self-concept, and academic achievement of culturally different gifted children. *SABE Journal, 1,* 18-25.

Esquivel, G. B., & Lopez, E. (1988). Correlations among measures of cognitive ability, creativity, and academic achievement for gifted minority children. *Perceptual and Motor Skills, 67,* 395-398.

Feuerstein, R., Rand, Y., & Hoffman, M. B. (1979). *The dynamic assessment of retarded performers: The Learning Potential Assessment Device: Theory, instruments, and techniques.* Baltimore: University Park Press.

Figueroa, R. A., Sandoval, J., & Merino, B. (1984). School psychology and limited-English-proficient (LEP) children: New competencies. *Journal of School Psychology, 22,* 131-143.

Florey, J., & Tafoya, N. (1988) *Identifying gifted and talented American Indian students: An overview.* Washington, DC: Office of Educational Research and Improvement.

Gardner, H. (1983). *Frames of mind: The theory of multiple intelligences.* New York: Basic Books.

Guilford, J. P. (1956). The structure of the intellect. *Psychological Bulletin, 53,* 267-293.

Guilford, J. P. (1967). *The nature of human intelligence.* New York: McGraw-Hill.

Haensly, P. A., & Torrance, E. P. (1990). Assessment of creativity in children and adolescents. In C. R. Reynolds & R. W. Kamphaus (Eds.), *Handbook of psychological and educational assessment of children: Intelligence and achievement* (pp. 697-722). New York: Guilford.

Hocevar, D. (1981). Measurement of creativity: Review and critique. *Journal of Personality Assessment, 45,* 450-464.

Hunsaker, S. L. (1994). Adjustments to traditional procedures for identifying underserved students: Successes and failures. *Exceptional Children, 61,* 72-76.

Institute for Behavioral Research in Creativity. (1968). *Alpha Biographical Inventory.* Greensboro, NC: Prediction Press.

Leiter, R. G. (1979). *Leiter International Performance Scale.* Chicago: Stoelting.

Lopez, E. C. (1994, March). *Errors made by interpreters during on the spot translations of WISC-R questions.* Paper presented at the meeting of the National Association of School Psychologists, Seattle.

Lopez, E. C. (1995). Best practices in working with bilingual children. In A. Thomas & J. Grimes (Eds.), *Best practices in school psychology III* (pp. 1111-1121). Washington, DC: National Association of School Psychologists.

Lopez, E. C. (1997). The cognitive assessment of limited English proficient and bilingual children. In D. P. Flanagan, J. L. Genshaft, & P. L. Harrison (Eds.), *Contemporary intellectual assessment: Theories, tests, and issues* (pp. 503-516). New York: Guilford Press.

Lopez, E. C., Esquivel, G. B., & Houtz, J. C. (1992) The creative skills of gifted culturally and linguistically diverse students. *Creativity Research Journal, 6*(4), 401-412.

Maker, C. J., Nielson, A. B., & Rogers, J. A. (1994). Giftedness, diversity, and problem-solving. *Teaching Exceptional Children, 27*(1), 4-19.

Marland, S. J. (1972). *Education of the gifted and talented. Report to Congress.* Washington, DC: U.S. Government Printing Office.

McCallum, R. S., & Bracken, B. A. (1997). The Universal Nonverbal Intelligence Test. In D. P. Flanagan, J. L. Genshaft, & P. L. Harrison (Eds.), *Contemporary intellectual assessment: Theories, tests, and issues* (pp. 268-280). New York: Guilford Press.

Melesky, T. J. (1984). Identifying and providing for the Hispanic gifted child. *NABE, 9*(3), 43-57.

Michael, W. B., & Wright, C. R. (1989) Psychometric issues in the assessment of creativity. In J. A. Glover, R. R. Ronning, & C. R. Reynolds (Eds.), *Handbook of creativity* (pp. 33-55). New York: Plenum.

Mistry, J., & Rogoff, B. (1985). A cultural perspective on the development of talent. In F. D. Horowitz & M. O'Brien (Eds.), *The gifted and talented: Developmental perspectives* (pp. 125-144). Washington, DC: American Psychological Association.

Mitchell, B. M. (1988). A strategy for the identification of the culturally different gifted talented child. *Roeper Review, 10*, 163-165.

New York City Public Schools. (1993). *Answers to frequently asked questions about limited English proficient (LEP) students and bilingual ESL programs: Facts and figures 1992-1993*. New York: Author.

Patton, J. M., Prillaman, D., & Van Tassel-Baska, J. (1990). The nature and extent of programs for the disadvantaged gifted in the United States and territories. *Gifted Child Quarterly, 24*, 94-96.

Payan, R. (1989). Language assessment for the bilingual exceptional child. In L. M. Baca & H. T. Cervantes (Eds.), *The bilingual special education interface* (2nd ed., pp. 125-137). New York: Merrill.

Pearson, C. A., & DeMers, S. T. (1990). Identifying the culturally diverse gifted child. In A. Barona & E. E. Garcia (Eds.), *Children at risk: Poverty, minority status, and other issues in educational equity* (pp. 283-296). Washington, DC: National Association of School Psychologists.

Ramirez, A. G. (1990). Perspectives on language proficiency assessment. In A. Barona & E. E. Garcia (Eds.), *Children at risk: Poverty, minority status, and other issues in educational equity* (pp. 305-323). Washington, DC: National Association of School Psychologists.

Rampaul, W. E., Singh, M., & Didyk, J. (1984). The relationship between academic achievement, self-concept, creativity, and teacher expectations among Native children in a Northern Manitoba school. *The Alberta Journal of Educational Research, 30*, 213-225.

Raven, J. C. (1958). *Standard Progressive Matrices*. London: H. K. Lewis.

Reis, S. M., & Renzulli, J. S. (1991). The assessment of creative products in programs for gifted and talented students. *Gifted Child Quarterly, 35*, 128-134.

Renzulli, J. S. (1973). Talent potential in minority group students. *Exceptional Children, 39*, 437-444.

Renzulli, J. S. (1995). Teachers as talent scouts. *Educational Leadership, 52*(4), 75-81.

Renzulli, J. W., & Reis, S. M. (1994). Research related to the Schoolwide Enrichment Triad Model. *Gifted Child Quarterly, 38*, 7-20.

Richert, E. S. (1985). Identification of gifted students: An update. *Roeper Review, 8*, 68-72.

Richert, E. S. (1987). Rampant problems and promising practices in the identification of disadvantaged gifted students. *Gifted Child Quarterly, 31*, 149-154.

Sattler, J. M. (1992). *Assessment of children intelligence and special abilities* (3rd ed.). San Diego: Author.

Smith, D. D., & Luckasson, R. (1995). *Introduction to special education: Teaching in an age of challenge* (2nd ed.). Boston: Allyn & Bacon.

Smith, J., LeRose, B., & Clasen, R. E. (1991). Underrepresentation of minority students in gifted programs: Yes! It matters! *Gifted Child Quarterly, 35*, 81-83.

Sternberg, R. J. (1988). A three-fact model of creativity. In R. Sternberg (Ed.), *The nature of creativity* (pp. 125-147). Cambridge, England: Cambridge University Press.

Taylor, I. A. (1975). A retrospective view of creativity investigation. In I. A. Taylor & J. W. Getzels (Eds.), *Perspectives in creativity* (pp. 1-36). Chicago: Chicago Aldine.

Torrance, E. P. (1963). *Education and the creative potential.* Minneapolis: University of Minnesota.

Torrance, E. P. (1969). Creative positives of disadvantaged children and youth. *Gifted Child Quarterly, 13*, 71-81.

Torrance, E. P. (1972). Predictive validity of the Torrance Tests of Creative Thinking. *The Journal of Creative Behavior, 6*, 236-252.

Torrance, E. P. (1974). *Torrance Tests of Creative Thinking: Norms technical manual.* Princeton, NJ: Personnel Press.

Torrance, E. P. (1978). Dare we hope again? *Gifted Child Quarterly, 22*, 292-312.

Torrance, E. P. (1980). *Thinking creatively in action and movement.* Bensenville, IL: Scholastic Testing Service.

Torrance, E. P. (1984). The role of creativity in the identification of the gifted and talented. *Gifted Child Quarterly, 28*, 153-156.

Toth, L. S., & Baker, S. R. (1990). The relationship of creativity and instructional style preferences to overachievement and underachievement in a sample of public school children. *Journal of Creative Behavior, 24*, 190-198.

U.S. Department of Education. (1994). *Summary of the Bilingual Education State Educational Agency Program survey of states' limited English proficient persons and available educational services, 1992-1993, Final Report.* Arlington, VA: Office of Bilingual Education and Minority Language Affairs.

Woods, S. B., & Achey, V. H. (1990). Successful identification of gifted racial/ethnic group students without changing classification requirements. *Roeper Review, 13*(1), 21-26.

Part 4

---

*Educational Interventions
and Programs*

Chapter 8

Educating the Culturally Diverse Child: An Integrative Approach

Charlene M. Alexander

Ball State University

Melissa D. Shuman-Zarin

Fordham University

This chapter focuses on helping educators find alternative ways to develop the creative ability of culturally diverse children in their classrooms. Torrance's (1963) model of creativity is presented as the theoretical framework for the discussion in this chapter. Torrance defines creativity as the process of: (a) sensing problems or gaps in information, (b) forming ideas or hypotheses testing, (c) modifying those hypotheses, and (d) communicating the results. This process, as he defines it, may lead to any one of many kinds of products; verbal or nonverbal concrete or abstract. For children, it may be the discovery of a new relationship in nature, a song, a poem, a story, or some unusual contraption or gadget. Although the literature has outlined the process necessary to arrive at creative products, little attention has been given to how children from culturally diverse backgrounds might use their cultural heritage in the process of creative development.

The purpose of this chapter is to broaden our concept of creative education so that students from diverse cultural backgrounds can see themselves reflected in the curriculum. Education has far too often followed methodology that has caused children from nontraditional backgrounds to feel left out of the process. Educational methodology must now make a move to reflect the richness of each child's cultural heritage in an attempt to enhance creativity in the classroom. Creativity should be implemented in the classroom as a matter of common practice rather than seen as it so often is as "different" methods used to work with "different" populations. If this new conceptualization can occur, then all children would find their creative self, which would enable them to bring their heritage into the classroom. Celebrating each child's cultural heritage enables all students to learn from each other, which, in turn, would allow them to accept and understand differences as a positive experience.

Creative forms of expression have been found to foster creativity, concept acquisition, self-concept, self-awareness, empathy, and interpersonal skills (Alexander & Sussman, 1995; Frasier, 1991; Griss, 1994; Hoyt, 1992; Kulka, 1987; Moran & Saxton, 1985). Frasier (1991) pointed out that there is an inextricable link between children's natural movement expression and their ability to communicate and problem solve creatively. It is with this in mind that we demonstrate how the incorporation of music, drama, dance, and food in the classroom will foster and enhance the child's natural abilities and talents that stem from their cultural heritage. Far too often teachers understand the process but feel limited in their ability to implement activities into an already restrictive curriculum (Biasini, Thomas, & Pagonowski, 1969; Wright, 1985). Subsequently, we have developed a list of activities that can be used to build a creative curriculum.

The goal of each activity is described along with the anticipated outcomes. A checklist is included at the end of each section for teachers to use following the activity. The activities and checklist were developed with Torrance's theory of creativity in mind. That is, students are encouraged to explore problems or conflicts, forms new ideas or revise earlier hypothesis that can be tested, and finally express this new knowledge utilizing whatever means of communication they deem appropriate. The checklist is adapted from Small (1955) Checklist for New Product Ideas and is a suggested tool to encourage student elaboration and creativity. The checklist should always be revised so as to focus on the present topic of discussion in the class. Furthermore, students should be encourage to generate as many examples of diverse populations as they can.

MUSIC

Music is a common shared element of all cultures. Introducing the content of music into the classroom can appeal to the expression of a diverse student body, as well as enable students to find creative outlets of expression.

Background music can be played in class during free periods. This can be a subtle way by which children and adolescent are exposed to a range of musical expression. It creates a more relaxed and less rigid learning environment. Students should be encouraged to bring in music that they feel reflects their ethnic group. The students should also be encouraged to explain to the group their particular choices of music, the cultural background of the music, and why they made this choice.

Music can also be used to accompany classroom lessons. Historical lessons are often reflected in the music of particular time periods. The lyrics of particular songs often tell stories of people, events, sociopolitical atmospheres, and cultures. Selecting appropriate timepiece music to accompany lessons and text materials could be a way to reach children who have more difficulty with text comprehension. It also makes the lessons more enjoyable and have more of an impact on the students. In addition, in some cultures it is often the music that teaches the history, not a textbook. Thus, the use of music becomes not only a way to reinforce interest, but also serves to further explore other creative methods that have been used to retell history.

Students should also be encouraged to seek out music they feel is appropriate to a presentation topic or that they feel reflects the tone of the material they are studying. For example, if a student is reading a particular book, he or she could seek out music that captures the essence of the book and might make comprehension easier. Furthermore, some students experience difficulties when they have to speak in front of their class. The use of music might decrease their discomfort level. If their anxiety is reduced, then they will be able to explain themselves in a more comfortable manner. It would provide a different experience then just standing up and talking in the front of the room.

Over a period of time students can be exposed to a variety of musical styles (i.e., classical, jazz, spiritual, rock, blues, country, folk,

Caribbean, religious, etc.). After each piece students could be encouraged to reflect what they liked or did not like about that particular style of music and how it impacted him or her. This exercise would enable students to learn not only about music, but also about themselves. Such examples of music exploration would also facilitate self-exploration.

Another way that music can be used to enhance creative expression and self-reflection is having students write while listening to music. Different types of music can be played for students while they are asked to write what feelings or thoughts it evoked. This can be done individually or in a group. For example, the leader plays a song with the theme of racial/ethnic harmony as an example for the group. Students are then put into groups of three to five to work on this assignment. Students are asked to present to the rest of the group the feelings, thoughts, and responses that the song evoked in the group. The program leader then debriefs students on themes that emerge, and the class develops a "wish list" for racial harmony in their neighborhood, world, and so on.

In addition, if a student has an interest in writing his or her own music, that student should be encouraged to do so. Students are asked to think of a song from their racial/ethnic background that talks about celebration. Students can participate individually or in a group. Each student or group then performs a chosen song for the larger group. The program leader identifies commonalties in the different racial/ethnic songs of celebration and shares this with the group.

Checklist

- Create a song that reflects similar feelings to the topic and explain how you developed it.
- Create a song that addresses the role of the family from a culture other than your own.
- Create a song that talks about the role of work and the different roles that individuals can take in the work environment.
- Create a song that talks about the differences and similarities among people from different cultures.
- Create a song that promotes the themes of peace/harmony among different peoples.

DRAMA

Drama, like music, is another creative medium that can be incorporated within an educational setting. Children typically learn about their environment by acting out themes, taking on the roles of different characters and so on. Therefore, encouraging the use of such pretend play with a culturally specific theme is a natural mechanism for a child to learn about his or her world.

Often literature is explored only in written form. Exploration of the particular literature utilizing visual means (i.e., video tapes, plays, movies, etc.) may allow for students to gain a new or clearer understanding of the presented material. This is especially important for students who have more difficulty with text comprehension.

Teachers can use plays to develop and facilitate group dynamics as well as to bring the material alive in the classroom. If students are in the process of reading a particular play for class, scenes should be acted out with a group discussion following the scene. Students should be encouraged to explore literal and creative presentations. The environment or tone of the room should be one that reflects the acceptance of both presentations.

Children can be encouraged to identify novels or works of fiction from their culture and adapt them into a skit. These skits would then be performed for class members. At all times, these interpretations should be as creative and as different as the students choose to make them.

The use of video in the class can also facilitate discussions about how the media represents different cultural experiences. This can aid students in better understanding both their peers backgrounds and the feelings evoked by their experience in the media. It can help students learn to discuss racism, bigotry, and discrimination.

Efforts to explore themes of racial identity can also be enhanced through the integration of drama in classroom lessons. For example, students can be assigned a particular topic and then be asked to explore any feelings that were evoked. They would then be asked to write any thoughts they had about the feeling that developed. Students could also be assigned a particular feeling such as sad, happy, mad, lazy, and so on. They would be asked to describe what that feeling means to them and what it is like to have that feeling. Then they would have to act it out physically, verbally, or vocally and act it out with their classmates. The goal would be to help the students explore how different feelings bring up different things in different people, and that based on our emotions we can interact in very different ways. This method can also be applied to cultural experiences. Students can explore what other cultural groups experience as they take on roles that are different from their own group and interact with their classmates based on their perception of those culture groups. Students can hopefully learn to negotiate between perceptions, stereotypes, and truths.

The use of drama games such as "machine" (i.e., in which one person initiates an act, followed by a second individual who builds on that act to construct a machine that works together) and "trust" (i.e., students work in a pair with one wearing a blindfold while the other partner walks him or her around the room, trusting that the partner would care for him or her) can be used to help the class learn to work together. This shows students that verbal communication is not the only method of achieving group cohesiveness.

Another way in which drama can be used to increase group development is through role play and improvisation. In the construction of skits, students can take on different roles that lead to the creation of the scene. Someone might be assigned the role of director, actor, playwright (if he or she is working on a novel), set designer, and so on. If the piece of work is to come together and be performed for an audience, the participants must learn to work with one another.

Skits can also be used to further explore lessons in history, sociopolitical environments, and different cultural experiences. Students can be asked to bring in stories or plays that they feel reflect something about their culture or heritage, or a culture or heritage they would like to explore further.

Video use should also be implemented to support books and plays that are being studied in the classroom. Students can be shown different ways that the media have interpreted literature and asked to explore the difference between the media interpretation and the literature. In addition, many pieces of literature, including "Romeo and Juliet," and "West Side Story," "Somewhere over the Rainbow" and "The Wiz," have been interpreted by different people utilizing different cultural backgrounds. If teachers can acquire different videos or plays of the same literature piece, students cannot only understand creative interpretation, but also gain an understanding of different cultural experiences.

Checklist

- Create a skit/play that reflects similar feelings to the topic matter.
- Create a skit/play that addresses the role of the family from a culture other than your own.

- Create a skit that talks about the role of work and the different roles that individuals can take within the work environment.
- Create a skit that talks about the differences and similarities between people from different cultures.
- Create a skit/play that promotes the theme of peace/harmony among different peoples.

DANCE

Dance is another creative medium practiced among all cultures. It can be a traditional tool used to reflect a group's feelings, ways of coping, celebrating, and resolving conflict.

Dance can be used to help students experience how different emotions affect their bodies. The teacher will begin by modeling this exercise for the students. The teacher will think of an emotion in a "scene" and will nonverbally communicate how he or she is feeling by adopting a single pose and expression that reflects this "scene" (e.g., the leader might be thinking of a time when he or she first left home and was feeling lonely or scared). Students have to guess what the teacher is trying to portray. The first to guess or come closest then does his or her own story or emotion.

A dance can be demonstrated for the group that identifies common wishes for racial/ethnic harmony. For example, a possible ice breaker activity can be included with two objectives: (a) to establish rapport and familiarity between students and between students and program leaders, and (b) for students to see similarities in the ways people have fun and to learn cooperation and joining. The program leader chooses three students to stay outside of the group. The rest of the group stands in a circle holding hands. Someone is chosen as leader, and he or she begins to weave in and out of the circle, while everyone continues to hold hands, until the group looks like a large pretzel. Now the students originally kept out of the group work together to get everyone disentangled. Every week different students are chosen so that everyone can experience what it feels like to lead and/or to disentangle.

To celebrate diversity, students will be asked to bring in one item from their home that they feel reflects their heritage. Students will also be asked to bring in a brief report, to be presented orally next session, of someone who they believe has contributed to the positive reputation of their racial/ethnic heritage. It is important to note that this can be someone alive or dead and can be from music, literature, politics, or other.

Examples can be used to demonstrate that conflict resolution is a cross-cultural phenomenon. Students are asked to identify music from their cultures that describe a conflict and how it this conflict is resolved. The music is performed or played for the entire class, and the student shares the conflict and its resolution with the group. Students are encouraged to dance out the conflict and the resolution. The group discusses the conflict and compares and contrasts it with the other cultures represented in the room. In addition, other students can then be asked to dance their interpretation of the same conflict and resolution.

The "Electric Slide" or the "Macarena" can be used to help students discover how difficult it is for persons entering a culture for the first time to understand and adopt its rules and mores. Students are taught the dance the "Electric Slide" or the "Macarena" by the teacher. Everyone is encouraged to participate until most of the students can accomplish it with relative ease. The teacher then discusses with the group: (a) how it felt to participate; (b) what prevented students from participating, and (c) what would encourage students to participate. It is explained that the dance is a metaphor for how it feels to enter a new culture. Students are then encouraged to share a dance from their own culture that the entire group may participate.

Checklist

- Create a dance that reflects a similar theme to the topic matter.
- Create a dance based on the study of a culture other than your own.
- Create a dance that reflects the differences and similarities between people from different cultures.
- Create a dance that promotes a theme of peace and harmony among different people.

FOOD

The use of food in a classroom cannot only be a way to introduce students to different cultures, but also to create group cohesiveness. Much of the foods we eat are often rooted in the tradition of a cultural group. Bringing food into the classroom can be a social means of learning. The following are suggestions on how food can be used in the classroom to learn about different cultures.

At the beginning of the school year students can be asked to find a food that is part of their heritage and prepare a little background information on the food they choose such as how it is traditionally prepared, eaten, in what setting, and so on. Then students can be assigned a Friday at some point during the school year when they will bring in the food for the class. Thus, each Friday the group will get to experience a little bit of heritage and have a social experience.

At the beginning of the school year students can be asked to find a food that is representative of a cultural group different from their own. They will be responsible for exploring the history behind the dish and presenting it to the class. Again, they would be assigned a particular Friday during the school year to bring in the food for the class and make the presentation.

Food can be used to complement lessons on history that focus on different cultural group's experience. That is, if the lesson is on Native Americans, students can be encouraged to explore what foods Native Americans ate and why, and they can try to recreate it for their classmates. As part of this, students can explore the foods by trying to make them in the classroom. This would also facilitate group work.

When holiday parties approach, classrooms should explore the different holidays that are occurring and try to bring in different foods to represent the various occasions.

Checklist

- Choose a new dish to share with your family and discuss with them their reaction to the food.
- Create dishes for the multiple ways that cultures work.
- Create a dish that reflects the culture of your school.
- Create foods for the celebration of peace.

CONCLUSION

In writing this chapter, we have set out to demonstrate that the aspects of one's culture that exist in everyday life can be developed and incorporated into an school-based curriculum. We highlighted specific activities that can be used to encourage a wide range of cultural experiences—music, drama, dance, and food. All the activities have been designed to encourage students' creativity as a means of learning and understanding. At the same time, the goal is to encourage the development of a curriculum that celebrates the strengths of a culturally diverse student population and promotes positive racial identity among students. We do not suggest that all activities will be appropriate for all classroom settings, rather, these are suggestions that we hope will encourage food for thought.

REFERENCES

Alexander, C. M., & Sussman, L. (1995). Creative approaches to multicultural counseling. In J. G. Ponterotto, J. M. Casas, L. A. Suzuki, & C. M. Alexander (Eds.), *Handbook of multicultural counseling* (pp. 375-384). Thousand Oaks, CA: Sage.

Biasini, A., Thomas, R., & Pagonowski, L. (1969). *Early childhood music curriculum*. Bardonia, NY: Media Materials.

Frasier, M. (1991). Disadvantaged and culturally diverse gifted students. *Journal for the Education of the Gifted, 14*, 234-245.

Griss, S. (1994). Creative movement: A language for learning. *Educational Leadership, 51*, 78-80.

Hoyt, L. (1992). Many ways of knowing: Using drama, oral interactions, and the visual arts to enhance reading comprehension. *The Reading Teacher, 45*(8), 580-585.

Kulka, K. (1987). David Booth: Drama as a way of knowing. *Language Arts, 64*(1), 73-78.

Moran, N., & Saxton, J. (1985). Working with drama: A different order of experience. *Theory into Practice, 24*(3), 211-218.

Small, M. (1955). *How to make more money*. New York: Pocket Books.

Torrance, E. P. (1963). *Creativity*. Washington, DC: National Education Association.

Wright, L. (1985). Preparing teachers to put drama in the classroom. *Theory into Practice, 24*(3), 205-210.

Chapter 9

The Quintessential Features of Gifted Education as Seen From a Multicultural Perspective

Ernesto M. Bernal
University of Texas-Pan American

INTRODUCTION

Much has been written about different aspects of gifted education, from the administration/management of these programs to the selection of teachers. Certainly the education of the gifted is not a facile matter. But neither is it so complex that it should serve to confuse the public or prevent a would-be adopter from attempting to accommodate gifted and talented children in the schools.

In this chapter we summarize the range of factors present in gifted education and then attempt to distill the quintessential features of the program. We do so, however, not from the point of view that all current features of gifted-talented (GT) education need to be preserved, but from the perspective that the social and economic exigencies of the 21st century will for the first time force the United States to find and appropriately educate all of its most able learners. Demographically speaking, this will include the GT

159

children from the United States' nondominant ethnic groups and those who are females (O'Connell-Ross, 1993). It is our hope that this radical change in the way GT educators conduct their business will also result in the full utilization of the diversity that naturally exists in groups of GT children so that homogenization and deracination will not occur, and that our nascent leaders will be able to forge at last a society in which all human beings are equal before the law and have equal opportunities to become educated and earn a living (Bernal, 1996b). To prepare GT programs that support this social ideal is not, we believe, nearly as difficult as maintaining the present system of GT education. Seen from the perspective of a multicultural ideal for the 21st century, it should be possible to simplify GT education, concentrating on the design and implementation of its quintessential features, and produce thereby an even more rigorous program for all the students whom we expect to become gifted adults.

IDENTIFICATION/SELECTION ISSUES

The historical practice in GT programs has been to identify only the highly achieved gifted children. This implies that we have largely excluded from this service those students with underdeveloped potential or handicapping conditions (Whitmore, 1980). Teachers usually nominate those students who are striving, conforming, high achievers from more or less traditional backgrounds, those who are "competitive" (see Thorkildsen, 1994). Children who are from the lower socioeconomic classes or who carry a label such as "special ed," limited-English-proficient (LEP), or migrant rarely have their names sent forward (Seidell, 1985); and teacher nomination is the most frequently used means of student identification ("Richardson Study," 1985). Schools that are stigmatized as minority or "Title I" schools are often not seen as places that spawn GT students (High & Udall, 1983).

Barkan and Bernal (1991) pointed out that the "most perplexing populations for traditional educators of the gifted to select and educate are the gifted children from language-minority groups" (p. 144), especially while they are still lacking proficiency in English. The upshot is that many intellectually eligible children are not nominated, much less identified or selected, until they are older, when they become proficient enough in English to be tested in that language. By that time, however, they have not received appropriate services for a year or more (usually more, in our experience) and may have already been functionally "tracked" because of their initial lack of English (see Diaz, Moll, & Mehan, 1986) into regular or even other compensatory programs. And even if they are nominated, the tests they must pass may be subtly but sufficiently biased to lower their estimated intelligence and achievement scores (see Fradd & Hallman, 1983) to the point at which they are not selected. In this author's experience (Bernal, 1985), even the brightest Hispanic children (as measured by IQ tests administered in English)—children with Weshler IQs in excess of 140—rarely do uniformly well (e.g., above the 98th percentile) across the different achievement subtests if they come from severely impoverished homes or have to attend several schools during the year due to their families' mobility.

Traditionally, status programs seeking to identify students have been able to maintain an exclusive posture by using multiple cutoffs (as opposed to multiple criteria) for inclusion. Using multiple critical scores—for example, requiring 97-percentile scores on both IQ and total achievement tests—is a practice that has great appeal and "face" validity. In reality it merely serves to screen out the bright but unevenly achieved and the well achieved but unevenly bright students (e.g., children whose composite Wechsler IQ falls just short of the critical score)—conditions that are not especially stable and that could be easily and normally corrected after the child would gain access to the GT program. Here it is important to keep in mind (a) that multiple cutoffs are rarely necessary in real life, in which total intellectual performance is what counts, as in creative productivity; and (b) that these procedures, for all their "face validity," have never been empirically validated (Bernal, 1990b).

Renzulli (1984) cautioned that "we must reexamine identification procedures that result in the total pre-selection of certain students and the concomitant implication that these youngsters are and always will be gifted" (p. 164). He rejected the notion that tests alone can determine who is gifted and who is not and maintained that gifted behavior can be developed in persons who do not necessarily meet the traditional critical scores on IQ and achievement tests.

The label "gifted" can actually be counterproductive to programming (Renzulli, 1987). The emphasis should be on "developing gifted behavior in the youngster who have the highest potential for benefiting from special services" (p. 61).

Some GT programs, meaning well, have responded to these inequities by establishing quasi-quota systems such as those advocated by Mitchell (1988) and Storlie, Bellis, Powills, and Prapuolenis (1978). Such adjustments, however, are based on traditional approaches to identification and basically consist of lowering the selection scores for children of nondominant ethnic groups in order to achieve a measure of equity in representation and opportunity. Bernal (1994) has opposed such systems because he feels that (a) they stigmatize the previously underrepresented populations, who are now included in greater numbers; and, more importantly, (b) they are based on traditionally defensible criteria that nevertheless produce too many false negatives such as that which exclude too many children who would succeed in GT programs if offered the opportunity, especially if these programs were multiculturally sensitive by design (see Matute-Bianchi, 1986; Ogbu & Matute-Bianchi, 1986).

The use of multiple criteria (vs. multiple cutoffs) has been a move in the right direction because this system allows for some (usually unspecified) compensation across a set of selection/identification variables. In such schemes, for instance, achievement data are frequently used in combination with IQ and reviews of student products, or, more recently, portfolios may play a part in the placement decision as well. These approaches to selection, although generally being more inclusionary, are in the author's experience still subject to cultural bias and are still dominated by the IQ test. The only basic difference between multiple criteria and multiple cutoffs, after all, is the willingness to interplay the variables. But unless one has empirical data based on multiple regression studies of a longitudinal nature to support the weights that these variables are assigned, and unless one uses this system strictly once it is set up, my experience has been that multiple criteria devolve into a "flexible" selection process that is fraught with inconsistencies and privilege.

Gallagher (1991) recommends "special programs" (e.g., talent pools), in which students "who show a high level of responsiveness would then [later] be placed in the standard program for gifted students" (p. 26). This is a moderate to conservative position because it is the child, essentially, that makes all the accommodation. Smith and Perez (1992) caution us against special efforts aimed solely at increasing the number of nondominant ethnic students in the GATE program because they believe that it does not produce any lasting changes in the way the gifted program operates: "Giftedness . . . expresses itself in groups of gifted students in a multitude of ways. We, in gifted education, should have written the book on equity" (p. 1). "One of the important responsibilities of gifted programs is to take risks in the development of potential" (p. 42). "Heavy reliance on tests alone [for identification] suggests a desire to avoid risks" (p. 42). Bernal (1992) would like to see a reconfiguration of the program so that the needs of all students are met, bilingual children do not lose their native language proficiency, and the mental health of minority children is not compromised through deracinating messages from teachers and the curriculum. Exum and Colangelo (1981) believe that nondominant ethnic children need to identify with their groups of origin as part of their personal identity development.

The method of bringing children into the GT program that this author supports is essentially eclectic, a method I believe fits the diversity of potential that those in the profession refer to as gifted. To implement this model one need only to replace the status practice of identification with the professional practice of selection. This practice involves the use of multiple criteria but does not stop there. Selection also utilizes talent pools for children who have demonstrated that they do well under accelerated instruction, be that in an English monolingual class or in a bilingual class. Figure 9.1 indicates one way of doing this through K-2 talent pools in districts with large numbers of LEP children. Note that (a) traditional testing criteria are applied late in the process to children who initially were deemed to succeed better at a regular educational pace, (b) a parallel bilingual GT program operates during these early years, and (c) most importantly, children in the bilingual GT program exit to a multicultural GT program, not to the regular educational program, in which they might languish while waiting to be nominated.

In order to focus less on identification and more on selection, keep the following key points in mind (see Bernal, 1990a, 1990b). First, no extant test or battery of tests measures giftedness per se, and the "cut score" for giftedness on IQ tests has never been validated. Focus on admission, not "identification," and validate your criteria against those who actually succeed or fail in the GT program.

Second, there are few manifestly gifted children, far too few to justify a program. Our only real justification for the GT program is the expectation that it will select potentially gifted children and produce more gifted adults. We need to understand that, in perhaps 99% of the cases, the children we identify are still too young to be manifestly gifted, that is, to make independent contributions to a profession or a field, contributions that cannot be ignored. And those that do are prodigies. Everybody knows about them, for they make news. There is no need to test them, just admit them. The rest of the children in GT programs are merely selected, although most of these are deemed to have been "identified gifted."

Third, a program's "standards" are not really concerned with admissions; standards for students are correctly applied at the point of exit or certification or graduation or other climacteric signifying some sort of completion or transition. Admissions and selection are the proper terms to use, not identification, and admissions criteria should guide the selection process, preferably one that has been

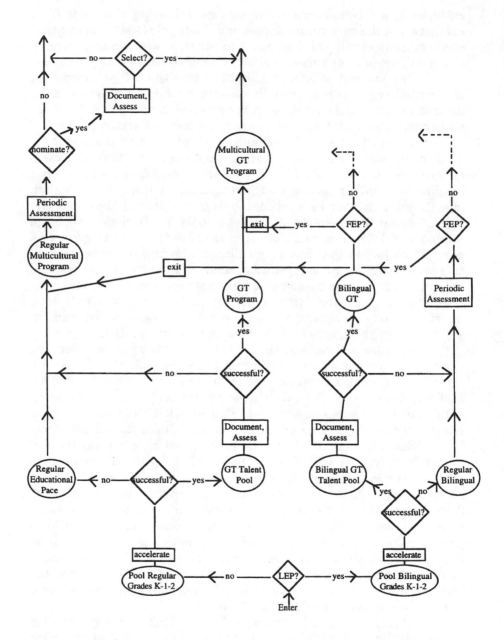

Figure 9.1. Parallel bilingual, GT, and regular programs: Meeting the needs of all children through multicultural education

validated through experience and focused on both the purpose of the program and the processes that it emphasizes.

Fourth, the other factor for success lies in programming, designing, and actually delivering a program that takes care of two concerns: (a) a program must build on the students' assessed characteristics—"must play to what they've got;" and (b) a program needs to "give 'em what they need," develop a strong knowledge or skills base, critical thinking and investigative and evaluative skills, a tolerance for ambiguity coupled with a dedication to excellence, the security to take intelligent risks and to be creative, the serenity to cope with failures constructively, and the ethical habit of seeking to do the right thing, not an obsession to do things right.

Fifth and finally, to be successful in the long run the GT program's staff members must commit themselves to the process of refining the program continuously. Evaluation and improvement are the proper exercises for experiencing the GT professionals' own gifts and talents.

What are the stakes of these admissions? The stakes are the GT program's resources. The bet is that the selected children and the GT teachers, with a little bit of honest effort, will make a little magic when they come together. And what should be left after the program's puff of smoke clears away? The product should be a bunch of gifted young men and women.

Keeping these points in mind, the GT staff and the GT teachers can design a system for admission and a curriculum that will do the job for all the bright children in the district. A commitment to serve all the children who are bright, who have potential for giftedness, says that the GT program is willing to work to produce results. I like to put it like this: The real purpose of the gifted program is to select children who are highly able learners for the purpose of producing gifted young adults. Conduct a talent pool that accelerates instruction, that hot-houses the flower pots to see which ones will germinate and blossom. Those who do are prime candidates for admission because they have authentically demonstrated their ability to succeed in the GT program, not just on IQ tests.

GT PROGRAM AS DEVELOPER OF A DIVERSE POOL OF TALENT AND INTELLIGENCE

Any GT program that wishes to include all high ability children must be willing to accommodate those who have what Baldwin (1987) calls "skill weaknesses." Do not be confused on this issue, however, for children from nondominant ethnic groups are not all "weak," in the achievement sense, and not all children from the dominant group are "strong." The questions here are (a) whether the GT program wishes to include all bright children—for example, disadvantaged children or handicapped children—or only those who are well achieved in every subject; and (b) how it would go about correcting their "weaknesses." Baldwin (1987) and O'Connell-Ross (1993) make the case that the GT curriculum should use these children's individual areas of strength to encourage the growth of less-developed skills. Baldwin (1994) cited the example of the Seven Plus program in Brooklyn, NY, as one that capitalizes on Gardner's "multiple intelligences" to identify and instruct a multiethnic, low-socioeconomic status student body. Goertz, Phemister, and Bernal (1996) described a Saturday morning program that provides broadening experiences to disadvantaged and advantaged GT students alike, and Kirschenbaum (1988) and Sisk (1993) described successful summer programs that provide for critical thinking, self-esteem, and academic development. To some extent these programs exist to promote giftedness among the disadvantaged, recognizing the reluctance of established GT programs to make any significant changes to accommodate these students (Spicker, 1993).

According to Bernal (1986c), the public schools would seem to have sheltered both regular education and GT from the need to make major adjustments to accommodate the characteristics of a changing school clientele. GT educators, for instance, fear compromising the nature of GT education and its "standards." Some educators worry that a more broadly based program would dissipate GT funds and make the program appear to be a "frill" (Silverman, 1993). But perhaps they fear the prospect of having to learn how to work with culturally and linguistically diverse (CLD) children in integrated settings in ways that will actually require the GT program to attract and motivate a more widely representative group of GT students: "Change is more palatable when we know how to proceed and can anticipate its effects on the educational institution" (Bernal, 1986c, p. 137). To avoid admitting more CLD students into the program, exclusionary GT education has been willing to sacrifice many White children whose achievement or IQ profiles are also "different." Heterogeneity among the potentially gifted students can have healthy effects on a GT program, "including curricular diversity and a less elitist image, without compromising excellence" (Bernal, 1986c, p. 143). These practices do not spell the end of GT education but the beginning of an exciting, rigorous curriculum.

Reis et al. (1993) reported that 95% of the teachers in the Curricular Compacting Study were able to identify high-ability students accurately. Although more complete data were not presented, it is clear that training has a positive effect on GT teachers' skill in finding eligible children from all ethnic groups.

Treffinger (1991) holds that a stronger definition of giftedness, based on our understanding of human talent and abilities, would shift the view away from tests of maximal performance to evidence for a potential for creative productivity. Such a change would make giftedness a complex, dynamic, and growth-oriented concept. The needed shift should be "in the direction of more flexible, inclusive, and instructionally oriented conceptions and away from using identification simply to include or exclude students from a particular category" (p. 445). In short, GT programs should move beyond talent identification to talent development by providing enriching opportunities that begin in the regular classroom and move toward a differentiated curriculum for highly able learners (see Stewart, 1985).

"Gifted programs can no longer simply serve those students who have actualized their talents" (Smith & Perez, 1992, p. 42). "Teaching gifted children requires . . . knowing how to modify what we do in classrooms so that the underrepresented gifted child functions as a vital participant" (p. 42). "Teaching the gifted should never have meant working with a [culturally] homogenous population" (p. 43). Bernal (1986b) believes that diversity within the gifted program also makes for a more exciting, more rigorous program that challenges the educators to grow as much as the students. It also lets students identify more closely with the school program they experience (see Ford & Harris, 1990). Indeed nondominant ethnic students need to discover that they can be successful on their own terms, that they do not have to "sound White" to be accepted into the program and feel their presence is appreciated (see Gregory, 1992). Part of the accommodation of GT students from nondominant ethnic groups is really no more difficult than accounting for a wide diversity of expression of talent, ability, and creativity (see Runco, 1993). Gallagher (1991) and Perez and Bernal (1996) described multicultural programs in two Big City school systems (Chicago and San Diego). Some of the Chicago programs have begun experimenting with bilingual programs, and San Diego has established a pre-K to grade 5 bilingual program in several schools with high concentrations of English-language learners with good results.

POSTMODERN: INCLUSIONISM WITH OR WITHOUT IDENTIFICATION

As early as 1962, Hilda Taba spoke about the adverse effects of homogenous grouping on GT students because of the isolation and competitiveness that this practice tends to create. More recently the negative effects of tracking students have been studied generally (Oakes, 1985), and the response of the profession has been inclusionism or the Regular Education Initiative, the attempt to integrate all students successfully into the regular classroom and to do away with all labels such as LD or gifted. The literature, however, is quite clear insofar as GT students are concerned: best results occur when GT students spend a significant amount of time studying together under the tutelage of a well-trained teacher (Allan, 1991; Kulik & Kulik, 1989; O'Neil, Gallagher, & Haycock, 1993; Reis, 1994). It is not yet clear that teachers will successfully work with a wide range of ability and a wide range of needs (Tomlinson, 1996). Compromises and adaptations still need to be studied (Gentry, 1996) for their impacts on GT and other students alike:

> The range of existing adaptions of school programs for gifted children is quite remarkable and sometimes obscures the fact that they were all attempts to meet these three specific problems: the wide range of ability, teachers' limitations in content areas, and teachers' lack of special methods. (Gallagher, 1985, p. 79)

INSTRUCTIONAL DELIVERY MODELS: ARRANGING THE DELIVERY OF GT INSTRUCTION

In-class Accommodation

One of the principal reasons for attempting in-class accommodation of the gifted is to avoid setting up a separate program that is elitist or exclusionary and that removes the most able learners from influencing other students in general classes (O'Neil et al., 1993), limits classroom teachers' willingness to meet individual needs, and impairs the creation of a classroom climate of inclusion and acceptance of human differences (Sapon-Shevin, 1994). Archambault et al. (1993), under the sponsorship of the National Research Center of the Gifted and Talented, surveyed a large group of third- and fourth-grade teachers in public and private schools with high concentrations of minority students to determine the extent to which

GT students receive differentiated instruction in the regular classroom. The results were disappointing but not unpredictable: Third and fourth grade teachers in all types of schools make only minor modifications in their regular curriculum to accommodate their GT students, and even those who did try to accommodate them did so only within the confines of their classrooms. Archambault et al. (1993) also concluded that regular classroom teachers in schools in which a gifted program is formally established serve their GT students no better than teachers in schools with no gifted program: "Unfortunately, in their zeal for equalitarian equality, schools have turned away from ability-based grouping even within classrooms" (Reis, 1994, p. 39). This movement coincides with the current rise of detracking or inclusionism (Reis, 1994), and this author suspects that as much support training would be required for the regular teacher to work with GT students as seems to be required for the regular teacher to work with disabled individuals.

Another form of in-class accommodation is within-class grouping or clustering (see Clark, 1983; Schuler, 1997), the second most popular programming option (Cox, Daniels, & Boston, 1985). Deliberate within-class grouping of GT students for instructional purposes has produced "positive academic effects" (Allan, 1991). This arrangement, however, contrasts sharply from in-class accommodation that does not provide for GT children to interact as a group as part of the learning experience provided. In some cases a peripatetic resource teacher works with the GT students in their classroom for a period of time on a regular basis. In other cases acceleration of these students can make room for enriching experiences within the regular school day (see Reis et al., 1993).

A mixed model is the Schoolwide Enrichment Triad. Renzulli and Reis (1994) have summarized some 15 years of field research on this model, which essentially provides two levels of enrichment to most students and a Type III for higher ability students that often involves resource rooms. It appears that Good and Brophy's (1984) proposal for a "stratified heterogeneous grouping" of students could also support the clustering and enrichment models by reducing some of the variability within classrooms while still mixing together moderately diverse levels of ability.

Good and Brophy's model has the advantage of apportioning different combinations of high, medium, and low achievers to different teachers so that all of them have a mix of all three *without* having the full range. Although all teachers would have to differentiate instruction in their classrooms, the degree of accommodation would not be nearly so great as one finds in the modern inclusionary classroom. In Good and Brophy's arrangement, however, not every teacher would have to be able to work with the gifted, although at least one in every three would probably need this training.

This author (Bernal, 1986b) advocates that the best compromise for elementary schools may result by deliberately assigning a cluster of GT students—a "critical mass" of four or five— to a classroom with an appropriately credentialed teacher. For most elementary campuses this would mean one teacher of the gifted per grade level. Such an arrangement, furthermore, would ensure GT students' continuity in an appropriately challenging program from year to year (see Maker, 1982) and would facilitate the designated teachers' planning together. Cluster grouping appears to be a cost-effective means of ensuring appropriate instruction in a moderately heterogeneous class environment (Gentry, 1996).

A related program, especially at the secondary level, is the special or advanced class (Allan, 1991). For middle and high schools, in which subject-matter specialists teach the courses, only the teachers of the advanced placement or honors courses would have to be organized to meet those students' needs and to update the curriculum, especially for honors courses, in which traditional subjects can be meaningfully integrated around themes and realistic problems (Bernal, 1996b). In this arrangement GT students remain in heterogeneous classes most of the day and take only those advanced courses for which they are deemed to have exceptional talent.

A few schools—for example, 8% in Texas (Gaddis-Davidson, 1993)—report using independent study to support GT students. If such efforts are regularized they can serve to give students a real opportunity to work on extended projects and develop personal contacts with experts. Teachers, however, need to stay involved in order to ensure growth in critical thinking and opportunities for the independent study to be shared with authentic audiences (Goertz, 1996).

Pullout Programs

Resource room "pullouts," or part-time special classes, is the most popular approach to GT education (Cox et al., 1985; Gaddis-Davidson, 1993) because one certified teacher can work with many GT children of different ages and diverse interests. This arrangement, however, is not without problems and faces many of the same criticisms of pullout programs generally. One of the principal difficulties has proven to be the attitude of the homeroom teacher, whose cooperation—and, preferably, collaboration—must be counted on if the GT students are not to suffer. For this reason some pullout programs are combined with regular classroom clusters of GT children, ensuring the work of the regular classroom teacher with a deliberately assembled cluster of GT students in the class (Clark, 1983).

Another form of a pullout program consists of regularly taking children to a special school or center for intense instruction or enrichment, usually on topics that can be covered in a day, or for specialized lessons such as art or music that are not offered at these children's neighborhood schools. These excursions are often referred to as Special Day programs.

Yet another type of pullout program involves concurrent enrollment in a community college or nearby university for the purpose of providing secondary-level GT students the opportunity to earn college credits while meeting high school graduation requirements (e.g., taking college-level courses in English literature, chemistry, and U.S. government) or to take advanced or specialized courses (O'Connell-Ross, 1993).

Clark (1983) emphasizes "flexible" groupings of GT students so that even the special GT class has some integrated classes for part of each day (see also Good & Brophy, 1984). One such arrangement in the Joplin Plan which requires that each core subject be taught at a designated time so that individual students' abilities may be better accommodated by assigning them to teachers of these subjects at different grade levels (Subotnik, 1998).

Out-of-Class Enrichment

Various extra-class arrangements have been made. Summer programs, including the Governor's school model (principally in the South), provide enrichment and in some cases acceleration. The program associated with the Study of Mathematically Precocious Youth at Johns Hopkins University (SMPY), for example, accelerates students in mathematics (Fox, 1977; see also Sisk, 1993). The Center for Academic Precocity at Arizona State University offers a full menu of enrichment courses for school-aged youth. There are also before-school and after-school and weekend programs; some such as the New Challenge (Goertz et al., 1996) provide thematic instruction in ethnically integrated settings on weekends, which permits GT children from different schools and districts to interact.

Mentorships work, especially when combined with independent study, but they require considerable effort to set up, maintain, and in some cases to qualify the mentors as good persons for the schools to recommend or recognize.

Full-Time Programs

Special GT classes operating full time within a school (including individualized classrooms with GT clusters), schools-within-schools, and special schools, with or without a magnet theme, constitute the basic four full-time options for ability-grouped GT students. These arrangements, of course, appear to be the most "elitist," but also offer the easiest ways to meet GT students' needs for mentoring, acceleration, and independent study. Some full-time programs presuppose the selection of students who excel in virtually every subject—a kind of special class for every class—but others, in the author's experience, are committed to introducing the brightest children to the most demanding and enriching classes, even if they do not all earn As in the process. This tacit accommodation to a limited form of diversity gives me hope for GT programs' acquiring ethnic diversity as well. As Whitmore (1980) has warned, "future research could prove that the regular classroom is the most restrictive environment for the gifted child . . . [particularly] if teachers are not helped to become more able to effectively individualize instruction" (p. 68). O'Neil et al. (1993) think that those who would do heterogeneous grouping need to explain how they plan to work with students "at the top and at the bottom" (p. 8). "The toll is . . . potentially great on a personal level for gifted students who must go without special services" (Tammi, 1990, p. 44).

The consensus among educators of the gifted is that a GT program must provide enrichment and acceleration (Tannenbaum, 1986). The latter allows children to move faster through the curriculum and to reach advanced levels of achievement (e.g., advanced placement) even before they enter college; the former provides experiences not ordinarily given to all students to broaden their lives and explore diverse career options (Feldhusen, 1991) that regular students would not realistically consider. Over the years (e.g., Allan, 1991; Kulik & Kulik, 1989; Pressey, 1966) it has been shown that GT students do not suffer from these experiences.

CURRICULUM AND METHODS: WHAT TO TEACH AND HOW TO TEACH IT

The bases of any attempt to design a truly "differentiated" curriculum for the gifted are the content and methods that are used (Bernal, 1986a, 1986c; Reis, 1994). Seven points about curriculum are developed here.

Acceleration

Acceleration of instruction, especially of the basic or critical elements defined for a grade level in elementary school or for subjects or blocks in secondary school, is one of the defining characteristics of gifted education. "Covering" these materials quickly (Reis et al., 1993), or integrating them almost casually into larger units of instruction, makes time in the schedule to allow for advanced studies and the exploration of skills and understandings that very able learners can handle at comparatively early ages and develop to advanced or subtle levels of sophistication by the time they are in high school (Feldhusen, 1989).

Higher-Order Thinking Skills, Critical Thinking Skills

There is a discipline to the acquisition of higher-order thinking skills, especially when these are expressed in a group setting such as a classroom. Questioning, brainstorming, hypothesizing, argumentation, and generalization—these skills can be explicitly modeled and taught (see Taba & Hills, 1965). One needs to leave room for students' styles and initiatives, however (Runco, 1993), else "our students will not greet the teaching of higher-level thinking with great joy" (Udall, 1992, p. 13). Students need to discover their abilities (Williamson, 1992), but calling on this natural tendency toward heterostatic explorations of their environments and their own abilities (Menninger, Mayman, & Pruyser, 1963) may occur more spontaneously in real or meaningful problems or issues in which solutions perforce involve several subject matters or traditional disciplines (Bernal, 1986b; McIntosh, Journal, & Meacham, 1992).

Computer Skills and Applications

A way to promote the development of essential computer skills and independent habits of work is to introduce computers to children—particularly the disadvantaged, who may not be able to access computers at home—as integral to their regular assignments (Trifiletti, 1985). Everything from word processing to computer simulations and imaging to searching distant databases is possible if the computers are connected to each other through local area networks and connected to the Internet and to e-mail. The ideal is to move children to the level at which they can learn independently and engage in academic "conversations" with mentors and other GT children in distant sites.

Thematic, Interdisciplinary Units of Instruction and Study

Content should be "organized around broad-based concepts, themes, and problems" (McIntosh et al., 1992, p. 3) such as the notion of "Change," instead of more "concrete" themes, such as "Puritans," which allow only the explorations of interconnections and are too teacher-centered.

For Bernal (1986b) this approach resolves to:

1. Solving real (not contrived or socially "distant") problems
2. Developing critical thinking skills, including expressible skills, questioning skills, and vocabulary
3. Avoiding the deracination of nondominant ethnic groups; more positively, teaching in and about the cultures represented in the classroom
4. Eschewing compensatory approaches for any underperforming gifted children.

So a better theme than "Change" might be "Local Ecological Problems" for elementary students, "School Rules: To Promote Character Development or Institutional Control?" for middle school classrooms, and "Immigration, Social Conflict, and Social Change: A Sociological History of the United States" for high school social studies. These are "hot topics" that would teach children to learn to think—and how to behave—under the pressures that attend controversy. To help them develop values and self-awareness, the social and affective consequences of being a high-level "producer or performer" need to be explored as well (Tannenbaum, 1986).

These practices, I believe (Bernal, 1986b, 1996b) may also help to broaden gifted students' academic repertoires by correlating their interests to other disciplines and through intense interaction with GT peers. As Tafolla (personal communication, December 22, 1996) put it: "I learned all these other things not to compete with my friends but to be able to understand what they were saying."

Enrichment

One important aspect of enrichment has to do with ensuring that GT students become aware of "significant value dilemmas, social alternatives, the implication of social trends and decision making at all levels of government" (Wasgschal, 1980, p. 9). This sounds a lot like moral education and could certainly lead to values-clarification experiences under the expectation that tomorrow's leaders need to know themselves, their motives, and their limitations, in order to provide a basis for continual growth in the personal domain (Tannenbaum, 1986) and to address larger social issues (Wasserman, 1981).

In a similar vein multicultural education can broaden the GT students' notions of lifestyles, values, demeanor, beauty, and creative expression: "All learning material should be accurately representative of racial and cultural groups in order to set in motion concepts of cultural diversity" (Ford & Harris, 1990, p. 31). Multicultural education that teaches in the culture, furthermore, allows the GT educator to recognize—indeed, to call forth—the cognitive and motivational repertoires of minority students (see Brown, 1988).

One of the best ways to enrich a curriculum for individual children is to find mentors for them (Fleming, 1985). In-depth learning, inspiration, motivation, and career development are all affected (Fleming, 1985). It is crucial that educated, minority role models for minority and non-minority children also be involved, but especially for minority GT children from at-risk backgrounds, who do not all believe that education can make a difference in their lives (Ogbu & Matute-Bianchi, 1986).

According to Valencia (1985), bilingual programs for GT limited-English proficient (LEP) students will allow them to demonstrate their language-based intellectual skills. More specifically, a developmentally appropriate bilingual program permits LEP children to continue to evolve the language genres necessary for school success in their stronger languages while acquiring English (see Heath, 1986). Bilingual options may also be offered to English monolingual children whose parents appreciate the value of a more classical education (Bernal 1991, 1992, 1998).

Creativity

Although virtually all programs for the gifted provide for some acceleration, enrichment, and advanced topics, not all programs, in this author's experience, provide for creative expression (Bernal, 1986c, 1994). Some provide "exercises," but few build into their curricula regular opportunities for GT students to undertake, pursue, and present original ideas and their issues (see Treffinger, Isaksen, & Firestien, 1983). Some programs, in fact, establish institutional cultures that militate against creativity, as often happens to students who are so grade-conscious that their anxiety levels move perceptively higher when they are asked to pursue a thought or invest energy in a project that is perforce somewhat ambiguous in form, whose outcome cannot be guaranteed, or that requires real discipline and effort to complete (a type of deferred grade gratification). For a student to construct a homemade illustration of a scientific principle for a junior science fair is not creative if he or she has already seen one and merely copies it. Coming up with an exemplar that is better, however, would be a real challenge, and the student may learn something of the spirit and the discipline of engineering in the process.

A curriculum design effort should ensure that every student completing every major unit of work has the opportunity to do some critical thinking, original writing, synthesis, or hypothesis testing, and that each semester each student present a "piece of work" to the GT faculty assembled. Such work may be sponsored or overseen by a GT teacher or by a designated mentor. Larger pieces may be coauthored by two or more students. The upshot, however, will be that outstanding pieces may be presented to authentic audiences or serve to interest other individuals or institutions in the GT students' work. Followup should be part of the job for the GT program's staff, who may serendipitously find new support for the program from sources, individual and corporate, outside of regular educational channels.

Exposure to Postsecondary Educational Options

One of the tenets on which this chapter is based is that all GT children need to be included in programs for the gifted and nurtured in appropriate ways, not just "educated." Many bright children, especially those from economically disadvantaged homes and neighborhoods and those from castelike minority groups (see Ogbu & Matute-Bianchi, 1986), set somewhat lower (McIntosh & Greenlaw, 1986) and often very concrete and circumscribed aspirations (Bernal, 1985) for themselves. Indeed several studies (e.g., Gregory, 1992; Matute-Bianchi, 1986) have documented the seemingly paradoxical belief among many minority students that rejects academic achievement as a coping strategy in school and elsewhere. Effective vocational guidance can and should be incorporated into classwork, whatever else is done in mentoring, so that students will understand the process of achieving professional status through postsecondary education, feel more confident about being admitted to college, know how to secure financing and how to apply for scholarships, and be able to select a college or university where they will feel less lonely and be better supported emotionally and socially (see McIntosh & Greenlaw, 1986). For many students this process is a deeply personal experience that requires considerable introspection and personal growth for its resolution (see Feldhusen, 1991; Fleming, 1985). If undertaken successfully, however, the experience is highly motivating to the students and helps them to internalize higher, better defined ambitions that are coupled to realistic plans for attaining them.

TEACHER SELECTION AND DEVELOPMENT

A teacher is, next to parents, the significant other in the life of a child. (Wasserman, 1981, p. 4)

Colangelo and Exum (1979) stress that effective and well-adjusted teachers of the disadvantaged gifted have a sense of humor, high levels of knowledge in their topical areas, well-developed problem solving and planning skills, high energy levels and enthusiasm, authenticity and empathy, a high tolerance for ambiguity, and an appropriate regard for discipline and control in the classroom. Among the other characteristics of successful teachers of the gifted are:

1. The strength of character to realize that on some topics the teacher will not be the most knowledgeable person in the class
2. Honesty in everything the teacher says to the GT students (Bernal, 1994).

Maker (1975) emphasizes three other points:

1. "an ability to relate effectively to the particular group of youngsters one is planning to teach" (p. 17)
2. "an openness to change" (p. 17)
3. "high regard for imaginative ideas, a respect for the potentialities of the individual, a high regard for the teacher's responsibility . . . and the group's responsibility to the child, and a belief in the importance of enhancing pupils' self images" (p. 18).

Runco (1993) warns teachers that some of the behaviors that GT children exhibit, including nonconformity, independence, and persistent questioning, are sometimes seen as hostile behaviors when exhibited by disadvantaged students.

PROGRAM EVALUATION

Although everyone agrees that programs for the gifted must be
accountable, especially in the case when the state or local district
provide special funds to support their operations, programs for the
gifted in the public schools remain largely unevaluated except in the
most general terms of keeping track of their students during the
current year of operation (see Tremaine, 1979). Unlike private
schools, who try to stay in touch with their alumni and thereby have
at least an informal system of evaluation, the public school GT
administrators tend to lose touch with their graduates and rarely do
longitudinal followups (Bernal, 1986a). (This author speculates that
this is due in large measure to the fact that the GT program in most
school systems tends to get diffused among the middle school's
special classes and particularly at the high school among honors and
advanced placement courses.) Gold's (1984) study in Cleveland is a
rare exception. As Traxler (1987) put it, GT programs often lack a
"determined" evaluation design.

Bernal (1986a) lists two major reasons why GT programs
appear to be reluctant to engage the evaluation process: (a)
evaluation could put the GT program's reputation at some risk; and
(b) methodologically, there are "certain unusual or special conditions
which have not always been taken into account" (p. 65). Tomlinson
and Callaghan (1993) also note the lack of evaluation skills among
GT program directors and the lack of funding for this purpose:

> Any program must be able to show that it is benefitting the
> population it is serving. This is a problem area for gifted education
> because the significance of services to gifted children may not become
> evident until they reach adulthood. Unless program evaluation can
> show trends toward positive effects . . . for the students, gifted
> programs cannot become defensible and cannot expect financial
> support from the legislature or local education agencies. Therefore,
> program evaluation is a major factor in the continuation of programs
> for gifted children. (Starks & Garcia, 1991, p. 24)

If GT programs are successful in securing greater allocations
of resources, it is almost certain that greater accountability in the
guise of formal evaluation will come about (Bernal, 1986a). Some
states are already planning the disaggregation of statewide
achievement test data that will show the performance of GT students
in the public schools.

Traditional models of program evaluation, developed largely
for compensatory educational programs, are not readily adapted to

GT education, in which many children produce "ceiling effects" on standardized tests designed for their age-grade level. Similarly, special efforts to convert obtained scores to true scores need be taken to prevent the feared "regression towards the mean" effect in repeated measurements such as pre-post tests (Bernal, 1986a).

The short-term nature of many program models also pose a problem, as does the lack of GT continuity across grade levels in many schools (Renzulli, 1980). The GT program itself may not be the principal, much less the determining factor in students' academic growth. Hence, in too many cases enough information cannot be gathered to serve neither the program's formative evaluation needs nor a district's or state department's needs for periodic sunset reviews or accountability.

THE QUINTESSENTIAL PRECIPITATE: THROUGH THE CENTRIFUGE

In 1975, Renzulli listed seven key features in programs for the gifted. Taking a few liberties in wording, these are summarized as follows:

1. Selection and training of teachers
2. Curriculum
3. Screening and identification procedures
4. Philosophy and objectives
5. Staff orientation to secure cooperation
6. Evaluation
7. Delineation of administrative responsibilities.

According to Bernal (1986b, 1994), the essential characteristics of programs for the academically gifted are:

1. Providing acceleration and enrichment
2. Teaching a curriculum that is cross-disciplinary/integrated and reality-based
3. Establishing a supportive, risk-taking environment
4. Providing regular, frequent opportunities for creative expression.

To these, a fifth point could be added: teaching children how to evaluate themselves (Maker, 1982). A sixth point, then, should be the ethnic integration of students in noncompensatory, rigorous, mutually enriching environments (see O'Connell-Ross, 1993).

Given these and the foregoing discussion, it would seem that the quintessential features can be abstracted as listed in the following sections.

Philosophy and Goals

The most dramatic, productive, and trenchant philosophical statements are truly simple (not facile). The one I prefer is, "Find all the able learners; help them to become gifted adults."

Selection and Training of Teachers

A review of experts' opinions about the characteristics of teachers would seem to suggest that teachers of the gifted should in many ways model the temperamental and mental characteristics of gifted adults. Aside from the more general characteristics of successful teachers, it seems that these teachers need to have high marks in the following:

1. An appreciation of other U.S. cultural groups' ways of relating and expressing themselves
2. Never losing sight of the motivational and interactive benefits of grouping GT children (see Feldhusen, 1989).

It is widely recognized that a philosophy of inclusionism presently permeates popular public education (Kulik & Kulik, 1989; O'Neil et al., 1993), and that any form of "tracking" is interpreted as detrimental to all children (Reis, 1994). Still it is clear that currently employed teachers, including many of those who have recently completed teacher education programs, are not well prepared to deal with the full-spectrum of ability in their classrooms (Tomlinson, 1996). Although some compromise may have to be reached in many districts between full-time or pullout GT programs and full-spectrum inclusionism, a reasonable and potentially effective clustering of GT students (Gentry, 1996) may be possible to implement to the benefit of all students and teachers. It is within such contexts that this author is willing to experiment with inclusionary instructional methods such as the Cooperative Integrated Reading and Composition and Team Accelerated Instruction models promulgated by Slavin (1990), as the presence of a critical mass of GT talent must first be assured.

Selection of Students

Multiple avenues for selection should be open to all students, including traditional means of selection, talent pool placements, and authentic assessments. It is likely that a district's commitment to find all the gifted children from the dominant ethnic group will result in a more nearly equitable representation of students from the nondominant ethnic groups as well (Bernal, 1998).

Curriculum: Acceleration, Enrichment, and Creative Expression

Enriching, broadening experiences such as structured field trips can be shared by both advantaged and disadvantaged students. Proper pretrip study and preparation can ensure a disciplinary grasp of important concepts and processes, and the trip itself and its aftermath can reinforce in-school learning (see O'Connell-Ross, 1993).

Acceleration makes amplitude or repertoire possible in academic preparation. Enrichment provides for diversity of experiences, the development of special talents of individuals, character development, and "polishing" or rounding out of personalities. Creative expression is central to the process, however, because this is the quality that differentiates the accomplished technician from the irrepressible visionary.

Modern programs for the gifted reflect a multicultural United States and a broadened linguistic environment. Private schools for the gifted, for example, frequently offer modern languages at the elementary and secondary levels. There is no good reason in this day to not offer selected modern languages to the brightest children in public schools and to do so in a way that complements the linguistic strengths of some non-dominant ethnic groups in the same schools (see Barkan & Bernal, 1991; Diaz et al., 1986; Perez & Bernal, 1996; Smith & Perez, 1992). Specifically, Bernal has proposed that GT and bilingual and modern language programs get together to provide a two-way bilingual option for academically gifted students (Bernal, 1991, 1998), an option that offers intensive modern language instruction to native speakers of English, while the limited English speakers who are native speakers of that same modern language begin their gifted program bilingually. Immediate or eventual integration of both groups would occur in a curriculum in which subject content—not just language—would be taught bilingually, producing highly fluent, literate bilinguals over the long run (Bernal, 1992, 1996b).

Outreach to Parents and Parental Involvement

This is particularly important as the base of students is expanded to include all able learners. A special committee of experienced parents may wish to divine a strategy for integrating parents from both dominant and nondominant ethnic groups as well as parents from non-middle-class backgrounds.

Instructional Delivery System

Provision must be made for a full- or part-time schedule in a separate facility or grouping arrangement that permits the GT students to learn from one another as well as from their designated teachers.

Career Guidance and Mentoring

This is especially important for meeting GT children's developmental tasks.

Delineation of Administrative Responsibilities

Every major aspect of the program needs to be assigned to someone on the GT program's staff.

Program Evaluation

One of the most important administrative functions of GT program staff is to conduct program evaluations, for it is through such efforts that the program can remain professionally and politically viable (Bernal, 1986a). Professional viability is achieved through formative evaluation, the process through which periodic evaluative results are "fed back" to the program's administrator and the program's principal stakeholders with the idea of taking corrective action (Lapan, 1989; Starks & Garcia, 1991; Tomlinson & Callaghan, 1993) or ensuring quality processes and products (Bernal, 1996a).

Among the most important administrative or programmatic functions to monitor is the continuity of the program. Do selected students receive GT instruction from year to year? Are GT students who exit the bilingual GT program reliably placed into the "regular" multicultural GT program, or do some of them languish in a non-GT placement? What kinds of transitions do GT students face when changing levels, for example, from elementary to middle school. As one can see, good descriptive studies are vital in documenting policy-related events and in sparking the level of interest necessary to take effective, corrective action.

Another feature worth monitoring on a continuous basis is the success of the selection process (Lapan, 1989). What is the gender and ethnic composition of the GT students? Can you break this down by grade level and school to see when the CLD students are identified? Looking at new admissions each year, is there a trend that can be discerned? How do the gender and ethnic proportions match up to the district's or the school's composition? Is there an objective here waiting to be articulated?

One of the most crucial aspects of the program has to do with the students' success. How many students who were invited to participate actually joined the program? What are the characteristics of the students who turned down the invitation (see Rivlin, 1978)? Are all of the students in the GT program making satisfactory progress—grades and achievement test scores? Were the GT teachers involved at the school level to take corrective steps to help the GT students who were showing weak results? Which measures seemed to help the most? Can the students who are experiencing difficulty be identified on the basis of selection criteria (i.e., can the selection process be improved)? Was there a special effort made to check on the progress of children who were admitted on less-than-clear consensus? Are there any local (campus) practices that are not in the best interests of certain students? Were the perceptions of the GT students and their parents and teachers taken into account in the evaluation (Gallagher, 1991)?

Evaluating aspects of the GT program such as continuity of services, student selection, and student success can be done in either sophisticated or informal ways. Informal means are sufficient, so long as the way of interpreting the results are valid. Basically, however, every major component of the program should be evaluated, including the effort to evaluate the program.

A minimally comprehensive evaluation (see Bernal, 1996a) should address:

1. Student outcomes, including longitudinal studies and followup studies of "alumni"
2. Implementation of the program delivery model, including continuity of services within campuses and expansion to all campuses
3. Implementation of the program's curriculum
4. School climate and expectations for the GT program
5. Anticipated outcomes based on objectives
6. Unanticipated outcomes, positive and negative
7. The search for and exposure of tacit beliefs and practices that facilitate or inhibit students' success

8. Disaggregation of student achievement and other
performance data to study impacts of the program
on subpopulations of students: gender, ethnicity,
and those with disabilities.

"This kind of evaluation can tie tacit practices, school climate,
and implementation success to student outcomes, and can therefore
serve to guide the next round of decisions about program
adjustments and modifications" (Bernal, 1996a, pp. 5-6).

There would appear to be nine quintessential features
necessary for GT programs to be implemented in a successful,
professional fashion. I opine that there are few programs for the
gifted that have incorporated all nine of these features, and that the
most effective programs I know are the ones that have come closest
to realizing this goal. These, in turn, are the ones that have several
professional staff assigned to their operation at least part time so
that some specialization or division of labor can take place. Although
it is true that GT programs can be run on a limited budget, it is not
true that GT programs can run themselves. Staffing is the 10th and
perhaps the most important quintessential feature of educational
programs for the gifted.

REFERENCES

Allan, S. D. (1991). Ability-grouping research reviews: What do they
say about grouping and the gifted? *Educational Leadership,
48*(6), 60-65.

Archambault, F. X., Jr., Westberg, K. L., Brown, S. W., Hallmark, B.
W., Zhang, W., & Emmons, C. L. (1993). Classroom practices
used with gifted third and fourth grade students. *Journal for the
Education of the Gifted, 16*(2), 103-119.

Baldwin, A. Y. (1987). I'm Black but look at me, I am also gifted.
Gifted Child Quarterly, 31(4), 180-185.

Baldwin, A. Y. (1994). The Seven Plus story: Developing hidden
talent among students in socioeconomically disadvantaged
environments. *Gifted Child Quarterly, 38*(2), 80-84.

Barkan, J. H., & Bernal, E. M. (1991). Gifted education for bilingual
and limited English proficient students. *Gifted Child Quarterly,
35*(3), 144-147.

Bernal, E. M. (1985, February). Preliminary analysis of Otis-Lennon
and WISC-R test scores of potentially gifted migrant students. In
S. Seidell (Chair), *Approaches to gifted migrant education.*

Symposium presented at the meeting of the California Association for the Gifted, Anaheim, CA.

Bernal, E. M. (1986a). Evaluation of programs for the gifted and talented. In J. Gallagher & R. D. Courtright (Eds.), *The World Council's annotated bibliography of gifted education* (pp. 65-72). New York: Trillium Press.

Bernal, E. M. (1986b, February). *Gifted program models.* Invited address to the Minority Gifted Institute, Kansas State Department of Education, Wichita, KS.

Bernal, E. M. (1986c). The implications of the curricular reform movement for gifted education generally and the culturally different gifted in particular. In L. Kanevsky (Ed.), *Issues in gifted education* (pp. 129-146). San Diego: San Diego City Schools, GATE Program.

Bernal, E. M. (1990a, October). Hispanic and language-minority students: Selecting able learners, producing gifted adults. In M. Frasier (Chair), *Manifestations of giftedness in different cultures: The mandate for change.* Symposium presented at the Council for Exceptional Children's Symposium on Culturally Diverse Exceptional Children, Albuquerque, NM.

Bernal, E. M. (1990b). The identification blues and how to cure them. *California Association for the Gifted Communicator, 20*(3), 1, 27.

Bernal, E. M. (1991, April). *A bilingual option for GATE: Expanding the talent pool for a new generation of leaders in the 21st century.* Invited address to the Arizona Department of Education's conference on Giftedness and the Limited English Proficient Student, Phoenix.

Bernal, E. M. (1992, November). The great debate: Introducing and maintaining pluralism in the education of the gifted. In J. Gallagher (Chair), *The great debate: Appropriate education for culturally diverse gifted students—pluralistic versus assimilationist approaches.* Symposium presented at the meeting of the National Association for Gifted Children, Los Angeles.

Bernal, E. M. (1994, April). *Finding and cultivating minority gifted/talented students.* Paper presented at the National Conference on Alternative Teacher Certification, Washington, DC. (ERIC Document Reproduction Service No. ED 391 345)

Bernal, E. M. (1996a, October). *Site-based decision-making: Achieving a new level of professionalism.* Keynote address at the Edgewood I.S.D.'s Second Annual Curriculum and Instruction Conference, San Antonio, TX.

Bernal, E. M. (1996b, November). *Will the complexion of GT education change? Demographics may revitalize the field.* Paper presented at the meeting of the Texas Association for the Gifted and Talented, Austin, TX.

Bernal, E. M. (1998). Could gifted English-language learners save gifted and talented programs in an age of reform and inclusion? *TAGT Tempo, 18*(1), 11-14.

Brown, R. (1988). Model youth: Excelling despite the odds. *Ebony, 43*(10), 40-48.

Clark, B. (1983). *Growing up gifted* (2nd ed.). Columbus, OH: Charles E. Merrill.

Colangelo, N., & Exum, H. (1979). Educating the culturally diverse gifted: Implications for teachers, counselors, and parents. *Gifted Child Today, 6*(1), 22-23, 54-55.

Cox, J., Daniels, N., & Boston, B. (1985). *Educating able learners.* Austin, TX: University of Texas Press.

Diaz, S., Moll, L. C., & Mehan, H. (1986). Sociocultural resources in instruction: A context-specific approach. In D. D. Holt (Ed.), *Beyond language: Social and cultural factors in schooling language minority students* (pp. 187-230). Los Angeles: California State University, Evaluation, Dissemination & Assessment Center.

Exum, H. A., & Colangelo, N. (1981). Culturally diverse gifted: The need for ethnic identity development. *Roeper Review, 3*(4), 15-17.

Feldhusen, J. F. (1989). Synthesis of research on gifted youth. *Educational Leadership, 46*(6), 6-11.

Feldhusen, J. F. (1991, May). Focus: Talent development. In J. L. Baytops (Ed.), *Project Mandala Concept Papers* (pp. 6-17). Williamsburg, VA: College of William & Mary, School of Education, Project Mandala.

Fleming, E. S. (1985). Career preparation. In R. H. Swassing (Ed.), *Teaching gifted children and adolescents* (pp. 340-373). Columbus, OH: Charles E. Merrill.

Ford, D. Y., & Harris, J. J., III. (1990). On discovering the hidden treasure of gifted and talented Black children. *Roeper Review, 13*(1), 27-32.

Fox, L. H. (1977). Sex differences: Implications for program planning for the academically gifted. In J. C. Stanley, W. C. George, & C. H. Solano (Eds.), *The gifted and the creative: A fifty-year perspective.* Baltimore: Johns Hopkins University Press.

Fradd, S., & Hallman, C. L. (1983). Implications of psychological and educational research for assessment and instruction of culturally and linguistically different students. *Learning Disability Quarterly, 6*(4), 468-478.

Gaddis-Davidson, L. (1993). *Advantages and disadvantages of program models for elementary gifted and talented education.* Unpublished master's thesis, the University of Texas-Pan American, Edinburg, TX.

Gallagher, J. J. (1985). *Teaching the gifted child* (3rd ed.). Newton, MA: Allyn & Bacon.

Gallagher, J. J. (1991a). Educational reform, values, and gifted students. *Gifted Child Quarterly, 35*(1), 12-19.

Gallagher, J. J. (1991b, May). Policy issues associated with the identification and serving of gifted "at risk" learners. In J. L. Baytops (Ed.), *Project Mandala Concept Papers* (pp. 18-27). Williamsburg, VA: College of William & Mary, School of Education, Project Mandala.

Gallagher, R. M. (1991, November-December). Programs for gifted students in Chicago public schools: Yesterday, today, and tomorrow. *G/C/T*, pp. 4-8.

Gentry, M. (1996, Spring). Total school cluster grouping: An investigation of achievement and identification of elementary school students. *Newsletter (National Research Center on the Gifted and Talented)*, pp. 8-11.

Goertz, M. J. (1996). *The center approach to meeting the individual needs of the gifted in the regular classroom*. Unpublished manuscript.

Goertz, M. J., Phemister, L., & Bernal, E. M. (1996). The new challenge: An ethnically integrated enrichment program for gifted students. *Roeper Review, 18*(4), 298-300.

Gold, S. (1984, March). Sixty years of programming for the gifted in Cleveland. *Phi Delta Kappan,* pp. 497-499.

Good, T. L., & Brophy, J. E. (1984). *Looking in classrooms* (3rd ed.). San Francisco: Harper & Row.

Gregory, S. S. (1992, March 16). The hidden hurdle: Talented Black students find that one of the most insidious obstacles to achievement comes from . . . their own peers. *Time*, pp. 44-46.

Heath, S. B. (1986). Sociocultural contexts of language development. In D. D. Holt (Ed.), *Beyond language: Social and cultural factors in schooling language minority students* (pp. 143-186). Los Angeles: Evaluation, Dissemination, and Assessment Center, California State University, Los Angeles.

High, M. H., & Udall, A. J. (1983). Teacher ratings of students in relation to ethnicity of students and school ethnic balance. *Journal for the Education of the Gifted, 6*(3), 154-166.

Kirschenbaum, R. J. (1988). One special program for secondary gifted students. *Excellence in Teaching, 6*(1), 14-15.

Kulik, J. A., & Kulik, C.-L. (1989). Effects of ability grouping on student achievement. *Equity and Excellence, 23*, 1-2, 22-30.

Lapan, S. D. (1989). Guidelines for developing and evaluating gifted programs. *Roeper Review, 11*(3), 167-169.

Maker, C. J. (1975). *Training teachers for the gifted and talented: A comparison of models*. Reston, VA: Council for Exceptional Children.

Maker, C. J. (1982). *Curriculum development for the gifted*. Rockville, MD: Aspen.

Matute-Bianchi, M. E. (1986). Ethnic identities and patterns of school success and failure among Mexican descent and Japanese-American students in a California high school: An ethnographic analysis. *American Journal of Education, 95*(1), 233-255.

McIntosh, M. E., & Greenlaw, M. J. (1986). Fostering the post-secondary aspirations of gifted urban minority students. *Roeper Review, 9*, 104-107.

McIntosh, J. E., Journal, P., & Meacham, A. W. (1992). Thematic, interdisciplinary curricula for secondary gifted students in English and social studies. *Update on Gifted Education, 2*(1), 2-5.

Menninger, K., Mayman, M., & Pruyser, P. (1963). *The vital balance*. New York: Viking.

Mitchell, B. M. (1988). A strategy for the identification of the culturally different gifted/talented child. *Roeper Review, 10*(3), 163-165.

Oakes, J. (1985). *Keeping track: How schools structure inequality*. New Haven, CT: Yale University Press.

O'Connell-Ross, P. (1993). *National excellence: A case for developing America's talent*. Washington, DC: U. S. Department of Education, Office of Educational Research and Improvement.

Ogbu, J. U., & Matute-Bianchi, M. E. (1986). Understanding sociocultural factors: Knowledge, identity, and school adjustment. In D. D. Holt (Ed.), *Beyond language: Social and cultural factors in schooling language minority students* (pp. 73-142). Los Angeles: Evaluation, Dissemination & Assessment Center, California State University, Los Angeles.

O'Neil, J., Gallagher, J., & Haycock, K. (1993, June). When ability grouping helps . . . and when it hurts: An interview with James Gallagher and Kati Haycock. *ASCD Curriculum Update*, pp. 7-8.

Passow, A. H. (Ed.). (1979). *The gifted and the talented*. Chicago: National Society for the Study of Education Yearbook.

Perez, R. I., & Bernal, E. M. (1996, March). *Project EXCEL: Gifted bilingual*. Paper presented at the meeting of the Southwestern School Boards Association, San Diego, CA.

Pressey, S. L. (1966). Acceleration: Basic principles and recent research. In A. Anastasi (Ed.), *Testing problems in perspective*. Washington, DC: American Council on Education.

Reis, S. M. (1994, April). How schools are shortchanging the gifted. *Technology Review*, pp. 38-45.

Reis, S. M., Westberg, K. L., Kulikowich, J., Caillard, F., Hebert, T., Plucker, J., Purcell, J. H., Rogers, J. B., & Smist, J. M. (1993, July), *Por quç no dejar a los estudiantes con habilidad superior comenzar la escuela en Enero? Estudio de la compactaciøn del curriculum* [Why not let superior students start school in January? A study of curriculum compacting] (V. I. Kloosterman & E. L. Hernandez, Trans., Research Monograph 94401). Storrs: The University of Connecticut, National Research Center on the Gifted and Talented.

Renzulli, J. S. (1975). Identifying key features in programs for the gifted. In W. Barbe & J. Renzulli (Eds.), *Psychology and education of the gifted.* New York: Irvington.

Renzulli, J. S. (1980). Will the gifted movement be alive and well in 1990? *Gifted Child Quarterly, 28*(2), 163-171.

Renzulli, J. S. (1984). The triad/revolving door system: A research-based approach to identification and planning for the gifted and talented. *Gifted Child Quarterly, 28*(2), 163-171.

Renzulli, J. S. (1987). The three-ring conception of giftedness: A development model for creative productivity. In R. J. Sternberg and J. E. Davidson (Eds.), *Conceptions of giftedness* (pp. 53-92). Cambridge, MA: Cambridge University Press.

Renzulli, J. S., & Reis, S. M. (1994). Research related to the Schoolwide Enrichment Triad model. *Gifted Child Quarterly, 38*(1), 7-20.

Richardson Study Q's and A's. (1985, January/February). *G/C/T*, pp. 2-9.

Rivlin, H. N. (1978). How can we teach the gifted and talented we do not reach? *Roeper Review, 12*(3), 6-11.

Runco, M. A. (1993). *Creativity as an educational objective for disadvantaged students* (Creativity: Research-based Decision-making Series, Report No. 9306). Storrs: University of Connecticut, National Research Center on the Gifted and Talented. (ERIC Document Reproduction Service No. ED 363 074)

Sapon-Shevin, M. (1994). *Playing favorites: Gifted education and the disruption of community.* New York: State University of New York Press.

Schuler, P. A. (1997, Winter). Cluster grouping coast to coast. *National Research Center on the Gifted and Talented Newsletter,* pp. 11-15.

Seidell, S. L. (1985, May). Gifted migrant education. *CAG Communicator,* pp. 14-15.

Silverman, L. K. (1993). The gifted individual. In L. K. Silverman (Ed.), *Counseling the gifted and talented.* Denver, CO: Love.

Sisk, D. (1993). A different approach pays off. *Gifted Child Today,* *16*(5), 13-16.

Slavin, R. E. (1990). Point-counterpoint: Ability grouping, cooperative learning and the gifted. *Journal for the Education of the Gifted,* *14*(1), 3-8.

Smith, E., & Perez, R. (1992, April). Cultural diversity in gifted education: A better chance at succeeding. *Journal of the California Association for the Gifted, 22*(2), 1, 42-43.

Spicker, H. H. (1993). *Final report of Project SPRING (Indian site): Special Populations Resource Information Network for the Gifted.* Bloomington: Indiana University Press. (ERIC Document Reproduction Service No. ED 365 067)

Starks, J., & Garcia, J. H. (1991, December). *Final report of the Gifted Evaluation Models (GEM) project.* Austin: Texas Association for the Gifted and Talented.

Stewart, E. D. (1985). Social Studies. In R. H. Swassing (Ed.), *Teaching gifted children and adolescents* (pp. 232-275). Columbus, OH: Charles E. Merrill.

Storlie, T. R., Bellis, D. D., Powills, J. A., & Prapuolenis, P. G. (1978). *The development of a culturally fair model for the early identification of gifted children* (ETS PR-78-8). Princeton, NJ: Educational Testing Service. (ERIC Document Reproduction Service No. ED 177 273)

Subotnik, R. F. (1998, June-July). *Special schools for talented children: Who should attend, when and why?* Paper presented at the Sixth Annual Institute on Creativity and Gifted and Talented Learners, Fordham University-Lincoln Center, New York.

Taba, H. (1962). *Curriculum development: Theory and practice.* New York: Harcourt, Brace, & World.

Taba, H., & Hills, J. H. (1965). *Teacher handbook for Contra Costa Social Studies, grades 1-6.* San Francisco: San Francisco State University.

Tammi, L. A. (1990, February 14). Programs for the gifted are not "elitist." *Education Week,* p. 44.

Tannenbaum, A. J. (1986). A proposed enrichment matrix for gifted children. In L. Kanevsky (Ed.), *Issues in gifted education* (pp. 17-42). San Diego: San Diego City Schools, Gifted & Talented Education Program.

Thorkildsen, T. A. (1994). Some ethical implications of communal and competitive approaches to gifted education. *Roeper Review, 1,* 54-57.

Tomlinson, C. A. (1996, Spring). Learning how new teachers relate to academic diversity in mixed-ability classrooms. *Newsletter (National Research Center on the Gifted and Talented),* pp. 6-7.

Tomlinson, C. A., & Callaghan, C. M. (1993). A planning guide for evaluating programs for gifted learners. *Quest, 4*(2), 1-4.

Traxler, M. A. (1987). Gifted education program evaluation: A national review. *Journal for the Education of the Gifted, 10*(2), 107-113.

Treffinger, D. J. (1991). Future goals and directions. In N. Colangelo & G. A. Davis (Eds.), *Handbook of gifted education* (pp. 441-449). Boston: Allyn & Bacon.

Treffinger, D. J., Isaksen, S., & Firestien, R. (1983). A preliminary model for creative learning. *Journal of Creative Behavior, 1*, 9-17.

Tremaine, C. D. (1979). Do gifted programs make a difference? *Gifted Child Quarterly, 23*, 500-517.

Trifiletti, J. J. (1985). Using computers to teach the gifted. In R. H. Swassing (Ed.), *Teaching gifted children and adolescents* (pp. 316-339). Columbus, OH: Charles E. Merrill.

Udall, A. (1992). Utilizing higher level thinking skills. *Update on Gifted Education, 2*(2), 8-14.

Valencia, A. A. (1985). Curricular perspectives for gifted limited English proficient students. *National Association for Bilingual Education Journal, 10*, 65-77.

Wagschal, H. (1980, February-March). Towards a new pedagogy for the humanities and social sciences. *Roeper Review*, pp. 7-9.

Wasserman, S. (1981). Teaching the gifted: Preparing tomorrow's leaders. *Roeper Review, 14*(1), 2-4.

Whitmore, J. R. (1980). *Giftedness, conflict, and underachievement*. Boston: Allyn & Bacon.

Williamson, J. (1992, Spring). Awakening the potential in gifted students. *Update on Gifted Education, 2*(1), 18-21.

Chapter 10

*Parents of Gifted Culturally Diverse Youngsters**

Joan Silverstein
Montclair State University

Parents play a crucial role in the life of a gifted youngster. They are generally the child's first teachers and remain as important sources of support, influence, and continuity throughout the different stages of a child's life (Christenson, Rounds, & Gorney, 1992; Roedell, 1989; Silverstein, Springer, & Russo, 1992; Takanishi, 1993). Together with extended family members such as grandparents, parents transmit family and cultural values, convey expectations, model desirable behaviors, provide direction and encouragement, and foster such important characteristics as persistence, achievement motivation, feelings of self-efficacy, and self-confidence (Davis & Rimm, 1989;

*I am extremely grateful to Bonnie Dirkson, a school psychology graduate student, who, through her thoughtful assistance, made an important contribution to the literature review.

   Research for this chapter was supported, in part, by released time provided by the Montclair State University Separately Budgeted Research Program and the Faculty Scholar Incentive Program and was enhanced by activities supported by the MENSA Education and Research Foundation/Montclair State University Workshop Series on Underidentified Gifted Youngsters.

Freeman, 1993; Strom, Johnson, Strom, & Strom, 1992; Tannenbaum, 1983; VanTassel-Baska, 1989b). Parents can also play a key role in identifying children's gifts and talents. Once the gifts are identified, parents can help guide their youngsters' choices, develop opportunities for peer interaction, and provide access to enrichment opportunities (Hines & Boyd-Franklin, 1982; Roedell, 1989; VanTassel-Baska, 1989; Webster, 1989). Therefore, it is important for professionals who care about gifted children to work collaboratively with parents and, when appropriate, with other extended family members.

Parents of gifted children often need support (Robinson, Roedell, & Jackson, 1979). Parenting a gifted child can be difficult: Giftedness is an ambivalent and misunderstood construct in many cultures and societies, including the United States. Consequently, when a child is identified as gifted, parents may react with multiple emotions including joy, pride, fear, and anxiety. Some may view giftedness as elitist, whereas others may be concerned that their child will be perceived as a "nerd" or an isolate. They may also feel incompetent, questioning their ability to parent a child who may be brighter than they are. They may also be concerned about the time, energy, and financial commitment required to foster talents (Davis & Rimm, 1989; Meckstroth, 1991; Rimm, 1991; Saunders & Espeland, 1991). Behavioral characteristics and vulnerabilities of some gifted children—including emotional intensity, extreme variability in development, perfectionism, overexcitability, stubbornness, excessive self-criticism, high levels of curiosity, alienation from the peer group because of different interests and cognitive levels, and incessant question asking—may also create challenges, resulting in high levels of parental exhaustion and stress (Friedman-Jenkins & Gallagher, 1991; Meckstroth, 1991; Roedell, 1984; Seagoe, 1974; Webb, 1993).

Parenting a gifted child can be even more complex when the family's cultural beliefs about giftedness differ from those of the dominant culture. Discrepant beliefs—in such areas as what constitutes giftedness and what constitutes acceptable behavior for gifted youngsters—can lead to confusion, stress, and conflict for parents and children at home, in school, and in the interaction between home and school. In some cases—when school professionals foster students' gifts and provide access to opportunities for students without including parents in the process—they can unintentionally alienate youngsters from their families and from their cultural values (Kirschenbaum, 1991). In order to prevent this unintended schism, it is important that professionals work closely and collaboratively with parents of gifted children.

Because children are part of a family system (Bronfenbrenner, 1979), it is crucial that parents not be excluded from the school's interventions with their children. In families and cultures in which extended family and kinship and friendship networks are important, extended family members—including "blood-related kin and persons informally adopted into this system" (Hines & Boyd-Franklin, 1982, p. 324)—can also be included as powerful supports for parents and youngsters. For example, grandmothers have been noted as key people who often transmit cultural and family values (VanTassel-Baska 1989a, 1989b).

This chapter begins with a review of aspects of the parenting role as it relates to raising a gifted child who comes from a cultural and/or linguistic background different from the dominant culture. Issues reviewed include child-rearing beliefs and cultural values, acculturation and biculturality, environmental factors such as poverty and adversity, and the role of extended family and friends as these issues relate to fostering parent-professional partnerships. Factors related to parent-school interactions and frameworks for conceptualizing interventions involving parents in school, home, and community is also discussed.

PARENTING ROLE

Cultural Factors

Cultural values play a mediating role in parents' understanding of the concept of giftedness and in their understanding and acceptance of interventions suggested by professionals. Different cultures have different worldviews (Zorman, 1991). For example, not all cultures value and promote individual excellence (Freeman, 1993). Cultural beliefs, values, and assumptions affect such aspects of the parenting role as communication; conceptualizations of problems and solutions; the meaning of parental actions, childrearing practices, and mediations between parent and child; as well as parental understanding and interpretation of interventions proposed by professionals (Hines, Garcia-Preto, McGoldrick, Almeida, & Weltman, 1992; Hundeide, 1992).

In order to effectively intervene with the parents of gifted children, it is important to understand and respect the "metaframes," the "cultural meaning system" implicit in the family's cultural heritage (Hundeide, 1992). "The tacit background of established cultural practices and contracts of interaction between caregiver and child" (Hundeide, 1992, p. 53) must be considered in order to understand the implications of parental behavior. For example, authoritarian forms of discipline, which are currently viewed negatively in the dominant culture, may have more positive connotations in traditional cultures in which they may be perceived as signs of love and concern (Bronfenbrenner, 1989; Dornbush, Ritter, Leiderman, Toberts, & Fraleigh, 1987; Hundeide, 1992). If this is the case, professionals' efforts to encourage a parent from a traditional culture to reject their own child-rearing practices and substitute those of the dominant culture may have unintended negative outcomes. For example, when a mother from a traditional culture is encouraged to praise routine child behaviors such as household chores, there may be negative ramifications: If both mother and child considered the chores to be the child's responsibility, then the praise may inadvertently communicate the message that the chores should no longer be considered the child's routine responsibility but should now be viewed as special behaviors deserving of praise and only performed when requested by the parent (Hundeide, 1992).

In order to work collaboratively with parents, it is important to respect their culturally based realities (Hundeide, 1992). For example, traditional societies often place more stress on the development of moral behaviors such as obedience and compliance, than on the promotion of advanced cognitive development (Hundeide, 1992). Similarly, parents from Japan, Taiwan, and China appear to have a culturally based belief system that may influence their interpretation of their child's academic functioning and lead to the exertion of more parental pressure for higher performance levels. Results in a survey (Lee, 1993) indicated that parents of students in these countries felt their children could still do better academically, despite already high levels of academic performance. This was in contrast to parents of students in U.S. schools who appeared to be far more satisfied with their children's current academic performance. The difference in viewpoints may be due to the belief in these Asian cultures that higher achievement is the result of hard work; these parents deemphasized the importance of innate ability, often viewed as a determining factor in U.S. schools (Lee, 1993). Values and behaviors—such as family centeredness, obedience to elders and to culture, and interdependence—that are central in many traditional societies, are in direct contradiction to values such as independence, question asking, and competition that is often fostered in U.S. school programs for the gifted. Individualistic, competitive behaviors are likely to be viewed by traditional families as disrespectful and are likely to be discouraged by parents. The pressure of conflicting values between home and school can lead to increased stress and the development of behavior problems in the children (Hines et al., 1992; Woliver & Woliver, 1991).

Acculturation and biculturality. Some of the stressors experienced by gifted children and their parents are related to acculturation and biculturality. The acculturation process occurs when immigrants make the transition "from the environment of their native country, with its social networks, familiar institutions, and customs to a foreign country with unfamiliar ways and confusing networks" (Kopala, Esquivel, & Baptiste, 1994, p. 352), resulting in major physical, social, and cultural changes. Biculturality is defined by Pinderhughes (1982) as "the ability to function in two worlds" (p. 114). Both acculturation and biculturality can create stress, emotional strain, and identity confusion for children and adults, but can also foster emotional strength and flexibility (Cohelo & Stein, 1980; Kopala et al., 1994; Pinderhughes, 1982).

Children experience acculturation stress "when there is a discrepancy between the child's cultural values and those encouraged in the dominant school culture in terms of behavioral style. . . . Behaviors that are adaptive according to the child's culture may be viewed as signs of maladjustment within the school context" (Kopala et al., 1994, pp. 97-98). Similarly, in cultures where families have experienced a history of racism—such as African Americans and non-White immigrants to the United States—family members may feel stressed as a result of attempts to reconcile and cope with divergent sets of values in a society in which they may not feel or be accepted as full members (Papajohn & Spiegel, 1975; Pinderhughes, 1982).

In order to fulfill their potential, gifted youngsters who are bridging two cultures need to simultaneously establish an identity as a member of their cultural group while also adapting some of the dominant culture's behaviors, values, and standards (Zorman, 1991). Youngsters' success in school may create conflicts for them and their families as they attempt the difficult balancing act of achieving higher social and educational status without betraying their cultural heritage (Bernal, 1979). In addition to societal racism, gifted African-American adolescents can also be faced with an additional form of isolation if they are ostracized and/or accused by peers of "acting White." This negative peer pressure can affect achievement motivation and contribute to underachievement in gifted youngsters (Ford, 1993; Zorman, 1991).

It is important that parents be able to serve as sources of stability and support for their youngsters when they are grappling with these conflicts and stressors. For example, Clark (1983), studying the lives of successful African Americans, found that a number of factors in the home environment contributed to school success. These included a positive parent-child relationship, clear parental expectations for behavior and performance, and considerable parental involvement in the child's education. In some cases parents will not need professional assistance in order to serve as supportive resources for their child. In other cases—such as when parents are grappling with their own stressors—parents and children may need support from the school and other professionals. It is important to distinguish between the two situations so that help is not imposed by professionals on well-functioning parents. No matter how well intended, unsolicited help imposed by professionals can be interpreted by parents as insulting and demeaning if it is viewed as implying that parents cannot function competently (Silverstein, Springer, & Russo, 1992).

In addition to dealing with their child's behaviors and reactions, parents may also be experiencing their own stressors related to the effects of acculturation and biculturation, including financial pressures, employment difficulties, and marital strains (Gonsalves, 1992; Kopala et al., 1994). They may also be stressed by contacts with school personnel regarding their child's school behavior, particularly if they are being told negative things about their child or about their parenting skills. To compound the problem, parents and children who have immigrated to the United States may no longer have the supports that were available to them in their home country. As parents begin to succeed, additional stressors may develop. For example, when a family achieves higher socioeconomic status, nuclear family members may be faced with two difficult choices: alienation from their family of origin, or a drain on family economic resources if they continue to support extended family members (McAdoo, 1977; Pinderhughes, 1982). Upwardly mobile parents are also faced with additional pressures such as risk of failure and the possible consequences of being perceived by the dominant culture as "deviant" or "reject" (Bernal, 1979, p. 397).

Effects of poverty. Poverty and its ramifications, extending over several generations, also can have a powerful effect on parent-child relations, child development, and talent development for gifted children. Adversity alone is not the problem. In fact, several studies of eminent individuals have noted that such factors as troubled homes, loss of a parent, poverty, and loss of economic and social status were not uncommon (Albert, 1980; Goertzel & Goertzel, 1962; VanTassel-Baska & Olszewski-Kubilius, 1989). Instead, the meaning attached to the adversity is a key factor: In studies comparing gifted achievers and underachievers and in studies comparing immigrants of equal ability and economic status, a critical difference between those who succeeded and those who failed was the meaning they attached to their adversity and their perception and interpretation of their situation. Factors identified as influencing success or failure in the face of adversity included internal versus external locus of control, attributions of success or failure to self or others, perception of the adversity as a positive or negative motivator, and perceptions of the effects of racism as modifiable or pervasive and immutable (Csikszentmihalyi & Beattie, 1979; Ford, 1993; VanTassel-Baska, 1989a).

The likelihood that adversity will negatively affect the relationships between parents and gifted children may be exacerbated in families in which several generations have been raised in poverty and in which parents have not had the academic exposure and the educational or employment opportunities potentially available to their youngsters. In these cases parents may not have the academic background or the economic resources to expose their children to experiences, skills, and concepts that make it possible to identify, foster, and support their children's gifts and talents (Zorman, 1991). Similarly, infant language development and exceptional early achievement depend substantially on adult stimulation and opportunities for verbal stimulation and practice, including parents talking with infants from birth and reading to children. Therefore, parental literacy and language fluency can affect parents' potential to stimulate their children's abilities and gifts (Freeman, 1993; Radford, 1990).

Parents serve as the primary mediators for their young children, providing them with ways to look at and make sense of their world within a cultural framework. The mediator, through the use of mediated learning experiences (MLEs), facilitates development of prerequisite cognitive functions and needs systems so that the child can become an independent and autonomous learner (Jensen & Feuerstein, 1987). MLEs play a major role in the transmission of culture from parent to child: "The MLE-deprived child is perceived as culturally deprived in the sense that the child has been deprived of his or her *own* culture" (Jensen & Feuerstein, 1987, p. 381; emphasis in original). As opposed to learning through direct exposure in which stimuli reach the child in a "fragmented, disassociated, and even random fashion" (p. 380), in mediated learning:

> Stimuli are selected by a mediator; their appearance is scheduled in time and organized in space; and they are framed by goals and attributes, regulated in intensity through repetition, and enhanced through being connected by purpose and imbued with meaning. The mediator serves as a powerful filter, assisting the child in structuring his or her experience, expanding experience to areas inaccessible to the learner through the sheer activation of sensorial systems, thereby instilling and enlarging need systems. (p. 380)

Parents' ability to be effective mediators is influenced by their own early and current experiences. For example, when parents themselves did not receive effective mediation when they were children, they are likely to lack the ability to mediate effectively with their own children (Feuerstein, Rand, & Rynders, 1988). Parents who are overwhelmed due to such factors as poverty or depression may also lack the emotional energy to serve as effective mediators. A cultural discontinuity—such as can occur when parents reject their own culture in favor of the dominant culture—can also be a powerful factor in depriving children of mediated learning. This sometimes occurs when parents immigrate and reject their own culture in an attempt to help their children assimilate. Cultural discontinuity can also occur when parents in a minority culture discontinue, or are forced to discontinue, the transmission of their own traditions and culture (Feuerstein et al., 1988).

Although factors such as poverty can play a role, the deprivation of MLEs is not due to economic circumstances or stress, but is the result of parental attitude and is strongly affected by parents having their own culture and being able to transmit it (Feuerstein et al., 1988; Freeman, 1993). Deprivation of their own culture can affect a parent's ability to mediate effectively in such areas as perception and attention, verbal and cognitive functioning, and motivation. This, in turn, affects child development and can impede the development of gifts, creativity, and talent (Freeman, 1993).

Culturally based child-rearing beliefs can also affect parents' ability to foster creativity and gifts. For example, when children's question-asking behavior is rejected or ignored, and when imaginative play and opportunities for sustained, creative activity are discouraged or punished, children's development will be negatively affected (Freeman, 1993; Strom et al., 1992). If children do not receive effective mediation in an atmosphere in which learning is appreciated and encouraged, it is far less likely that their gifts and talents will be identified and stimulated.

The content and type of mediation required varies with developmental changes in the child's cognitive capacities and needs, but the necessity for mediation continues throughout the child's development (Freeman, 1993). For example, when gifted and talented students are ready to choose a college program and career, Bernal (interviewed by Kirschenbaum, 1991), proposed that youngsters need a mediator to "help them take an analytical perspective with regard to choosing a career" (p. 41) and to help them examine their choices. Youngsters from poor families often choose careers for reasons such as individual or family financial pressures, job security, or fulfilling parental desires. These gifted adolescents may be limited in their choices by the careers they see around them in their family and circle of friends and may not be aware of their options (Kirschenbaum, 1991). Because these youngsters often are the first in their family to attend college, their parents—despite their hopes and expectations for higher education for their child—may not be able to provide firsthand advice about such activities as college admissions and college planning (Kirschenbaum, 1991; VanTassel-Baska, 1989b; VanTassel-Baska, Patton, & Prillaman, 1991).

When parents do not have the information they need to guide and teach their child—whether it be about college choices or sixth grade mathematics—their relationships with their children, including their ability to support and encourage their child, can suffer (Kirschenbaum, 1991; Sarason, 1996; Silverstein, Springer, & Russo, 1992). As Bernal noted:

> Parents of gifted students may be concerned about messing something up with their children. For example, it's not unusual for a gifted child in 6th grade to know more math than the parents ever learned. At that point, their confidence in their ability to help their child diminishes rapidly. They're afraid to give wrong advice and do something that might "hurt" their child somehow. (cited in Kirschenbaum, 1991, p. 44)

When professionals provide information to youngsters without also presenting the knowledge to their parents, this can result in an informational discrepancy that places the parents in a weaker position, further eroding parental self-confidence and authority. In families in which parents do not speak English, parental authority may already be undermined because youngsters often serve as translators for their parents and go-betweens with bureaucracies (Harry, 1992). To compound the problem, gifted children may already be treated like miniature adults if they have advanced verbal skills and advanced cognitive abilities. This can be destructive to a sense of security and role clarity for both parents and children. Therefore, it is important to empower parents by providing them with information, skills, and resources to build up their confidence and "to maintain their position as knowing adults" (Kirschenbaum, 1991, p. 44), so they can serve as primary mediators for their children. If they are given the support and information they need, parents can work collaboratively with professionals rather than being excluded from their child's education. Parents can then be full partners in the decision-making process, ensuring that interventions aimed to encourage giftedness in youngsters will be congruent with the family's values rather than breaking the family apart.

PARENT-SCHOOL RELATIONSHIPS

Parental Role in Identification of Giftedness

Parents, as their youngster's first mediators and teachers, can be valuable sources of information about their child's gifts and talents (Roedell, 1989). This information can be useful for both the identification and the assessment of giftedness. Children's gifts and talents may not be evident in the classroom for several reasons: Gifted children may hide their ability in order to conform with their peers, or they may perform like their average peers unless they are placed in challenging situations at school. Therefore, their gifts and talents may not be directly observed by teachers. Young gifted children's performance may vary and may not be evident in the classroom. Children from diverse cultural and linguistic groups may demonstrate characteristics valued in their culture, but not identified as gifted in the dominant culture. Therefore, it is important that parents be encouraged to share information about exceptional skills such as fluent reading ability in a young child or talents and interests they may have observed at home, so that the skills can be fostered at school.

When children are assessed for giftedness, the testing session provides a restricted sample of behavior and ability. In contrast, parents can provide multiple samples of the child's behavior in a variety of settings and conditions. Information can be solicited through assessment procedures such as interviews, surveys, written descriptions of child behavior, and the development of portfolios of their child's work (Davis & Rimm, 1989; Meckstroth, 1991; Roedell, 1989). Clearly, parental input is valuable. However, similar to the findings of Silverstein, Springer, and Russo (1992) and Harry (1992) for parents of disabled children, parents' observations about gifted children tend to be ignored by professionals who may assume that their own observations are more professionally valid (Meckstroth, 1991; Roedell, 1989).

Because cultural conceptions of intelligence and giftedness differ, parents from different cultures may not view their child as gifted according to the standards of the majority culture and may not request an evaluation of their child for a gifted program (Hundeide, 1992; Scott, Perou, Urbano, Hogan, & Gold, 1992; Webster, 1989). In order for parents to be able to identify their child's abilities, share information with professionals, and make informed choices, they need information about characteristics of giftedness and programming options for gifted youngsters, as well as information about how to navigate the system to obtain services (Robinson et al., 1979; Roedell, 1989; Strom et al., 1992).

A public education program can alert parents to characteristics of giftedness, inform them about parental and children's rights, and provide information about programming options for gifted students (Scott et al., 1992). Adapting suggestions from Kopala et al. (1994), parent consultants recruited from different cultural groups represented in the school district could lead informational sessions for parents whose children are being considered for gifted programs. The sessions could address such topics as cultural differences in identification of giftedness, assessment of giftedness, procedures for entering gifted programs, and methods to foster giftedness at home and in school. Additionally, as Bernal has suggested (cited in Kirschenbaum, 1991), parents from different cultural groups can be involved in school committees that solicit nominations and collaborate in developing programming. This may encourage parents of minority youngsters who otherwise might not take an active role in identification and advocacy for their gifted child.

Supporting parents during and after the identification process. Once the youngster is identified, parents may differ in their acceptance of the child's giftedness. Parents also may have varied attitudes toward giftedness, including negative, skeptical, and critical; highly positive; or overidealized. Parental concerns can include anxieties that the gifted label will inflate the child's self-esteem or fears that the child will be viewed as elitist. Parents may also be confused about how they can best meet their child's special needs and worried about their ability to parent a gifted or talented youngster (Friedman-Jenkins & Gallagher, 1991; Hackney, 1981; Rimm, 1986). Parents may also worry about the effect of the label on nonidentified siblings. In fact, when only one child is identified as gifted in a family, problems can develop for the other siblings, particularly if the parents do not appear to value the other siblings' accomplishments or devote inordinate amounts of time, energy, and money to the identified child (Cornell & Grossberg, 1989; Webb, 1993). However, identification can also be a positive, "organizing force, shaping the family's corporate personality and structuring family relations to actualize the potential of every family member" (Friedman-Jenkins & Gallagher, 1991, p. 260).

After the child is evaluated, it is important that professionals continue to work collaboratively with parents. The more that parents are included as informed members of the team working with their child, the less likely that they will feel disenfranchised and alienated from their youngster and the school. After testing is completed, the feedback conference between parents and school personnel can play a crucial role in how parents view their gifted child and can begin the process of developing a home-school partnership in which parents can fully contribute to their child's educational programming. In order to build a collaborative relationship between parents and professionals, it is important that the conference be a dialogue, not only eliciting information from parents, but also encouraging them to contribute to the planning and development of goals and interventions (Friedman-Jenkins & Gallagher, 1991).

Rather than presenting a "gifted-nongifted dichotomy" (Meckstroth, 1991, p. 98), parents need to be helped to understand the specific manifestations of giftedness—including special abilities, interests, sensibilities, personality, temperament, concerns, needs, and areas of variability in development and behavior—so they can appreciate their child's unique individuality (Meckstroth, 1991). In order to develop appropriate parental expectations, it is important that parents realize that giftedness does not imply consistent development in all areas. A review of the tests used during the assessment would also help parents to understand the nature of the findings. For example, a discussion of the structure of the cognitive tests and subtests might help them realize that an IQ score is not a unitary concept. Parents' own stereotypes about giftedness could also be explored to help them understand and appreciate their child as a whole child, and they should be urged not to focus solely on academic achievements or on test scores (Davis & Rimm, 1989; Meckstroth, 1991). Parents whose children are tested but not placed in the gifted program may also need support (Friedman-Jenkins & Gallagher, 1991).

Similar to the findings of Silverstein et al. (1992) for parents of disabled children, little information is typically shared with parents after the identification process is completed (Colangelo & Dettman, 1983; Friedman-Jenkins & Gallagher, 1991). It is important that information continue to be provided through consultation, readings, parent groups, and other programmatic activities because parents may not be able to understand, retain, and process all the information given in the initial feedback session.

PARENT SCHOOL RELATIONSHIPS AND PROGRAMMATIC INCLUSION OF PARENTS

Fostering Collaborative Relationships

Programs for gifted youngsters need to make available opportunities for collaboration, support, and access to resources for parents. Robinson et al. (1979) advocated a strong parent component for programs for gifted preschool children. Similar outreach is equally important for parents from minority cultures (VanTassel-Baska et al., 1991) because these parents may not be familiar with the dominant culture's concept of giftedness and may not have access to information and resources to help their child. Collaborative relationships can assure that parental input is sought and welcomed so that parents are not alienated from the youngsters as a result of the gifted program.

Collaboration is a cooperative and nonhierarchical venture based on shared power and authority, in which power is based on knowledge and expertise rather than role and function (Kraus, 1980). The collaborative relationship is egalitarian and trusting, with an emphasis on "reciprocity of influence" (Tyler, 1983, p. 388) and persuasion rather than unidirectional influence and coercion. Consequently all partners change and gain as a result of the collaboration (Parsons & Meyers, 1984; Rosenfield, 1987; Tyler, 1983). Professional and parent each bring a unique perspective and different type of knowledge and expertise that is not readily available to the other (Silverstein et al., 1992).

A positive parent-school relationship is also important for gifted youngsters because it models parental respect for education (Rimm, 1990, 1991). When parents and school engage in conflict and assume rigid positions—even if both parties feel their stance is in the child's best interest—the results may be detrimental to the youngster's emotional development and learning. Particularly during adolescence, gifted students whose parents are in conflict with the school may stop perceiving school personnel as legitimate authorities and may stop viewing school as a vehicle for learning. The possible result is student underachievement, insecurity, and unhappiness and the consequent reduction of opportunities for success (Gelcer & Dick, 1986; Rimm, 1991). In contrast, school interventions are more likely to be effective when parents are included as partners together with school professionals (Christenson, Rounds, & Franklin, 1992). For example, Sizemore (1989) found that when administrators worked with parents, teachers, and students to make high academic expectations the top priority, African-American students' school achievement increased.

To enhance positive parent-school interactions, it is important that the parents' cultural values be respected. For example, when working with parents from Hispanic cultures, it is important that professionals acknowledge and reciprocate values such as *respeto* [respect], *dignidad* [dignity], *personalismo* [personalism], *honor,* and *confianza* [trust], all of which "reflect a tradition of respect for the individual that requires the expression of an explicit deference from one person to another" (Harry, 1992, p. 29). In order to help school professionals understand how to most effectively work with parents from diverse cultures, Kopala et al. (1994) have suggested that parents from those cultural groups could serve as consultants to school personnel. Possibly, school professionals could utilize parents of gifted children as parent consultants.

Several interacting factors can distance the parents of gifted youngsters from schools: Parents may have had negative experiences with other professionals such as pediatricians or may have had prior adversarial relationships with school personnel who did not provide appropriate programming for their gifted child. In addition, economic pressures and other outside demands may reduce the time and energy parents can devote to school activities and may diminish the priority parents can put on involvement in school activities. These pressures and demands are compounded by survival issues for families who live in poverty. Parents also may lack information and skills in working with school professionals, or they may lack knowledge about giftedness and gifted education and about how to appropriately plan for their child. In addition, parents who have experienced school difficulty and parents who have immigrated from other countries may fear school personnel. Adding to their anxieties, parents may be intimidated by their child's giftedness (Friedman-Jenkins & Gallagher, 1991; Meckstroth, 1991).

School personnel, in turn, may fear contact with parents because they generally are not trained to work collaboratively with parents (Sarason, Davidson, & Blatt, 1986). School professionals may discount parents' abilities to contribute and may limit parental involvement to roles such as classroom assistant, homework assistant, and field trips. Schools may also restrict programming for gifted students (Friedman-Jenkins & Gallagher, 1991). In some lower income districts teachers and administrators may concentrate much of their energy and attention on children at the lower academic levels and ignore or overlook potentially gifted children (Zorman, 1991). Because parents from some minority cultures tend not to identify their children as gifted, low teacher expectations can result in students' gifts and talents going unrecognized. Similarly, if school professionals' expectations are low, they may be unresponsive to parents who approach them about gifted potential in their youngsters. In either case, talent and potential can be wasted and lost.

Culturally based attitudes and behaviors also may prevent parents from becoming actively involved in relationships with school professionals. For example, Bernal (cited in Kirschenbaum, 1991) noted that Hispanic parents tend to relate passively to schools and other authorities. This passive approach stems, in part, from a cultural valuing of modesty over assertiveness and a trust in people in authority to determine the best course of action. Consequently, rather than take an aggressive or assertive advocacy stance, most Latino parents tend to use indirectness and politeness, try to lend support to the school, and wait for professionals to take the initiative. Generally, by the time these parents react angrily, they are truly enraged, and it may be difficult to begin a collaborative relationship (Kirschenbaum, 1991). Therefore, it is important to find culturally congruent ways to help Latino and other minority parents to advocate for their children.

Levels of Parent-Professional Interventions

School interactions and interventions with parents of gifted children can take place on several levels: individual, group, and systems. Professionals can work collaboratively with individual parents during activities such as assessment and program planning. Parents can participate in support and informational groups and training programs. At a systems level, professionals can collaborate with individuals and organizations in the community who interact with parents of gifted youngsters.

Individual interventions. Several principles adapted by Friedman-Jenkins and Gallagher (1991) from Dunst and Trivette's (1987) model can help guide professionals to enable and empower parents of gifted youngsters. These suggestions include: (a) offering assistance that is reciprocal, (b) promoting "parents' natural resources and support networks," (c) conveying "a sense of cooperation and joint responsibility for meeting needs and solving problems," (d) promoting "parents acquiring behavior that reduces their need for help," and (e) helping to "increase parents' beliefs in themselves as causal agents in producing and maintaining desired changes" (pp. 265-266).

Stein (1983)—surveying Latino parents of youngsters with disabilities about lack of parental participation in conferences to develop Individualized Educational Programs—identified several barriers that may affect parental participation in school conferences: transportation problems, work pressures, time conflicts, child care concerns, and language difficulties. Parents also trusted school professionals and deferred to their opinions. These factors seem equally relevant to parents of gifted youngsters.

Some of Stein's (1983) suggestions to deal with these concerns included: (a) conducting meetings and presenting school communications in the language most comfortable for the parents, (b) encouraging parents to ask questions and offer information and suggestions about their child, (c) training bilingual facilitator to assist parents in becoming partners, (d) considering and respecting cultural differences and similarities and discussing the consequences of these differences and similarities openly as part of the developing collaborative relationship, (e) encouraging parents to participate in school, (f) helping parents to participate in their children's school program by clearly explaining parental and child rights and responsibilities and discussing educational programs and resources, (g) providing transportation and child-care services when parent participation at a school meeting is required or desired, and (h) working with community representatives and agencies to develop strategies to involve parents and other community members more actively.

When all efforts at collaboration fail, parents need to be supported by professionals in advocating for their gifted children through due process and mediation (Karnes & Marquardt, 1991). Parents may need information such as understanding of the assessment process, knowledge of legal rights and regulations, and examples of curricular and programmatic alternatives. Demystification of due process proceedings, assistance in mediating with school professionals, and skills in serving as child advocates may be helpful (Silverstein et al., 1992).

Group interventions. Parents of gifted youngsters may feel isolated, with few opportunities to talk with other parents of gifted children (Webb, 1993). Parent groups and training sessions—run by school personnel or parent consultants similar to those suggested by Kopala et al. (1994)—can provide opportunities for parents to gain support and information. Topics can include characteristics and identification of giftedness; child-rearing issues with gifted children, including variability in development, setting appropriate standards, supporting emotional growth, and discipline; fostering positive peer relationships; sibling relationships; effective parent-child communication; school, home, and community enrichment activities and community resources; curriculum, educational placements, and programming; parent and child rights; books related to giftedness; and planning for the future (Friedman-Jenkins & Gallagher, 1991; Meckstroth, 1991; Strom et al., 1992; Webb, 1993).

Parent group discussions can decrease the sense of isolation (Robinson et al., 1979) and may "help to normalize many behaviors and provide a sense of perspective, as well as to give many specific and concrete behavioral suggestions for parenting and educating gifted children" (Webb, 1993, p. 534). Contrary to the experiences of parents of children who are not gifted, parents of gifted children rarely have informal opportunities to discuss child rearing with other parents of gifted youngsters. Other parents may not be sympathetic or understand the issues faced by parents of gifted children (Webb, 1993). Where appropriate, members of extended families and friendship relations should also be considered for inclusion in planning and interventions to provide support and reduce feelings of isolation (Hines et al., 1992).

Outreach programs to parents of potentially gifted children—modeled on those suggested by Kopala et al. (1994) to deal with issues of acculturation—could help prevent feelings of isolation, provide education and support to parents, and encourage collaborative parental and family participation. Activities could include home visits, invitations to the school, parties, and picnics; and school orientation programs. Educational programs could also help parents to understand the role they can take in fostering giftedness. For example, some parents of infants and young children may not be aware of the importance of such activities as talking with their infant, reading to their young child, and encouraging exploration and curiosity (Strom et al., 1992).

It is important that these interventions be conceptualized in a manner that shows respect for parents' competency, experience, and knowledge and treats parents with dignity. For example, parents may feel offended if they are told they need training in activities that they consider to be a natural part of their parenting role (Silverstein et al., 1992).

Systems interventions. Organizations in the community and professionals involved with children and parents should also be contacted and invited to work collaboratively with school personnel and parents. At times they will need information and training about giftedness so they can serve as supportive resources to parents of gifted youngsters. Webb (1993) advocated for educating and involving pediatric professionals, including pediatricians, and psychologists, day care center staff, and others who work with gifted children and their parents. Using a model suggested by Kopala et al. (1994) for acculturation, church leaders and other community leaders and organizations could be utilized for outreach to identify gifted children and as resources for parent education.

Parents also need professionals' support, encouragement, and collaboration in order to generate preventive systemic changes through activities such as lobbying for the development of legislation and for the development of programs in school and community. In addition to support and collaboration, professionals can provide training, information about resources such as state and national organizations for gifted children, and access to networks of resource people. By joining together, parents, professionals, and community leaders can be a powerful force to help gifted children reach their fullest potential.

REFERENCES

Albert, R. (1980). Family positions and the attachment of eminence: A study of special family positions and special family experiences. *Gifted Child Quarterly, 24,* 87-95.

Bernal, E. (1979). The education of the culturally gifted. In A. H. Passow (Ed.), *The gifted and talented: Their education and development* (Part I, pp. 395-400). Chicago: University of Chicago Press.

Bronfenbrenner, U. (1979). *The ecology of human development: Experiments by nature and design.* Cambridge, MA: Harvard University Press.

Bronfenbrenner, U. (1989, June). *The ecology of cognitive development: Research models and fugitive findings.* Paper presented at the annual symposium of the Jean Piaget Society, Philadelphia.

Christenson, S.L., Rounds, T., & Franklin, M. J. (1992). Home-school collaboration: Effects, issues, and opportunities. In S. L. Christenson & J. C. Conoley (Eds.), *Home-school collaboration: Enhancing children's academic and social competence* (pp. 19-51). Silver Spring, MD: National Association of School Psychologists.

Christenson, S. L., Rounds, T., & Gorney, D. (1992). Family factors and student achievement: An avenue to increase students' success. *School Psychology Quarterly, 1,* 178-206.

Clark, R. (1983). *Family life and school achievement: Why poor black children succeed or fail.* Chicago: University of Chicago Press.

Cohelo, G., & Stein, J. (1980). Change, vulnerability, and coping: Stresses of uprooting and overcrowding. In G. Coelho & O. Ahmed (Eds.), *Uprooting and development: Dilemmas of coping with modernization* (pp. 19-40). New York: Plenum.

Colangelo, N., & Dettman, D. (1983). A review of research on parents and families of gifted children. *Exceptional Children, 50,* 20-27.

Cornell, D. G., & Grossberg, I. N. (1989). Parent use of the term 'gifted': Correlates with family environment and child adjustment. *Journal for the Education of the Gifted, XII,* 218-230.

Csikszentmihalyi, M., & Beattie, O. (1979). Life themes: A theoretical and empirical exploration of their origins and effects. *Humanistic Psychology, 19,* 45-63.

Davis, G., & Rimm, S. (1989). *Education of the gifted and talented* (2nd ed.). Englewood Cliffs, NJ: Prentice-Hall.

Dornbush, S., Ritter, P., Leiderman, P., Toberts, D., & Fraleigh, M. (1987). The relation of parenting style to adolescent school performance. *Child Development, 58,* 1244-1257.

Dunst, C. J., & Trivette, C. M. (1987). Enabling and empowering families: Conceptual intervention issues. *School Psychology Review, 16,* 443-456.

Feuerstein, R., Rand, Y., & Rynders, J. (1988). *Don't accept me as I am: Helping "retarded" people to excel.* New York: Plenum.

Ford, D. (1993). An investigation of the paradox of underachievement among gifted Black students. *Roeper Review, 16,* 78-84.

Freeman, J. (1993). Parents and families in nurturing giftedness and talent. In K. Heller, F. Monks, & A. H. Passow (Eds.), *International handbook of research and development of giftedness and talent* (pp. 669-683). Oxford: Pergamon.

Friedman-Jenkins, R. C., & Gallagher, T. (1991). The family with a gifted child. In M. Fine (Ed.), *Collaboration with parents of exceptional children* (pp. 257-273). Brandon, VT: Clinical Psychology Publishing Company.

Gelcer, E., & Dick, S. (1986). Families of gifted children: Achievers and underachiever. In K. K. Urban, H. Wagner, & W. Wieczerkowski (Eds.), *Giftedness: A continuing worldwide challenge* (pp. 447-459). New York: Trillum.

Goertzel, V., & Goertzel, M. G. (1962). *Cradles of eminence.* Boston: Little Brown.

Gonsalves, C. (1992). Psychological stages of the refugee process: A model for therapeutic interventions. *Professional Psychology: Research and Practice, 23,* 382-389.

Hackney, H. (1981). The gifted child, the family, and the school. *Gifted Child Quarterly, 25,* 51-62.

Harry, B. (1992). *Cultural diversity, families, and the special education system: Communication and empowerment.* New York: Teachers College Press.

Hines, P., & Boyd-Franklin, N. (1982). Black families. In M. McGoldrick, J. Pearce, & J. Giordano (Eds.), *Ethnicity and family therapy* (pp. 84-107). New York: Guilford.

Hines, P., Garcia-Preto, N., McGoldrick, M., Almeida, R., & Weltman, S. (1992). Intergenerational relationships across cultures. *Families in Society: The Journal of Contemporary Human Services, 73,* 323-338.

Hundeide, K. (1992). Cultural constraints on cognitive enrichment. In P. S. Klein & A. Tannenbaum (Eds.), *To be young and gifted* (pp. 52-69). Norwood, NJ: Ablex.

Jensen, M., & Feuerstein, R. (1987). The Learning Potential Assessment Device: From philosophy to practice. In C. Lidz (Ed.), *Dynamic assessment: An interactional approach to evaluating learning potential* (pp. 379-402). New York: Guilford.

Karnes, F., & Marquardt, R. (1991). *Gifted children and legal issues in education: Parents' stories of hope.* Dayton, OH: Psychology Press.

Kirschenbaum, R. J. (1991). An interview with Ernesto M. Bernal and Particia Hays. *The Gifted Child Today, 14,* 40-46.

Kopala, M., Esquivel, G., & Baptiste, L. (1994). Counseling approaches for immigrant children: Facilitating the acculturative process. *The School Counselor, 41,* 352-359.

Kraus, W. A. (1980). *Collaboration in organizations: Alternatives to hierarchies.* New York: Human Sciences Press.

Lee, S. (1993). Enhancing achievement through expectation and effort. In Urban Education Project (Ed.), *Restructuring to educate the urban learner: Invited papers* (pp. 19-22). Philadelphia: Research for Better Schools. (ERIC Document Reproduction Service No. ED 375 220)

McAdoo, H. (1977). Family therapy in the Black community. *Journal of the American Orthopsychiatric Association, 47,* 75-79.

Meckstroth, E. (1991). Guiding the parents of gifted children: The role of counselors and teachers. In R. Milgram (Ed.), *Counseling gifted and talented children: A guide for teachers, counselors, and parents* (pp. 95-120). Norwood, NJ: Ablex.

Papajohn, J., & Spiegel, J. (1975). *Transactions in families.* San Francisco: Jossey-Bass.

Parson, R. D., & Meyers, J. (1984). *Developing consultation skills.* San Francisco: Jossey-Bass.

Pinderhughes, E. (1982). Afro-American families and the victim system. In M. McGoldrick, J. Pearce, & J. Giordano (Eds.), *Ethnicity and family therapy* (pp. 108-122). New York: Guilford.

Radford, J. (1990). *Child prodigies and exceptional early achievers.* London: Harvester Wheatsheaf.

Rimm, S.B. (1990). *How to parent so children will learn.* Watertown, WI: Apple.

Rimm, S. (1991). Parenting the gifted adolescent—special problems, special joys. In M. Bireley & J. Genshaft (Eds.), *Understanding the gifted adolescent: Educational , developmental, and multicultural issues* (pp. 18-32). New York: Teachers College Press.

Robinson, H., Roedell, W., & Jackson, N. (1979). Early identification and intervention. In A. H. Passow (Ed.), *The gifted and the talented: Their education and development* (pp. 138-154). Chicago: University of Chicago Press.

Roedell, W. (1984). Vulnerabilities of highly gifted children. *Roeper Review, 6,* 127-130.

Roedell, W. (1989). Early development of gifted children. In J. VanTassel-Baska & P. Olszewski-Kubilius (Eds.), *Patterns of influence on gifted learners: The home, the self, and the school* (pp. 13-28). New York: Teachers College Press.

Rosenfield, S. (1987). *Instructional consultation.* Hillsdale, NJ: Erlbaum.

Sarason, S. B. (1996). *Revisiting "the culture of the school and the problem of change."* New York: Teachers College Press.

Sarason, S. B., Davidson, K. S., & Blatt, B. (1986). *The preparation of teachers: An unstudied problem in education* (rev. ed.). Cambridge, MA: Brookline.

Saunders, J., & Espeland, P. (1991). *Bringing out the best: A resource guide for parents of young gifted children.* Minneapolis: Free Spirit Press.

Scott, M., Perou, R., Urbano, R., Hogan, A., & Gold, S. (1992). The identification of giftedness: A comparison of white, Hispanic and Black families. *Gifted Child Quarterly, 36,* 131-139.

Seagoe, K. M. (1974). Some learning characteristics of gifted children. In R.A. Martinson (Ed.), *The identification of the gifted and talented* (pp. 20-21). Ventura, CA: National/State Leadership Institute on the Gifted and the Talented.

Silverstein, J., Springer, J., & Russo, N. (1992). Involving parents in the special education process. In. S. L. Christenson & J. C. Conoley (Eds.), *Home-school collaboration: Enhancing children's academic and social competence* (pp. 383-407). Silver Spring, MD: National Association of School Psychologists.

Sizemore, B. (1989). The algebra of African-American achievement. In National Alliance of Black School Educators (Ed.), *Effective schools: Critical issues in the education of Black children* (pp. 124-149). Washington, DC: National Alliance of Black School Educators.

Stein, R. C. (1983). Hispanic parents' perspectives and participation in their children's special education program: Comparisons by program and race. *Learning Disability Quarterly, 6,* 432-439.

Strom, R., Johnson, A., Strom, S., & Strom, P. (1992). Designing curriculum for parents of gifted children. *Journal for the Education of the Gifted, 15,* 182-200.

Tannenbaum, A. (1983). *Gifted children: Psychological and educational perspectives.* New York: Macmillan.

Takanishi, R. (Ed.). (1993). *Adolescence in the 1990s: Risk and opportunity.* New York: Teachers College Press.

Tyler, F. B. (1983). The resource collaborator role: A model for interactions involving psychologists. *American Psychologist, 38,* 388-413.

VanTassel-Baska, J. (1989a). Characteristics of the developmental path of eminent and gifted adults. In J. VanTassel-Baska & P. Olszewski-Kubilius (Eds.), *Patterns of influence on gifted learners: The home, the self, and the school* (pp. 146-162). New York: Teachers College Press.

VanTassel-Baska, J. (1989b). The role of the family in the success of disadvantaged gifted learners. *Journal for the Education of the Gifted, 13,* 22-36.

VanTassel-Baska, J., & Olszewski-Kubilius, P. (1989). Introduction. In J. VanTassel-Baska & P. Olszewski-Kubilius (Eds.), *Patterns of influence on gifted learners: The home, the self, and the school* (pp. 1-6). New York: Teachers College Press.

VanTassel-Baska, J., Patton, J., & Prillaman, D. (1991). *Gifted youth at risk: A report of a national study.* Reston VA: Council for Exceptional Children.

Webb, J. (1993). Nurturing social-emotional development of gifted children. In K. Heller, F. Monks, & A. H. Passow (Eds.), *International handbook of research and development of giftedness and talent* (pp. 525-538). Oxford: Pergamon.

Webster, E. C. (1989). Gifted and talented minorities. *Psychotherapy in Private Practice, 7,* 115-131.

Woliver, R., & Woliver, G. M. (1991). Gifted adolescents in the emerging minorities: Asians and Pacific Islanders. In M. Bireley & J. Genshaft (Eds.), *Understanding the gifted adolescent: Educational, developmental, and multicultural issues* (pp. 248-257). New York: Teachers College Press.

Zorman, R. (1991). Identification and nurturance of young disadvantaged gifted children. In R. Milgram (Ed.), *Counseling gifted and talented children: A guide for teachers, counselors, and parents* (pp. 161-178). Norwood, NJ: Ablex.

Chapter 11

Evaluation of Gifted and Talented Programs

John C. Houtz
Susan McCann Brown
Fordham University

We are in an era of increased efforts to respond to individual differences in learning. All population groups are involved: children, adolescents, and adults in every stage of life. All types of settings have experienced the need for specialized programs: schools and after-school programs, hospitals, social service agencies, community centers, clinics, and private business and industry. The kinds of human characteristics and conditions for which specific programs have been developed are extensive. A short list includes school learning and performance difficulties, emotional and behavioral problems, health treatment, job training, family functioning, personal growth and development, social competence, age-related adjustment difficulties, intellectual giftedness, and special talent development.

We are also in an era of critical evaluation of these programs. Despite their variety, evaluation is a common problem these programs all share. Are they effective? Are they worth the time and money we spend on them? There may be hundreds of variables contributing to a program's functioning. How are the effective variables to be separated from the ineffective ones? All the time, effort, and creativity focused to change some human condition or skill has to be measured and compared to the amount of change actually achieved. The common problem experienced by every program manager is that of how to determine whether the program works well enough to justify its continuation.

This chapter deals with the evaluation of educational programs for gifted and talented youngsters from different cultural, ethnic, and/or language backgrounds. Material is presented in four sections. First, a brief discussion of gifted education in general is presented. Still unresolved in the field are issues concerning the underrepresentation of minority and culturally different pupils and methods to identify them fairly for gifted/talented programs. Second is a discussion of evaluation itself as a field of inquiry. Both quantitative and qualitative models have developed and been promoted as appropriate ways to gather the necessary information to answer questions of program effectiveness. The third section details a variety of specific evaluation designs, statistical techniques, and qualitative evaluation models. Finally, the fourth section presents recommendations for program evaluations and the application of one model—Daniel Stufflebeam's (Stufflebeam et al., 1971) CIPP model, for context-inputs-processes-products, which offers considerable flexibility and structure for evaluation of gifted/talented programs that serve a variety of goals and purposes as well as possess numerous and complex educational components.

GIFTED AND TALENTED EDUCATION TODAY

Education for gifted and talented pupils in schools has made significant progress in the past half-century (Clark, 1992; Colangelo & Davis, 1997; Gallagher & Gallagher, 1994; Khatena, 1992). There is greater awareness by educators, parents, and community leaders of the need for such programs. There is a greater understanding of the cognitive and social-emotional abilities of gifted/talented pupils and greater knowledge of instructional and supportive services that can help meet these needs. There is more specialized training for teachers and counselors of the gifted/talented, but much remains to be done (Torrance, 1986). There continue to be unresolved debates, both about the philosophy and educational practices of gifted/talented programs. Many individuals continue to argue that educational resources should be allocated to the "less able" (e.g., the learning disabled, disadvantaged, physically challenged, etc.) child rather than to the highly able child. A common feeling is that the gifted pupil will achieve "in spite of" whatever obstacles are encountered, whereas the less able child requires assistance. Helping the more fortunate smacks to some in our U.S. culture of promoting elitism rather than the egalitarian values of democracy. This resistance is often seen among parents and community leaders who are concerned about high taxes to pay for such programs while they read stories of pupils receiving diplomas but who cannot find jobs because they have not mastered basic skills such as reading and arithmetic.

Even among supporters of gifted/talented education are researchers and educators who differ on methods of instruction for the gifted/talented. Some such as Julian Stanley (1976) believe strongly in acceleration of gifted/talented pupils through the regular school curriculum at faster rates. Gifted pupils are best served by being exposed to more advanced material—as early as they can handle it (Sowell, 1993). Often this means that they can skip grades, take advanced, "honors" classes, or attend special programs and schools.

Other gifted/talented educators such as Joseph Renzulli (1977) believe that gifted/talented pupils benefit most from different types of learning experiences as opposed to being given "the same material at earlier ages." This broad approach is often termed *enrichment* in contrast to acceleration. Renzulli's "Enrichment Triad Model," for example, relies on any number of types of individual and group activities that are "above and beyond" the regular school curriculum. Students of the literature, however, have come to realize that clear definitions of enrichment and acceleration do not always exist. Extreme programs are easy to identify, but many programs rely on both approaches. Their instructional activities combine exposure to advanced material in special subject areas (acceleration) with "supplemental," "pull-out" activities (enrichment) for some students in addition to regular class placement with "nongifted" pupils for other aspects of the school curriculum.

The literature of gifted/talented education shows benefits for both types of programs (Daurio, 1979; Feldhusen, 1991; Khatena, 1992; Torrance, 1986). So the debates are bound to continue. As with other educational interventions, there are too many variables to control in gifted programs to guarantee that unequivocal findings will result. Each program may be designed and developed with general principles in mind but for specific purposes, specific pupil populations, unique school and community contexts, and particular instructional inputs and educational outcomes. So many of these factors, their interactions, and their effects on pupil outcomes remain poorly or incompletely understood. Thus, evaluation of such programs becomes critically important if the literature is to move forward and provide better guidance for future program planners and researchers.

Identifying Gifted and Talented Minority Pupils

One of the most important issues in gifted/talented program evaluation concerns inclusion of minority pupils (Bernal, 1980, 1981; Borland, 1997; Passow, 1972; Renzulli, 1973; Taylor, 1968; Torrance, 1969, 1977, 1986). Many programs designed for the gifted and talented enroll fewer children from minority backgrounds than would be expected based on relative proportions of such children in the overall school population (Baldwin, 1987a, 1987b; Clark, 1992; Ford & Harris, 1990; Kitano, 1991; Kitano & Perez, 1998; Maker, 1987; Richert, 1987). African-American and Hispanic children and children from socioeconomically disadvantaged backgrounds continue to be underrepresented in most gifted/talented programs (Chinn & Hughes, 1987; Ford & Harris, 1994).

The reasons for such underrepresentation have been highlighted by these and other authors. The most often-cited explanation is the use of specific cutoff scores on standardized intelligence and achievement tests, whose validity for such minority populations is questionable. Other reasons cited include outright bias or, at best, insensitivity on the part of teachers to children from different cultural backgrounds, misunderstanding of the causes of underachievement among minority pupils, differences in learning styles and cultural values associated with schooling, lack of advocacy on these children's behalf from teachers or parents, or less active involvement by minority parents in their children's education (Bernal, 1979, 1990; Ford & Harris, 1994; Scott, Perou, Urbano, Hogan, & Gold, 1992). A literature is growing on the effectiveness of different assessment instruments and techniques for identifying gifted and talented minority children (Ford & Harris, 1990; 1994; Frasier, 1997; House & Lapan, 1994), but none of the special problems described here has been solved.

Enlightened designers of gifted/talented programs have taken special precaution to develop and apply assessment methods that improve the access of minority pupils to such programs (Baldwin, 1994; Fetterman, 1986; Maker & Schiever, 1989; Stone, 1992). Several of these methods include identification of a pool of minority students based on extensive reviews of achievement data over several year periods, meetings with parents of pool members for information and recruitment purposes, automatic inclusion of pool pupils in the testing program (as opposed to reliance on continued requests from teachers or parents), and the use of specialized assessment personnel to review all decisions (Woods & Achey, 1990). Programs have included staff development activities to increase teachers' awareness of minority pupils' potential and to increase expectations for their success in such programs. Programs have conducted outreach activities to enlist parent and community support to increase the number of nominations of minority pupils. Technical characteristics of standardized intelligence and achievement tests have been scrutinized and statistical manipulations made to eliminate or correct for as much cultural-, language-, or learning-style bias as is possible. Local instruments (teacher, peer, or parent nominations and rating scales, for example) have been developed, with local norms, so that predictions of future success in gifted/talented programs have greater validity. Screening processes are overseen by experts in measurement and cultural bias and by representatives from minority groups whose children are being served. These and other procedures have been employed to respond to the need for equal access to gifted/talented education.

The Fetterman (1986) report is a good example of the progress of a gifted program evaluation through a politically charged community atmosphere. The Peoria program initially was found by Illinois State authorities to discriminate against minority children because a much lower percentage of Black students were selected for the program (grades 4-8, homogeneous grouping, an enrichment model but with considerable advancement of the traditional curriculum into high school subjects) compared to the overall percentage of Black pupils in the district schools when compared with White pupils. State funding was at risk of being eliminated, so the district undertook an extensive evaluation of its referral, assessment, and selection criteria and procedures as part of an overall evaluation of the program.

Peoria hired an external evaluator with a positive reputation in the area of equal educational opportunity. A careful review of the screening process was initiated. Peoria actually had been using more assessment devices than the minimum recommended by the state and had been adhering to the published State Education Department guidelines for gifted/talented selections. Standardized intelligence and achievement test data, teacher nominations, past grades, and individual ratings were being used. Furthermore, some of the testing and ratings assessments were conducted by expert, local university personnel.

But further analysis revealed potential problems and led to recommendations for change. Teacher referrals of minority pupils were very low. Minority parents complained of teachers' low expectations for their children. Acknowledging this issue, staff development activities were developed to increase teachers' awareness of gifted behaviors, especially in minority children. Teachers with better "track records" of predictive validity of their nominations were recruited to aid in the in-service program. The selection committee makeup of teachers and other school personnel was changed to include representatives from predominantly minority schools. All these changes were intended to increase the pool of minority candidates.

The rating form of student characteristics was judged out of date and with little reliability. From the research literature, revisions were made and piloting of the modified form was undertaken. Several technical revisions were made to the administration, scoring, and interpretation of the standardized intelligence and achievement tests. The evaluation noted a few problems ranging from deviations from the standard administration directions for these measures to the type of pencils used to mark answer sheets. Additional recommendations were made concerning the use of raw scores rather than percentiles and modifications to the weights given to different measurements in the selection process. Finally, the discretionary power of administrators in selecting replacement pupils for those students who voluntarily left the program was greatly curtailed.

The Peoria evaluation went on to examine the community context of the gifted/talented program and attributed to this context a large measure of explanation for the underrepresentation of minority students. The city of Peoria was not ethnically or socioeconomically integrated. The report concluded that there were large areas of de facto segregation of minority subpopulations, with substantially different (lower) levels of educational achievement. The evaluator also examined a nearby city's (Evanston) gifted program for help in understanding the origins of the great disparity in White-Black program enrollment. Evanston's program, which had better enrollments of non-White pupils, had a significant focus on visual and performing arts, whereas Peoria's program was exclusively focused on high ability/high academic achievement. Peoria made substantial changes to its selection procedures, but was not able to change the achievement focus of its program as a result of the evaluation.

What can be learned from the Peoria case is that there are many things that can be done to safeguard the principle of "equal access" to gifted/talented programs through careful development of selection criteria and assessment methods. These precautions can enhance the pool of minority candidates and insure that their applications will be processed fairly. But larger societal issues of racial and/or socioeconomic discrimination in educational opportunity that limit the pool in the first place may be beyond the scope of any one educational program. Assessing community values, attitudes, and realities is a political and pragmatic necessity for most gifted/talented programs, but directors of gifted/talented programs should keep in mind that their programs may not be able to address larger issues of social injustice or inequality. The best they may aim for is a solid justification of their program's goals vis-à-vis the needs of their pupils and the demonstrated technical, psychometric, and instructional soundness of their assessment practices. This, they may hope, will gain them continued community support.

Talent Development

Alternative views have been developed in response to minority recruitment and other issues in gifted/talented education. The work of John Feldhusen (1993, 1993/1994, 1995) and the Resource Center for the Gifted and Talented at Purdue University is a case in point. Rather than continuing to focus on the concept of giftedness, Feldhusen argues that our focus should shift to the term *talent*, which has generally been used to refer to exceptionality in the arts or other aesthetic endeavors. For most people, *gifted* implies a focus on intelligence testing and traditional academic achievement. Associated with this term, too, is the *baggage* of biased standardized testing and distrust of the idea of educating an "elite" cohort of individuals. If we drop the term *gifted,* Feldhusen argues, we free ourselves from this excess baggage and can turn our attention to development of any number of different talents that humans possess.

The talent development approach, according to Feldhusen, focuses our attention on the strengths of each and every child. The direction of educational, psychological knowledge of individual differences in the past 50 years has been that of affirming human diversity rather than limiting it. We now have substantial theories and research establishing the wide range of human intellectual and performance abilities—talents—that can be measured and nurtured. An emphasis on individual talents throughout the school years helps to avoid the traditional biases of typical intelligence tests that often exclude nonmajority culture pupils. Talent development methods ensure the encouragement of many skills and abilities required in a thriving, pluralistic society. Equal valuation of individuals' differing talents helps to avoid the worry of supporting an education of an "undemocratic," elite group of citizens.

Griffin (1992) described the efforts of "A Better Chance, Inc.," a national academic talent search agency whose primary mission is to identify minority pupils with academic potential and to assist them in finding appropriate schooling to help them realize their full potential. The criteria used by this agency are broader than intelligence and achievement tests. In addition to the typical performance indicators such as test scores and personal information obtained from students, parents, and teachers, "A Better Chance, Inc." obtains evidence of such things as pupils' sense of self, independence of mind, questioning attitude, willingness to take risks, and perseverance. Broadening the criteria for identifying minority gifted pupils is consistent with modern psychological theories of intellectual and social-emotional development and the talent development approach advocated by Feldhusen.

PROGRAM EVALUATION

Evaluation methodology is a young field, perhaps no older than 25 years. Authors and "groundbreakers" in the field have identified the 1970s as the birthing decade. Various textbooks, handbooks, and journals first appeared on the scene. Writers tried to define the new field, distinguish it from other disciplines, and propose new models or ways of conceptualizing the tasks of evaluation. One now famous definition offered by Daniel Stufflebeam et al. (1971) was that evaluation was the act of acquiring information in a systematic way for the purpose of aiding decision making. This is an important definition because it served at the time to illustrate a possible major distinction between educational research and evaluation.

Historically, experimental research methodology (or "impact assessment," as Rossi & Freeman, 1989, describe it) was the most readily accessible theory and methodology available to the program developers of the 1960s. The publication, in 1963, by Donald T. Campbell and Julian Stanley, of "Experimental and Quasi-experimental Designs for Research" in the first *Handbook of Research on Teaching* was a significant milestone. It was notable because their chapter appeared to organize a complex set of principles (e.g., randomization, comparison groups, internal and external validity) into a coherent framework, and it reached a great many people who were in turn responsible for training researchers. But, as Stufflebeam and others pointed out, the overreliance on quantitative and statistical designs in evaluation studies limited the types of information and activities open to program evaluators. There were other purposes for conducting evaluations and alternative, qualitatively oriented models that could guide program evaluators.

Guba and Lincoln (1989) have claimed that evaluation science has actually progressed through four different generations, each characterized by different concerns and methods. The first two generations concerned themselves with measurement and description, paralleling the development of formal scientific principles and technologies in the last quarter of the 19th century and the first half of the 20th. The third generation was spurred by the perceived need to use these technologies to make judgments of the worth of programs. This generation, for Guba and Lincoln, dates from the post-Sputnik era, when we began to use publicly supported programs on a massive scale to influence broad social goals. For Lincoln and Guba and others concerned with the methods and purposes of program evaluation, each of these generations made significant progress but has outlived its usefulness. The current, fourth generation holds greater promise for further advancement. The foci of fourth-generation evaluation are the stakeholders in the program—those individuals and their beliefs and concerns that create and sustain the context, or milieu, in which the program functions and is judged. Stakeholders are the users of the program, those individuals who experience it or are affected by it. Their claims, concerns, and issues are the organizational factors of fourth-generation evaluation. Objective, statistical realities of experimental methods (a first- to third-generation technology) may not be the most appropriate methods for fourth-generation evaluation. Rather, qualitative methods—interviews, naturalistic observations, case studies, and conferences among all involved parties—may yield better data from which to understand what contributes to program success. All the more important for fourth-generation evaluation is the ability of program evaluators to be fully involved in a program, from inception to development, implementation, and conclusion (Renzulli & Smith, 1979).

Multiple Purposes of Evaluation

Anderson and Ball (1978) described six types of decisions for which program evaluation data may be collected: (a) to collect information to contribute to decisions about program installation; (b) to collect information to contribute to decisions about program continuation, expansion, or "certification"; (c) to contribute to decisions about program modification; (d) to obtain evidence to rally support for a program; (e) to obtain evidence to rally opposition to a program; or (f) to contribute to the understanding of basic psychological, social, and educational processes. The first purpose is often termed *front-end* analysis. Assessing the need for a new program would be one example. School officials could survey potential users, constituents, "stakeholders," or benefactors (such as parents, teachers, community leaders, or pupils themselves) to discover their views about the need for a gifted/talented program or the types of objectives for the program, services, or components that could be provided.

The second purpose is what many people commonly think of as the purpose of program evaluation—gathering data for judging whether a program should continue, be extended to a greater number of people, or otherwise given some "stamp of approval" such as official accreditation by a government agency or professional group. A functioning gifted and talented program typically gathers data on pupil test scores, grades, satisfaction ratings (from pupils, parents, teachers, etc.), competitive prizes or honors won, outstanding projects, creative productions, and so on. These types of information are periodically reported to the stakeholders and decision makers to establish the effectiveness or worth of the program. Positive data that impress the decision makers (e.g., parents, community leaders, taxpayers) may convince everyone involved that the program should be funded for another year or expanded to include additional pupils.

The evaluation conducted for the second purpose is often termed *summative evaluation* (Bloom, Hastings, & Madaus, 1971; Scriven, 1967) because its focus is on gathering end-product or output data. In contrast, the third purpose of program evaluation is often termed *formative evaluation* because its focus is on gathering information that will be used to change or modify a program—to improve it. Gifted and talented program evaluations do this as well, although perhaps not to as great a degree. How are all the program components functioning? Did the identification process work well? Are the assessment procedures or instruments doing what was intended? For example, are enough gifted minority pupils being selected? Other questions for formative evaluation might include the effectiveness of staff development activities, the content of the coursework developed for pupils, or the methods of instruction.

The fourth and fifth purposes deal with the advocacy of a program. Individuals who support or who are critical of special programs would seek information to convince others of their position. Clearly, parents of gifted and talented pupils may be strong advocates of programs that are intended to address the superior abilities of their children. They would be first to demand action from school officials when the regular school curriculum fails to hold their children's interests or develop their abilities and talents to the fullest. On the other hand, as mentioned earlier, there also may be opponents of special programs for gifted/talented pupils who will cite data in support of discontinuing such programs.

A recent addition to program evaluation practice has been the gathering of data on the "cost-effectiveness" (Rossi & Freeman, 1989) of programs. Advocates of programs can point to the expenses required to establish and operate a particular program compared to the "dollar-values" of the outcomes or benefits of the program, or the "costs" of not addressing the special needs of gifted/talented pupils. These costs might include lost wages and benefits to society for continued underrealization of potential, costs for counseling unhappy pupils, costs associated with disruptiveness or other socially maladaptive behavior caused by pupil boredom or misguided creativity. The design and implementation of a gifted/talented program may cost hundreds or even thousands of dollars per pupil, but the benefits to individual pupils and society at large in terms of school achievement, college admission, entry into professions, and lifetime success (as opposed to juvenile delinquency, crime, unemployment, poor health care, etc.) may exceed hundreds of thousands of dollars.

Finally, program evaluation data also may be used for research. We may learn from test scores, observations, interviews, surveys, anecdotal records of various kinds, and other types of data why some program components worked well or not. We may see relationships among psychological variables and processes that we have seen before in the literature and/or that support one theory or another. We may discover new relationships or see contradictory evidence in some cases. Evaluation data can lead us to generate new hypotheses as to how and why our program functioned as it did. An example might be learning from parent involvement in their children's gifted/talented program that such parental support translated into supplemental activities beyond the classroom and greater achievement and positive regard for the program among pupils. Another instance could be discovering a connection between staff development activities specifically directed for a gifted/talented program and classroom instruction that transferred beyond the special program to other teachers and classrooms. A third example might be using data from the assessment and instructional components of a gifted/talented program to examine the relationship between cognitive and emotional development. How, for instance, do gifted/talented youth feel about their special talents? What non-academic problems are they experiencing and how are they attempting to handle them?

Models of Program Evaluation

As there are multiple purposes, researchers and evaluators have proposed multiple models of how to go about gathering information to address these purposes. Worthen and Sanders (1973, 1987; Worthen, Sanders, & Fitzpatrick, 1997) noted that different models exist because individuals have different philosophical and ideological views of evaluation. Two of these views include to what degree one believes that evaluation information is (or can be considered) objective or subjective or whether the value of a program should be judged on the basis of its effects on the largest group of pupils or on each individual pupil (House, 1983a, 1983b). Worthen and Sanders have characterized models of program evaluation along House's (1983a) objective/utilitarian versus subjective/intuitionist-pluralist dimension. Objectives- and management-oriented models sit at the objective/ultilitarian end of the continuum, whereas naturalistic and participant-oriented evaluations sit at the other end. In between are other models such as consumer-oriented, expertise oriented, and adversary-oriented. Figure 11.1 displays this continuum.

The gifted/talented literature reflects this continuum as well. The classic, quantitatively oriented experimental research model would seem to apply to gifted/talented program evaluation for purposes 2, 4, and 5. For these purposes objectives for the program and its evaluation often are clear, criteria for success or failure are accepted generally, and stakeholders are definite in their opinions and needs. However, at the other end of the continuum is "fourth-generation evaluation." Stakeholders are not so self-confident or self-assured, criteria for success are more diverse and/or controversial, and program objectives may be less clearly defined and understood. For evaluation purposes 1, 3, and 6, therefore, more subjective, individualistic, context-based evaluation methods may be the most appropriate.

What we can conclude is that as the field of evaluation has grown, there has been a natural progression from reliance on a few, traditional experimental and quantitative methods to acceptance and use of a wider variety of qualitative techniques and models alone or in combination with quantitative methods. For gifted/talented evaluations this is a positive development. As stated earlier, the gifted/talented literature to date has served best to illustrate how complex the issues are, and an expanding evaluation methodology can only help improve the quality of evaluation research in the area.

EVALUATION DESIGNS AND STATISTICAL METHODS

Traditional "quantitatively oriented," objective/utilitarian wisdom consistent with the design of good experiments is that effective

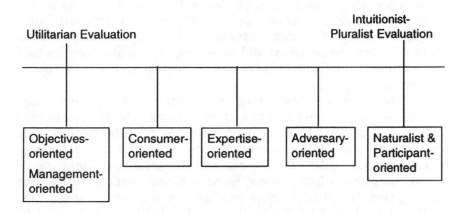

Figure 11.1. Distribution of six evaluation approaches according to objective/utilitarian vs. subjective/intuitionist-pluralist approaches

Reprinted from *Educational evaluation: Alternative approaches and practical guidelines* (p. 79), by B. Worthen, J. Sanders, & J. L. Fitzpatrick, 1997, New York: Longman. Copyright 1997 by Addison-Wesley-Longman. Reprinted by permission.

program evaluation requires that the new program must be compared with a control group—a group that receives no program or receives an alternative program of already established effectiveness (Campbell & Stanley, 1963; Gall, Borg, & Gall, 1996). If the evaluator assures us that the program and control groups are "equal" in all critical respects prior to the onset of the program, then we can measure the effects of the program after it concludes. By comparing program and control groups on the relevant "dependent variables," the evaluator can obtain a statistical decision as to the program's effectiveness.

Unhappily, too many "evaluations" of educational programs are similar to that of a recent one made by Kolitch and Brody (1992). These individuals identified mathematically precocious first-year college students through their high SAT scores. The purpose of the research was to evaluate the effects of early acceleration of mathematics content in school. Survey questionnaires were sent to a small number (69) of students, which asked for their opinions as to the usefulness and effectiveness of their various precollege math educational experiences and current and future math activities and plans. The authors performed detailed and careful analyses of the types of precollege experiences, grade-level and gender analyses, and students' satisfaction and/or perceived problems. But without a comparison group of similar students who did not have these various early acceleration instructional experiences, nothing can be said about a causal relationship between acceleration and later success in mathematics.

No doubt students' perceptions of their past experiences and current activities are important and interesting data. In fact, Kolitch and Brody made extensive recommendations regarding educational planning for such students and the development of accelerative learning opportunities for mathematically gifted students (recall evaluation purpose 3). However, these recommendations rest on the assumption (implied in this evaluation but not tested) that acceleration has led for these pupils to later success (measured by grades, credits, major, extra-curricular activities, career choice, etc.) in college. This connection cannot be inferred from the "preexperimental" design used (Campbell & Stanley, 1963; Cook & Campbell, 1979).

Kingsley (1986) reported the results of a questionnaire sent to 11 participants of an extracurricular enrichment program for high school students. The program was funded by a private foundation and included field trips to excavations of historic sites in the community and peer tutoring of elementary students by the high schoolers. The questionnaire solicited students' ratings of satisfaction with program activities and suggestions for improvements. The results can be of significant use to others planning similar programs, but no conclusions can be drawn as to the positive benefits of the program. There was no comparison group. There is nothing to counter the argument that these students might have developed on their own, without any special program at all, greater knowledge and understanding of local history and culture, leadership skills, responsibility, and so on.

Similarly, Baldwin (1994) reported an evaluation of a large gifted program in one school district in New York City, with significantly more minority enrollees (Black, Hispanic, and Asian) than White pupils. The program involved districtwide staff development and instructional changes in numerous schools along the model of talent proposed by Howard Gardner. Evaluation of the effects of the program, however, was confined to pre- and posttest teacher ratings of student characteristics (flexibility, originality, elaboration, commitment, performance, etc.). Statistically significant Fall-Spring gains were reported, but without a control comparison group, who can say that these children would not have improved on their own naturally?

The famous "null hypothesis" states that there is no difference expected in performance between program and comparison groups. To be more precise, the two groups are expected to be "samples" selected randomly from the same population of all possible subgroups of a population. If the program has no impact, this is a valid hypothesis. The evaluator's hope, however, is to discard the hypothesis of no difference—to reject the null hypothesis. Campbell and Stanley (1963) identified three "designs" that provide maximum internal validity (that is, the chance that one's comparisons are uncontaminated with alternative variables that will explain the observed differences). These designs are:

1. The randomized control-group design, wherein pupils are assigned randomly to program and no-program (or alternative program) groups
2. The randomized, pretest-posttest control group design, which is identical to the first design, with the addition of pre-measures administered before the program begins
3. The randomized, pretest/no pretest, control group design, otherwise known as the Solomon (for King Solomon) Four-Group Design, which is a combination of the first two designs.

These designs all employ random assignment of subjects to groups (program groups and controls or alternative treatments). The second and third designs use pretests administered prior to treatments to gather data on the equality of all groups. The third design adds a comparison of groups (both treatments and controls) that receive pretests and groups that do not, on the theory that experiencing pretests somehow affects individuals' subsequent performance in treatment. However, for long-term interventions in school settings, little evidence for the "pretest sensitization effect" has been observed (Willson & Putnam, 1982).

However, the "randomization" requirement of these three designs often is not possible in real educational settings. Additionally, comparison or control groups may not be possible either. Schools implementing programs are primarily responsible to their pupils and may not be able to withhold programs from some pupils for the sake of experimental rigor. To respond to these realities, Campbell and Stanley (1963) and Cook and Campbell (1979) recommend several other, "quasi-experimental" designs that evaluators can apply. These include:

4. The separate-sample, pretest-posttest control group design. No randomization is possible, but a second group is available and willing to receive pretests only or pretests plus some "placebo" or alternative treatment that can be compared to the program being evaluated.

5. The "wait-list," pretest-posttest control group design. Randomization may or may not be possible, but all members of a program's "target" population must be given the program. So the evaluator selects some pupils to begin the program at a certain time and others to wait for a "second round" of the program later. The "wait list" group serves as a comparison group for the first group. Its pretest occurs at the time of the first group's posttest so a statistical comparison can be computed.

6. The "time series," or "regression discontinuity" design. In this design no comparison or "wait-list" group is possible at all, but the pupils receiving the intervention are assessed several times prior to and after the program is administered. The pre- and postmeasures are taken at regular intervals to provide information as to the "normal" growth rates (i.e., amount of change between each of the pre-measures or each of the postmeasures) before and after the program. If the growth rate changes substantially between pre- and postmeasures, an inference can be made as to the effects of the intervention (Glass, 1988).

Although these designs have the potential for less internal validity than the true experiment (in which randomization is used), with adequate care in their application, valid conclusions ultimately can be drawn from the results of the comparisons. There are statistical techniques that can be applied to help program evaluators design their evaluations and analyze their findings to insure the greatest internal and external validity possible. These are discussed in the sections that follow.

Power Analysis

There are some drawbacks to traditional hypothesis testing that have become more apparent over the years of application to program evaluations. Hypothesis testing is an all-or-nothing situation. The resulting Pearson r, Student's t, or Fisher's F, for example, either are or are not statistically significant. There is no such thing as a result that "approaches" statistical significance, even though such phrases can be found in published papers, not-so-idle professional correspondence and conversation, and even textbooks. Often, psychologists, psychiatrists, counselors, or educators are reluctant to accept the null hypothesis that their well-designed and well-intended programs are useless just because a table of critical values has "told" them they must. It is hard for them to accept that all their good efforts, energies, instincts, and training have not made a difference in the quality of people's lives.

In fact, the null-hypothesis testing model has not been a very good model for decision makers. Jacob Cohen (1988, 1990, 1992) has published work that examines the concept of statistical power. *Power* is defined as the probability of finding truly significant differences, that is, statistically significant differences that are also true. When we test the null hypothesis and reject it at the 5% level of significance, what we are saying is that we are willing to tolerate a 5% error rate. Our result will be significant because of our intervention 95 times out of every 100 times that we employ it. But, as Cohen notes, we never do our experiment 100 times; we rely on just one experiment and have faith our result is one of the 95, not one of the five.

Cohen has argued that much of the published literature of the day has ignored the factors that would make the power of a study large such as a large sample size, small standard deviations in the measures employed, and the "size of the intervention effect." Because of this, many studies conducted and eventually published had low levels of power, say, perhaps 50%. This meant that about half the studies published in the fields he reviewed were reporting significant differences that were false ones.

The use of power analysis for the design of program evaluations is clear. In addition to internal validity, we are concerned with the external validity (Bracht & Glass, 1968; Gall et al., 1996) of our comparisons. External validity refers to the generalizability of our results to different populations or conditions. If statistical significance is obtained in traditional hypothesis testing, there is no guarantee that one significance will be repeated with additional comparisons. To avoid the risk of a Type II error (failure to observe a true, or replicable, difference between program and control groups), program evaluators need to review the literature of prior similar interventions, compute what are termed "effect sizes," then estimate the effect size of the proposed program and use Cohen's formulas and tables to identify the required sample size for the desired level of power. For example, if the evaluator decides that an 85% chance of finding a truly significant difference in favor of the program is the minimum he or she will accept, Cohen's tables will show how many pupils need to be assigned to treatment and comparison groups for various levels of expected effect size. If evaluators need to recruit additional pupils, they should do so. Otherwise they run the risk of obtaining spurious statistical significance. Sample size is extremely critical to statistical power. In spite of exceptional diligence in conducting their studies, program evaluators often have too few subjects in their treatment and comparison groups to yield powerful statistical results.

Statistical Methods for Measuring Program Effects

If a traditional experimental or quasi-experimental design is employed in a program evaluation, various statistical procedures can be used to judge the significance of program effects (the so-called dependent variables). Most common among these are the *t*-test, analysis of variance, and analysis of covariance (Winer, Brown, & Michels, 1991). However, newer methods include metaanalysis, regression, and path analysis (Pedhazur & Schmelkin, 1991). These techniques are applicable to a wider range of evaluation questions or purposes and can be applied when traditional evaluation designs cannot be or are not used.

The t-test. Of great interest to researchers and evaluators is the direct measurement of growth, or change in behavior, from pretreatment to posttreatment. Five of the six designs described earlier employ pretests and posttests of outcome measures. The *t*-test is used when the evaluator needs to compare only two groups (e.g., intervention vs. control or intervention 1 vs. intervention 2) or one group that has a pretest before the intervention and a posttest after the intervention concludes. The former is often termed the independent samples *t*-test and the latter *t* is typically referred to as a paired-difference or correlated *t*-test and involves the consideration of pre- to posttest gains or changes in the dependent variable (Wampold & Drew, 1990).

Analysis of variance. When more than two groups are involved, however, analysis of variance is the statistical technique most often used (Winer et al., 1991). ANOVA techniques have been the "workhorse" of statistical procedures for decades. The advantages of ANOVA procedures are that many variables can be studied in addition to the intervention, many groups can be included in the evaluation, and the interactive effects of treatments and these *ex-post-facto* or "control" variables can be measured as well (Iverson & Norpoth, 1976). The study is only limited by the realities of sampling and assignment of subjects to groups.

A recent example is that of Marsh, Chessor, Craven, and Roche (1995), who reported the effects of a gifted program in two studies of Australian pupils. Their design was simple—a gifted group and a comparison sample. A number of variables were studied; hence, a multivariate analysis of variance was used. Age and gender were included as main effects in addition to group, so numerous interaction effects were examined. Of further note is the overall purpose of Marsh et al.'s study, which examined the self-concept of pupils rather than academic achievement. Of Anderson and Ball's (1978) six evaluation purposes, the Marsh et al. study appears to be aimed at number six—adding to our understanding of basic psychological relationships. Marsh has written about a "Big Fish, Little Pond" theory that there are negative effects of segregation of gifted students in special programs. Removed from the general population, gifted learners may begin to feel less confident in their academic abilities due to their contact only with students who are equally academically successful. As a result of being "big fish in a little pond," so to speak, gifted learners will begin to experience failure more often when comparing themselves to other gifted learners rather than the general population. Marsh et al.'s results suggest such a decline in academic self-concept but not in nonacademic self-concept. Thus, this evaluation of a gifted program helps to increase our understanding of social comparison and self-concept theory.

If the evaluation design has no pretest, a matching or randomization procedure for subject assignment to intervention and control or comparison groups is sufficient to permit the general assumption of group equality prior to the intervention. Then, the ANOVA can be computed on the postintervention measures. Logically, if the assumption of group equality can be made at the beginning of the intervention, and there are statistically significant (and statistically powerful) effects on the posttest, significant change can be inferred. All that remains is the computation of post-hoc means comparisons tests such as the Scheffé, Newman-Keuls, Duncan, Tukey, and so on (Klockars & Sax, 1986; Winer et al., 1991). If more than two groups are involved in the significant main effect, for example, or interaction effect of the ANOVA, then post-hoc tests are necessary to identify which pairs of means differ significantly from one another. In interpreting complex interactions, post-hoc tests are especially helpful because they can show the differences to be due to main effects or true interactive effects. Actually, interactions have a higher priority for interpretation because they contain more data than simple main effects (Campbell & Stanley, 1963; Winer et al., 1991).

In the Marsh et al. studies, gifted pupils were initially identified for the special program using teacher nominations and academic achievement criteria. But for the actual samples of pupils used for the evaluation, Marsh et al. matched pupils on age, gender, and IQ. Pretests of self-concept were taken, and repeated measures MANOVAs were computed so that the change from time 1 to time 2 could be evaluated. There were several statistically significant interactions as well as main effects.

An alternative ANOVA procedure that has been applied to measuring change if a pretest is included in the design is the repeated-measures ANOVA. The "repeated measure" is, of course, the pretest and posttest scores. If the F for the "repeated" factor is statistically significant, we can infer change has occurred. This method is seen in the literature, but it does have its drawbacks. Because subjects are being compared with themselves (i.e., pretest-posttest), the estimates of error variance used to compute F-ratios may be smaller than would be expected in the general population. Thus, the smaller error estimate leads to an artificially high F-ratio. In other words, the significant statistic that obtains may not be a true result (a Type I error). A recommendation can be made that the repeated measures ANOVA would be better applied to posttest-to-retention-test intervals rather than pretest-to posttest intervals. In the former situation, no intervention occurs in the interval between measurements and, therefore, the possibility of a Type I error is less harmful to the evaluation. The evaluator can compensate for this error, somewhat, by increasing the criterion for significance from, say, .05 to .01 or .005.

Nested design ANOVA procedures can be applied for situations in which some factor in the evaluation does not or cannot occur in conjunction with other factors. For example, different teachers may work with different pupil groups in the program. Teachers may not have been assigned to groups of students randomly, and the evaluator desires to separate teacher effects from the other effects of the program. The teacher effect is said to be nested within the program effect. The resulting ANOVA gives a measure of how important it is to have a particular teacher as well as how important it is to have the program at all.

Analysis of covariance. Analysis of covariance is another choice for measuring change. If pretests are included in the design,

ANCOVA uses the pretest as a covariate to correct for possible group differences prior to the intervention. Such correction can be very powerful, but it comes at a price. Covariance is a more delicate technique than regular ANOVA in that violations of the mathematical assumptions undergirding the technique can lead to spurious results (Elashoff, 1969; Glass, Peckham, & Sanders, 1972; Wildt & Ahtola, 1978). Therefore, it is up to the evaluator to justify the technique's use. Before computing ANCOVA, F-tests should be computed on the pretest measures alone to determine the extent of preexisting group differences (for these particular tests, alphas of .15 or .20 rather than .05 should be used to maximize the power of the test). Intercorrelations should be computed between pretest and posttest scores for each group in the study and for the total sample. Clearly, if no pretest differences are observed, ANCOVA is not necessary. If very low correlations between pre- and posttests are obtained, the pretest will not be a useful covariate, and if very high correlations are obtained, ANCOVA results will be unreliable. (Other techniques, such as regression analysis [RA], can be applied and are discussed shortly.) ANCOVA is recommended only when the pretest-posttest correlations are moderate (.30-.60) and relatively homogeneous across the different groups in the evaluation. If homogeneity is not observed, ANCOVA should not be used.

Despite the previously described ANOVA methods, the measurement of change remains a controversial subject (Harris, 1963; Linn & Slinde, 1977; Willet, 1988). One of the most widely used methods for assessing change has been the use of simple change scores (i.e., difference scores between pre- and posttests for each subject), and this technique has engendered much disagreement. Change scores are then compared from one group to another to test the hypothesis that the intervention was more (or less) effective. Recall that the paired t-test described earlier involves a difference or "change" score.

The chief criticisms of change scores involve their supposed unreliability and insensitivity to detecting treatment effects equally well for subjects at different levels of initial performance. Some statisticians have gone so far as to suggest that those researchers wishing to measure change should rephrase their research questions (Cronbach & Furby, 1970). Recently, however, change scores have received a qualified vote of confidence (Willet, 1988). Suffice it to say, the debate will continue. A reasonable recommendation for evaluators is that change scores can be used in conjunction with other analyses. Evaluators should make the computations and include them in their reports together with means and standard deviations of each group on pretests and posttests, correlations between pre- and posttests for each group, and complete descriptive data on subjects and procedures of sampling. Other techniques such as ANOVA and ANCOVA should be computed as well. If all statistical tests point in similar directions, conclusions may be drawn. If the findings from different analyses conflict, then further work is needed. In any event, such data will be a positive contribution to other researchers and evaluators working in the field.

   Metaanalysis. In recent years the idea of evaluating many research studies to assess their common findings has become popular. The technique is called "metaanalysis" (Asher, 1991; Glass, 1977; Light & Pillemer, 1984). As a tool to this end, the concept of "effect size" has become one of the most useful concepts to be applied to such evaluations. In theory, effect size is a measure of how strong an effect a particular intervention is likely to have. Treatments that differ in only a few, trivial components will have similar effect sizes, but treatments that differ substantially in important components should have measurably different effect sizes. A statistically significant difference between an intervention and no intervention should imply a practical, worthwhile difference in effect size.

   A most common measure of effect size is the mathematical difference between the intervention group with the largest mean on the dependent variable and the mean of the control group, divided by the standard deviation of the performance of the control group (Asher, 1991; Glass, 1977). This is, in a sense, a standardized difference score and can then be compared to the percentages of the familiar normal curve. For example, an effect size of 1.0, or a full standard deviation, means that a person scoring at the 50th percentile on the dependent variable before treatment may now be expected to perform at the 88th percentile after experiencing the treatment. The effect-size statistic has shed a great deal of light on apparently conflicting results from many studies.

   Vaugh, Feldhusen, and Asher (1991) conducted a metaanalysis of nine studies comparing the effects of so-called "pull-out" programs for gifted/talented pupils. Pull-out programs are administrative arrangements in schools in which students remain in heterogeneous classes for most of the curriculum, but are "pulled out" into homogeneous groupings for some special schoolwork such as creative problem-solving training, enrichment activities, advanced work in some subject area, and so on. The nine studies identified by Vaugh et al. used either true or quasi-experimental designs to measure such things as achievement gains, self-concept, creativity, critical thinking, or other aspects of higher level thinking. The authors observed, contrary to expectations of critics of the pull-out model, small to moderately positive effect sizes in these studies. Vaugh et al. concluded that pull-out programs can be useful and effective for some gifted pupils.

Kulik and Kulik (1991) have studied the effects of ability grouping and the gifted for more than a decade. They have analyzed the results of several dozen studies comparing the effects of homogeneous grouping of gifted students, notably in accelerated instructional programs. The results of their analyses show positive effect sizes for this method as large as those for pull-out programs. Gifted program designers and evaluators can take heart. One can reasonably conclude from this literature that no one type of gifted program is likely to be best, and certainly more research is warranted.

The use of regression techniques. One of the most popular statistical techniques available today for research and analysis is regression (Darlington, 1990; Edwards, 1985; Kerlinger & Pedhazur, 1973; Pedhazur & Schmelkin, 1991). Regression analysis (RA) is based on the following mathematical model, known as the General Linear Model (GLM):

$$Y = b_0 + b_1X_1 + b_2X_2 + b_3X_3 + \text{.......} + b_kX_k + e$$

The GLM proposes that a variable, Y, can be known (or predicted) by some linear combination of other variables, Xs, plus random error, e. Because we can never know error, the best the mathematicians can do for us is predict Y from just the Xs, or independent variables. Through matrix algebra and calculus we can solve the previous equation (or more accurately, a series of equations), without the error term, for a set of b's such that the difference between the actual Y scores of the group and the predictions of the Ys, using the b's and Xs, is the smallest it can ever be.

Regression analysis works in the following way. The program director/evaluator collects measures of pupil characteristics, program characteristics, relevant school climate characteristics, and other variables of interest. These are the possible predictors of the criterion or outcome measure—student achievement, attitude, personal growth, and so on. A regression equation is then computed (with the aid of statistical computer packages, of course). What obtains from the equation are at least two important pieces of information. First is an overall index that tells how good the prediction is. How close did all the Xs come to predicting Y accurately. This index is the multiple R, a correlation between the actual and predicted Y scores for all the clients. It is interpreted just like a regular Pearson r. The larger the correlation, the better is the prediction.

The second piece of information concerns the b's, or regression coefficients. Each one can be tested against the null hypothesis that it is equal to zero. If this hypothesis is rejected, one knows that the "X" to which the b is "attached" is statistically significant to the prediction. That "X" variable is a very important element in the program. When the b's are then standardized by the RA, they can also be compared directly. One can tell which of the "Xs" are more or less important than other "Xs." Some of the program components may be more or less important than others. With regression analysis, there is a way to examine this.

Regression analysis can be applied to program evaluation in several ways and provides much useful information about the workings of the program under scrutiny. If the evaluation design employs a comparison group, regression can be used to test the significance of the treatment in a fashion similar to the traditional null-hypothesis model, but with a number of advantages. If the evaluation employs only a single treatment group (that is, all pupils receive the program), regression techniques in the form of path analysis (Kerlinger & Pedhazur, 1973; Pedhazur & Schmelkin, 1991) can be performed that will give the evaluator a better idea of the causal linkages between or among program variables and outcomes (more of this type of analysis follows in a later section).

If the evaluation study employs a comparison group, two models of RA can be chosen, depending on the way in which subjects are selected for the treatment. The two models are known as Regression Projection and Discontinuity, respectively (Judd & Kenny, 1981). If subjects are chosen for the treatment and comparison groups on a random basis or are not different on some pretest measures, then the Regression Projection model compares the treatment group's actual posttest mean score with the mean posttest score predicted for the comparison group from the comparison group's pretest scores. The logic here is that the comparison group's predicted performance represents the amount of gain that will naturally occur under a no-treatment situation. If the treatment group's actual posttest mean is larger by a statistically significant amount, one may conclude that the treatment was effective.

An alternative to this procedure is the Regression Discontinuity model, which tests the difference between the intercepts of the treatment and comparison groups' regression lines at the point that represents the cutoff score (if there is one) on the pretest measure. One major disadvantage of this model is that if one suspects the actual benefit from the treatment to be unevenly shared (e.g., the lowest scorers benefitting more than subjects scoring just below the cutoff), the discontinuity model may not show significance.

This is because the regression lines would not be parallel over the range of pretest scores. The major advantage of the discontinunity approach is that it makes use of both groups' actual scores to compute prediction lines and thus is considered more conclusive.

Karnes, Shwedel, and Lewis (1983) used the regression discontinuity design to evaluate the short-term effects of early programming for young, gifted, handicapped children in preschool. Cutoff scores for classification of creative functioning (the outcome) on a variety of teacher and student measures were determined, and predicted scores of children for pre- and postintervention conditions and for treatment and comparison children were computed. Significant differences between pre- and postscores were observed at the cutoff points. Karnes et al. appeared to have different regression slopes (b-weights) as well, but did not offer further analysis.

Clearly, the GLM can be applied to evaluation designs, including the traditional true and quasi-experimental designs such as the pre-post control group, the nonequivalent control group, and the interrupted time-series designs (Judd & Kenny, 1981). McCain and McCleary (1979) described several modifications of the regression method for use with time-series experiments. The overall advantage of the regression approach, in general, is that more than one pretest measure or program measure can be used to make the predictions. Typical gifted/talented programs collect data from several sources for purposes of initial screening and pupil selection, include numerous educational components, and often measure several outcomes. Regression analysis offers a sound way to use these data and obtain meaningful information concerning how all the elements work together.

Path analysis. As stated earlier, however, many evaluations cannot involve comparison groups. Yet there is the need to make judgments concerning causal relationships between treatment and outcome. Path-analytic procedures (Kerlinger & Pedhazur, 1973; Pedhazur & Schmelkin, 1991) offer some help, but there is a special requirement. Evaluators must break out of their traditional set for evaluation and design their programs in new ways. Path analysis depends on a model, or theory, of how different program elements relate to each other. This model must be specified before the program is implemented. All the elements, preprogram measures, in-process treatment measures, subject variables, treatment variables, and so on must be measured.

A set of paths, or predicted relationships, is developed prior to the program's implementation. After the data are collected, path coefficients (similar to regression coefficients or correlations) are computed. These coefficients represent the effects of one variable on another, without the effects of other variables in the model being involved. In other words, the concept of a path is like an identified "causal" relationship. For this reason, path analysis is often referred to as causal modeling. The advantages of path analysis are that it depends on a strong theory of how or why a treatment works and that causes can be inferred. The special costs for conducting path analysis are that program developers have to have the model or theory in the first place and have to collect a variety of data to test the paths in the model. A simple pretest-posttest design will not do.

Duran and Weffer (1992) used path analysis as part of an evaluation of a program for talented immigrant Mexican-American students. Path coefficients showed a strong effect for family educational values, which led to students' participation in a special math/science enrichment program, which, in turn, led to substantial improvement in achievement test scores. The study was longitudinal in nature and involved data collection of student background variables, pre-high school achievement, high school academic coursework, employment, homework, and attendance (absence) as well as participation in the enrichment program. From literally dozens of possible causal paths among all these variables, Duran and Weffer were able to identify meaningful relationships that contributed to the school success of these students.

Nonparametric methods. This statistical discussion cannot end without some mention of nonparametric methods. All that has been described here involves dependent measures that are assumed to be measured on an interval scale (Edwards, 1985). This is one of the important mathematical assumptions underlying the use of the most powerful statistical methods,such as the t-or F-tests and Pearson correlations used in analysis of variance and regression. In education and psychology great liberties often are taken by assuming that our measures are true interval scales. Usually this is not the case—most of the measures used to assess intellectual and other cognitive abilities, affective traits, interests, attitudes, motivations, and so on are ordinal scales at best. Statisticians have written extensively about the effect on the power (the accuracy and generalizability) of our results if this assumption is violated. In most cases in which large numbers of subjects are involved, the effects of not meeting the assumption of interval measurement are nil. But if sample size is small, the effect can be substantial. Thus, program evaluators with small studies should become familiar with the nonparametric methods that parallel t-tests, F-tests, and Pearson correlations (see Ferguson & Takane, 1989).

If the dependent variable or variables in a program evaluation are nominal (categorical data), the chi-square statistic is indicated (Roscoe, 1975). The chi-square procedure is especially useful when gifted/talented programs use multiple indicators of success rather than achievement or other test scores. Multiple indicators might include numbers of credits taken in a subject area, numbers and types of extracurricular activities engaged in, reduction in dropout or increase in attendance rates, involvement in community service or other volunteer activities, college majors or professions chosen, awards, honors, number of patents, publications, or other activities or accomplishments that indicate that program participants have developed talents, increased motivation, or improved attitudes. The use of multiple indicators is one of several strategies that is recommended for the design and evaluation of gifted/talented programs for culturally different pupils (House & Lapan, 1994) when program developers wish to deemphasize the use of standardized tests.

Qualitative "Fourth-Generation" Approaches

Now that the traditional, quantitative methods have been reviewed, it is time to return to an earlier theme of this chapter. What we wish to involve the reader in in this section is an alternative way of thinking about evaluations. As mentioned earlier, modern views of evaluation conceive of the task in a broader fashion than simply an experimental comparison of treatment and control groups (Anderson & Ball, 1978; Berk, 1981; Guba & Lincoln, 1981, 1989; Rossi & Freeman, 1989; Worthen, Sanders, & Fitzpatrick, 1997). For "fourth-generation" evaluation it is important to gain a richer, fuller understanding of how programs affect the lives of people involved in them.

For example, Enersen (1993) used qualitative methods to evaluate a Summer residential program run by the Gifted Education Resource Institute at Purdue University. Students (and their parents) who had attended the program for several summers were interviewed as to their perceptions of their summer experiences and the effects on their social and emotional as well as academic growth. The goal of the evaluation was to understand whether and/or how the program was meeting previously unmet needs of these gifted students (13- to 18-year-olds). Analysis of the extensive interview data showed that the summer program provided these students with many opportunities for reflecting on their own growth, both academically and personally, individually and in relationships with others. In turn, these opportunities served to reduce anxieties and generate strong, positive feelings about the program.

As stated earlier, many models of evaluation design have been defined and suggested in the literature as alternatives to the traditional experimental method. For example, Stufflebeam et al.'s (1971) CIPP model requires information about the context of the program, the resources that input to the program, and the process of the program's implementation in addition to traditional data about program outcomes or products. What distinguishes these approaches is a focus on the broad impact of particular programs, from inception and development to implementation, completion, and followup. All interested parties, or stakeholders, may be involved—not just the deliverers and receivers of the direct services, but also the program administrators, community leaders and legislators who support (or are critical of) the program, families of subjects, the general public, and any special individuals or groups for whom the program may have direct or indirect effects. Models such as Stufflebeam's offer detailed consideration of all the energies and activities that contribute to a program's operation.

Modern views of evaluation place the evaluator within the program development and implementation process (Berk, 1981; Guba & Lincoln, 1981, 1989; Renzulli & Smith, 1979; Rossi & Freeman, 1989). Rather than an aloof "outsider" who examines program records long after the last client leaves the program, the modern evaluator helps to plan the program from the beginning. Even before the program takes shape, a needs assessment or context evaluation may be conducted, for example, to better assay the prevailing problems and people's current reactions to the problems. It may take a systematic process of fact finding, opinion gathering, and analysis before any problem can be defined clearly enough to form a basis for subsequent program development. If specific needs are defined, additional questions arise as to available resources or "inputs" to build and carry on an appropriate program. If cost effectiveness is to be considered, appropriate program outcomes need to be defined, and someone has to examine alternatively available programs before the decision is made to proceed.

With clear objectives, a better program and a process for its implementation and progress monitoring can be developed. This process insures that corrective feedback can occur during the program so that major errors will be less likely to occur and minor ones will be easily repaired. The evaluator does not disappear for the 8 weeks, 12 weeks, or whatever time it takes to implement the treatment. Regular program staff meetings occur, for example, which review the interim measures (whatever they may be—formal and informal, staff or client interviews, questionnaires, progress records, probe trials, etc.). Thus, this process insures that treatment will be evenly and consistently applied, and any subsequent outcome measure will have the greatest psychological connection to what went on before it.

In addition to such things as constructing or selecting tests, running statistical analyses on the computer, or interpreting any statistical significances, the evaluator helps to select the model of evaluation suitable for the type of program. The evaluator helps to identify the needs for which the program is directed, the objectives that the program can reasonably address, and the process by which the program is developed, implemented, and monitored. In short, the evaluator is part of the program.

RECOMMENDATIONS FOR EVALUATING GIFTED/TALENTED PROGRAMS

In the final section of this chapter we make specific recommendations for the design and conduct of program evaluations for gifted/talented programs that are targeted to minority and culturally diverse pupil populations. We organized our recommendations according to four aspects of gifted/talented programs: (a) conceptualization, (b) design, (c) implementation, and (d) analysis.

Conceptualization

The conceptualization stage involves the development of program goals and the selection of a model for program evaluation. Consistent with the modern view of program evaluation as integral to program design and development we recommend that program evaluation be an item on the agenda of program developers and managers from day one. Program evaluators help identify the special needs for the program among the target population and assess the views of relevant "stakeholders" in the program in the larger community. Program evaluators can help to develop specific program goals and objectives, define *giftedness* and *talentedness,* select instruments and develop procedures for identification and assessment, and help to relate assessment practices to instructional program components. Program evaluators help develop timelines and target dates for the program, identify needed resources, and assist in planning for staff development and training activities. Program evaluators may take notes and keep records of all activities prior to the actual implementation of the program because these data may be essential to the overall evaluation model that is selected.

Design

Design activities include the plan for data collection and analysis. For many of the evaluation objectives described by Anderson and Ball (1978), qualitative models provide a greater variety of possible methods and techniques than does the traditional experiment. Notable among these models is Stufflebeam et al.'s CIPP model. For gifted/talented programs the CIPP model offers a flexible evaluation design that can accommodate a wide range of issues and program variables. For example, for the program context data can be obtained concerning the process of goals development, stakeholder opinions as to the needs for the program, school and community philosophies of education, prior experiences with special programs, general school and community resources, and other factors that could impact the program that "characterizes" the overall program milieu. For example, in this case school personnel, parents, and community leaders may discuss and decide whether to focus the program on intellectual giftedness, Gardner's (1983) multiple intelligences approach, Feldhusen's (1993) talent developmental approach, or use another model.

For input evaluation, data can be collected regarding specific "gifts" and "talents" of pupils, school achievement levels, school resources, teacher training and experience, other school-based support services such as counseling and vocational development activities, specific community resources that will be used in the program, levels of parental involvement and support, curriculum, scheduling, and physical characteristics of the school and/or classrooms. In this case program developers would decide what procedures to follow to insure that minority and culturally different pupils were afforded equal opportunities for program inclusion (Bernal, 1990). House and Lapan (1994) suggest several questions for program evaluators to ask at this point. They include:

1. Is the proportion of minority students selected . . . very nearly the same as the population from which they were drawn?
2. Are there students who were not selected who might be better served by the special program?
3. Are there students who were selected who might be better served outside the program?
4. Are the procedures for selection systematically excluding any students who should be in the program?
5. What is the relationship between the identification procedures and student access in the special program? (p. 458)

In this case evaluators may contribute by assisting in the analysis of factors that are known to influence minority and culturally different pupils' actual performance and ability to profit from the various instructional components that are part of the special program. For example, Ford and Harris (1990, 1994) discussed the effects of different learning styles, motivation, value systems, expectations, and other factors on minority students' achievement. With this knowledge program planners have a basis for selecting and/or modifying instructional conditions or variables that will complement pupil characteristics rather than conflict with them.

For process evaluation, data would be collected on a continuing basis throughout the program to monitor the progress of various program components. Recall the assumption that no one type of program for gifted/talented pupils may be best. For example, Getzels and Dillon (1973) identified numerous program elements for gifted pupils. Among them were summer classes, Saturday classes, nongraded primary schools, grade skipping, early school admissions, college courses for high school students, college credit for high school courses, special classes in some subjects, visiting resource teachers, alternative curricula in regular classes, extracurricular in- and out-of-school activities, counseling, individual tutoring, independent study, mentoring, parent training, to name a few. This diversity continues (Gallagher & Gallagher, 1994; Torrance, 1986). Good programs may involve both enrichment or accelerative components and may switch from one type of activity to another at various times or for different subject areas. How do pupils respond to the different components of the program? How are teachers responding? Are support services functioning? Are curricular experiences being carried out as designed? This stage of the CIPP program evaluation, more than any other, illustrates the benefits of alternative evaluation models. Typically, the experimental model's strengths lie in end-product evaluation. Process evaluation asks questions regarding the actual functioning of the program's components.

Recall Anderson and Ball's (1978) third evaluation purpose—to gather data to improve the program. Process or "formative" evaluation provides information about the program as it operates so that changes can be made during the program to improve poorly functioning aspects, to discontinue components that simply are not working, to enhance those factors that are working well, or to introduce new components that address new objectives or needs. Program designers can use periodic surveys, questionnaires, interviews, or observations to assess teacher, pupil, and parent reactions to the program and its specific activities. Classroom and/or instructional interactions can be observed to study the implementation of specific learning and teaching strategies, success of particular assignments, attitudes toward the program, or socioemotional support systems (teacher-pupil interrelationships, peer-group relationships, social skills development, crisis interventions, etc.).

Carter and Hamilton (1985) reported on the use of formative, process-oriented evaluation methods with a gifted program in the Greeley, CO schools, grades 3 to 5. The main technique used was content analysis (i.e., examination of written/printed materials) of the following program components: definition of giftedness, educational philosophy, identification procedures and criteria, program goals and objectives, student goals and objectives, curriculum, personnel, budget, and evaluation.

Finally, for product evaluation, program designers would be deciding the different types of outcome measures to be included in the gifted/talented program. Do the program's goals include both affective as well as cognitive outcomes? Is higher grade point average a goal? Is leadership in school activities a goal? Is community service a goal? Is advanced placement in college a goal? Is later professional success in careers a goal? Our recommendation to program developers is that multiple outcomes be assessed. Given the often controversial nature of gifted/talented education, we suggest that multiple outcome measures will provide stronger evidence for supporters who may have to convince others of the desirability of supporting such programs. For example, Shapiro (1985) reported on the evaluation of a program designed to prepare academically talented but economically disadvantaged minority high school students for entry into medical and health science professions. A variety of indicators of skill development, attitude, and career orientation were used to evaluate the effectiveness of the various program components.

Carter and Hamilton (1985), House and Lapan (1994), Kitano and Perez (1998), Renzulli and Smith (1979), and others recommend that gifted program evaluators make use of quantitative, outcome-oriented, summative designs and measures in conjunction with a formative, process-oriented, qualitative approach. This combination should provide the strongest possible evidence to support continuation and improvement of gifted/talented programs. The CIPP model, as a supplement to the traditional experimental model of program evaluation, provides a comprehensive design for gathering a wide range of information on relevant program components. Figure 11.2 represents the CIPP model applied to gifted/talented programs.

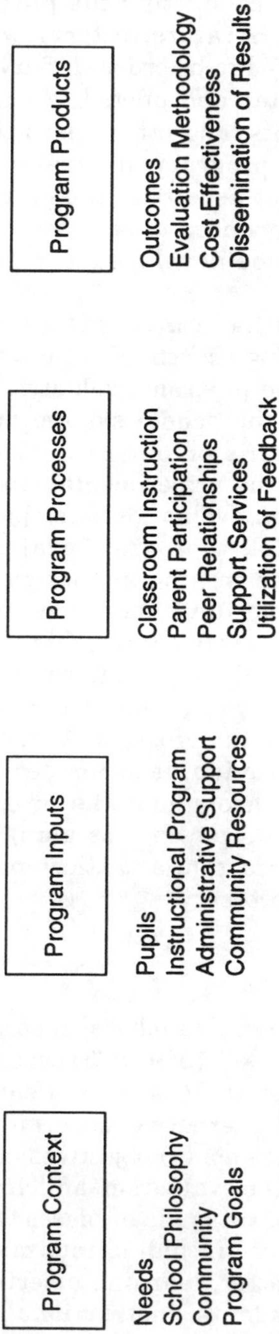

Program Context

Needs
School Philosophy
Community
Program Goals

Program Inputs

Pupils
Instructional Program
Administrative Support
Community Resources

Program Processes

Classroom Instruction
Parent Participation
Peer Relationships
Support Services
Utilization of Feedback

Program Products

Outcomes
Evaluation Methodology
Cost Effectiveness
Dissemination of Results

Figure 11.2. Stufflebeam et al.'s (1971) CIPP model applied to gifted/talented programs for minority and culturally different pupils

Implementation

Implementation refers to the activities of conducting the program evaluation. Data collectors (test administrators, interviewers, observers, etc.) need to be trained. Tests need to be ordered. Surveys, questionnaires, and so on need to be written and piloted. Meetings with stakeholders, school personnel, parents, and others need to be held to prepare them for aspects of the program, its evaluation activities, and to keep them informed about aspects of the program during its operation. Record-keeping systems need to be determined. Database management systems need to be developed and made ready.

Most gifted/talented programs have a coordinator or director—a person responsible for monitoring aspects of the program as it functions. Often this person is not the program evaluator. The evaluator may be another person from the school system or an outside consultant selected because of his or her expertise in statistics or research. This is one legacy of the "experimental model." However, if a modern approach to program evaluation is employed such as Stufflebeam's (1971) CIPP model, a program evaluator should be part of a team of people involved in program design and operation. As discussed earlier, context and input data need to be collected from the earliest days of program development. Otherwise much of these data are gathered as "recollections" or "after-the-fact" information. To record process data, as well, requires careful preparation in advance of the actual start of the program. And, since the basic purpose of evaluation is to provide data for decision making, having a team-based approach throughout the program provides additional support and "thinking power" for using the accumulating information as "checks" on program activities and for recommendations for ongoing changes, if necessary.

Analysis

Finally, the last stage of program evaluation is analysis, reporting, and use of the evaluation results. Robert Stake (1969/1973) described a suggested format for final evaluation reports. It is general enough to accommodate both the experimental and alternative models if they are employed. It includes the following sections: (a) objectives of the evaluation (including audiences served by the evaluation, anticipated decision to be made about the program, and rationale or biases of the evaluators); (b) specification of the program (including information about educational philosophy, subject matter, learning objectives, staff goals, instructional procedures, students, instructional and community setting, and school or other standards for judging quality); (c) program outcomes (such as opportunities and experiences provided students, student gains and losses, side-effects and bonuses, and costs); (d) relationships and indicators (which are congruences, real and intended, of program goals and outcomes, contingencies, causes and effects, and trend lines and comparisons); and (e) judgments of worth (values of the outcomes, relevance of specific values to program needs, and usefulness of the evaluation information gathered).

Other writers include similar things in their report recommendations. Worthen and Sanders (1987; Worthen, Sanders, & Fitzpatrick, 1997) offered a checklist of 24 criteria to consider in preparing and publishing written evaluation reports. They also made suggestions for oral reports to different audiences. Guba and Lincoln (1981) cautioned that different audiences may have different values and different prior knowledges and perspectives of the same program. Therefore, evaluators need to ascertain the values and expectations of the different audiences and attempt to prepare meaningful reports appropriate to each group.

Certainly, the CIPP model provides considerable information to fill out and "fill up" a thorough evaluation report. In addition to statistical comparisons of end-product and some types of process data, there are notebooks, memos, minutes of meetings, and other documentation that support a discussion of the program's objectives and guiding philosophies. There may be anecdotal information of individual cases, systematic observational data, interviews, and survey responses collected from students, their teachers and parents, and other school and community people that provide insights into the functioning of program components and explain actual statistical results from test scores or other outcome measures, both cognitive and affective.

One suggestion for gifted program evaluators and evaluation team members is to use a method often termed *triangulation* (Guba & Lincoln, 1981); that is, to obtain several different types of information for each key point (or objective) of the program or the evaluation plan. A simple example might be to interview several different people about an issue concerning the program—students, teachers, parents, administrators, and so on. Another example might be to obtain immediate feedback from pupils and other stakeholders at the conclusion of a program (or a particular component of a program), then do some form of followup at a later date with an alternative measurement method. Surveys of attitudes and judgments as to program effectiveness could be administered at the end of a school year, but the same pupils could be followed next year to examine their academic test scores, grades, choices of elective credits or majors, outside interests, or other "products" that would be desired long-range effects of gifted programs. As we have mentioned several times, it is important to obtain data from key stakeholders—students, teachers, parents, community leaders, and so on. Obviously, if multiple data sources are sought, multiple data-gathering methods employed, and multiple types of data collected, evaluators can try to "converge" these data to each of the important evaluation questions or purposes (Frasier, 1997; Kitano & Perez, 1998).

Of special note in this phase of program evaluation is the organization and analysis of cost-effectiveness data (Haller, 1974; Rossi & Freeman, 1989; Worthen & Sanders, 1987). From the beginning and planning stages of program evaluations, there should be some concern for gathering information about the relative costs and benefits of the program. But, in the analysis phase, these data must be put in some perspective. Typically, costs are dollar amounts associated with the development and implementation of the program. How much time did the program require? How many personnel were involved? What were their salaries? Were there expenses for staff development? Consultant fees? Curriculum development costs? Additional instructional supplies? Expenses for tests and instruments for identification of gifted pupils? Expenses for the interviews and observations and surveys and questionnaires to measure outcomes? Expenses for additional recordkeeping, statistical analyses, report writing, dissemination activities, and so on? One could even include the "expense" incurred by the redirection or "lessening" of resources away from the "nongifted" pupils, if such has occurred.

However, it often is much harder to assign "dollar figures" to actual benefits of gifted/talented programs. There is little to guide program evaluators, for example, in assigning dollar amounts to changes in test scores. We can count test score increases, number of extra credits earned, number of extracurricular activities engaged in, number of patents filed for, college admissions, awards, jobs, and more, but we usually have to rely on general social values when describing these potential benefits. There are data regarding expected earnings of college and non-college-educated individuals, of various occupations and professions, and of costs associated with crime, hunger, and disease. But the average educator and gifted program manager is not able to translate these data into meaningful statements to stakeholders about the "dollar benefits" of particular programs.

Nevertheless, it probably is a good idea to collect cost data as part of an overall evaluation plan. What the program manager can do is compare these costs with the costs of other programs in the same or nearby schools serving other students—for example, special educational services for the physically, emotionally, or cognitively challenged, and other gifted programs. It may be of use to decision makers to know how much their own gifted/talented program "costs," given the number of students or parents served, when compared with similar data for a variety of other programs. One would expect that favorable comparisons would not lessen support for the particular gifted/talented program being evaluated.

A final aspect of an evaluation analysis concerns recommendations and dissemination of information about the evaluation (Anderson & Ball, 1971; Guba & Lincoln, 1981; Worthen, Sanders, & Fitzpatrick, 1997). How will the results of the evaluation efforts be used? Who will be making decisions? Who will benefit from the evaluation? Who will be using the data to make program revisions? It would be a shame to do the work of evaluation only to have the report filed away on a shelf gathering dust. Modern evaluation models place a high priority on the usefulness of evaluations. Program evaluators involved with the program from the very beginning will have a good idea as to who are the decision makers, what types of decisions are to be made, and when and how the results of the evaluation may be applied. Program evaluators, with multiple types of information, should be able to write clear recommendations that are well supported and address the practical concerns of the decision makers. This will increase the chance that results will be applied in a manner consistent with the objectives of the program.

In summary, Tables 11.1 through 11.4 present questions from each of the four CIPP areas (context, inputs, process, and product), which may be used to guide the development and implementation of gifted/talented program evaluations. The questions are categorized within each area according to the issues presented in Figure 11.2.

CONCLUSIONS

This chapter reviewed a number of issues concerning the evaluation of gifted/talented education programs. The knowledge bases of gifted/talented learners and programs, of program evaluation as a field of inquiry, minority and culturally different gifted/talented pupils, traditional research and statistical methods, and modern evaluation models focusing on the concerns of program stakeholders are all relevant. After an analysis of these issues, the following conclusions are offered.

Table 11.1. Questions to Guide a Context Evaluation of a Gifted/Talented Program.

Needs

1. Who are the stakeholders for this program?
2. How many pupils (actual number, percentage of total school/district enrollment) would be served by this program?
3. What is the need in the community for types of workers? What are the values of the community (with regard to family, work, education, etc.)?
4. What minority and culturally different populations require service? How salient are issues of equity and equal opportunity?

School Philosophy

5. What special factors characterize the schools? What is the school's reputation?
6. What is the general educational philosophy of the schools?
7. How does a gifted/talented program relate to the school's goals or philosophy?
8. What types of curricular programs already exist in the schools?

Community

9. What factors characterize this community? What is the community's recent history or current issues?
10. What is the view of community leaders and parents regarding additional educational expenses for a gifted/talented program?
11. What is the experience of the community and school with other special education programs?
12. How active are parents in the community?
13 What are competing demands (educational, financial, etc.) on the schools?
14. What exists in the local press that would support (or argue against) any special program?

Program Goals

15 What are the exact goals—both primary and secondary—of the program? Who formed the goals? Why are they important? Do program goals need to be developed, clarified, communicated?
16. What is the purpose of the program evaluation? To start a new program? Review an old one? Improve the program? End it?
17. Who will be "paying" for this evaluation? Public or private funds? What are the expectations regarding dissemination of results of the evaluation?

Table 11.2. Questions to Guide an Input Evaluation of a Gifted/Talented Program.

Pupils

1. How will a pool of potential pupils for the program be selected? What are the selection criteria or weights assigned to different measures?
2. What tests, questionnaires, surveys, and so on are available, reliable, and valid for this program and these pupils? Who will evaluate them? Who can instruct others in their use? Are local instruments needed? Who will construct them and pilot them?
3. What are the achievement levels of the pool of potential pupils for this program? At grade level? Above? Below? What trends exist?
4. What special characteristics of the pupils in the pool are there? Age levels? Gender issues? Ethnic, racial, or socioeconomic issues? Language differences?
5. What special aptitudes or abilities characterize the pupils in the pool? Gardner's seven "intelligences"? Specific talents? Specific school subject areas?
6. What do pupils think about the need for or components to a special program?

Instructional Program

7. What is the program model? Acceleration? Enrichment? What are the possible program components?
8. What are the qualifications of the instructional staff? Experience with the gifted/talented? Training? Is there staff development?
9. What are the physical resources in the schools? Equipment? Supplies? Room?
10. How flexible are existing schedules to accommodate to new activities?
11. What time pressures constrain the program?
12. Are personnel motivated?
13. Are there legal conditions that can accommodate a new program? Union rules for teachers? Court mandates? Public or private lawsuits?

Administrative Support

14. What is the ability/experience of the school's administrative and support staffs?
15. What is the makeup and ability/experience of the program management and evaluation team?

Community Resources

16. What are special resources of the community that can contribute to a gifted/ talented program? Extracurricular activities? Field experiences? Mentors?
17. What outside expertise is available to contribute to the program? Local colleges/universities, private foundations, etc.?

Table 11.3. Questions to Guide a Process Evaluation of a Gifted/Talented Program.

Classroom Instruction

1. What is the philosophy or instructional model being followed?
2. What is the level of pupil involvement in their own curriculum? Planning? Monitoring? Evaluating?
3. What is the school day like for gifted/talented pupils?
4. How do teachers plan the instructional program for gifted/talented pupils?
5. What instructional methods are employed? What materials and techniques are used?
6. What types of assignments are given? How much homework, independent learning, or projects are assigned?
7. How often should classes be visited? What things should be observed? Which observation methods should be employed? Should there be training to collect observations?
8. What kinds of questions should pupils and teachers be asked periodically about the progress of the program? How should the questions be asked? In large or small groups? Individually? Interviews? Surveys? How often?

Parent Participation

9. How do parents involve themselves in their children's program?
10. How can parents become involved?
11. Is there regular opportunity to meet with parents to discuss the program? Obtain feedback from them?

Peer Relationships

12. How are peer interactions among gifted program pupils? Opportunities for social activities, cooperative learning, growth in non-academic areas?
13. How are gifted/nongifted pupil interactions during the program? In school? Out of school?

Support Services

14. How often and what types of counseling or special services are employed for gifted/talented pupils?
15. What recordkeeping and data management systems exist to support the program? How well do they work? Do they need modification?
16. Who monitors the budget?

Utilization of Feedback/Formative Evaluation

17. How do pupils and other stakeholders "feel" things are going?
18. How can the program be changed while it operates to respond to the information gathered in response to the above questions?
19. Are there periodic meetings to review progress? Who should join these meetings?
20. Can ineffective practices easily be stopped and better practices substituted? On whose authority? What support for change is necessary?

Table 11.4. Questions to Guide a Product Evaluation of a Gifted/Talented Program.

Outcomes

1. What are the expected outcomes of this program? Who wants them? Parents? Teachers? Pupils?
2. What gains in achievement are desired or expected from the program? How should the gains be measured?
3. Is creativity a desired outcome? How should it be measured?
4. Is social competence a desired outcome? How should it be measured?
5. Is personal development (self-concept, character, morality, etc.) a desired outcome? How should it be measured?
6. What are long-term program outcomes? College? Careers? Productivity in life?

Evaluation Methodology

7   Who will design, administer, and score the instruments needed for measuring program outcomes?
8. Are existing measures reliable and valid for use in this program? Who can help determine this?
9. Can there be followup for graduates of the program?
10. What is the evaluation design? An experimental or qualitative model?
11. Is there a comparison group? How can one be found or formed? Can internal validity of the eventual comparisons be assured?

Cost Effectiveness

12. What are the costs, in dollar terms, for running this program?
13. Can dollar amounts be fixed to real or potential benefits of this program?
14. How do the costs of this program compare with other, similar programs?

Dissemination of Results

15. Who will analyze and integrate all the data from the evaluation?
16. Does the information gathered correspond to the objectives of the evaluation and the goals of the program?
17. Who will use the results of the evaluation? Parents? Administrators? Teachers? Pupils? For what purposes?
18. How should the results of the evaluation be published or otherwise disseminated? Written reports? Oral presentations? Other media?

First, a commonly accepted approach to program evaluation has been the use of some quasi- or true experimental design, involving control or comparison groups and pre-, post-, and followup testing. However, there are a number of statistical methods, such as power, regression, and path analysis that could be applied to gifted/talented program evaluations that would increase the power and usefulness of evaluation results. We should improve our research and statistical skills if we are to gather more meaningful results that will persuade policymakers and the public to support gifted/talented education.

Second, evaluation research has come of age as a field. That means we, as professional educators, have an obligation to become aware of how this field can contribute to our own work. If we consider how much of our effort goes into the development of what we hope are effective interventions to help people, then we surely must not want that effort to be wasted. There are a number of qualitative evaluation models now available for gifted program developers to use when quantitative methods are not possible or to supplement traditional quantitative, experimental designs. These models guide information gathering on a wide range of program components that can lead to important decision making by program stakeholders. Program designers and evaluators should become aware of these models and learn to apply them to increase the chance that their efforts on behalf of gifted/talented pupils will have a positive impact.

REFERENCES

Allan, S. (1991, March). Ability-grouping research reviews: What do they say about grouping and the gifted? *Educational Leadership*, pp. 60-65.

Anderson, S., & Ball, S. (1978). *The profession and practice of program evaluation*. San Francisco: Jossey-Bass.

Asher, J. (1991). Meta-analysis. In N. Buchanan & J. Feldhusen (Eds.), *Conducting research and evaluation in gifted education* (pp. 220-241). New York: Teachers College Press.

Baldwin, A. (1987a). I'm Black but look at me, I am also gifted. *Gifted Child Quarterly, 31,* 180-185.

Baldwin, A. (1987b). Undiscovered diamonds: The minority gifted child. *Journal for the Education of the Gifted, 10,* 271-285.

Baldwin, A. (1994). The Seven Plus Story: Developing hidden talent among students in socioeconomically disadvantaged environments. *Gifted Child Quarterly, 38,* 80-84.

Berk, R. (1981). *Educational evaluation methodology: The state of the art*. Baltimore: Johns Hopkins University Press.

Bernal, E. (1979). The education of the culturally different gifted. In A. H. Passow (Ed.), *The gifted and talented: Their education and development. The 78th Yearbook of the National Society for the Study of Education Part 1* (pp. 395-400). Chicago: The University of Chicago Press.

Bernal, E. (1980). *Methods of identifying gifted minority students.* Princeton, NJ: ERIC Clearinghouse on Tests, Measurement, and Evaluation.

Bernal, E. (1981). *Special problems and procedures for identifying minority gifted populations.* New Orleans, LA: Creative Educational Enterprises. (ERIC Document No. ED203652)

Bernal, E. (1990). The identification blues and how to cure them. *CAG Communicator, 20*(3), 1, 27.

Bloom, B., Hastings, J., & Madaus, G. (1971). *Handbook of formative and summative evaluation of student learning.* New York: McGraw-Hill.

Borland, J. H. (1997). Evaluating gifted programs. In N. Colangelo & G. Davis (Eds.), *Handbook of gifted education* (2nd ed., pp. 253-266). Needham Heights, MA: Allyn & Bacon.

Bracht, G., & Glass, G. (1968). The external validity of experiments. *American Educational Research Journal, 5,* 437-474.

Campbell, D., & Stanley, J. (1963). *Experimental and quasi-experimental designs for research.* Chicago: Rand-McNally.

Carter, K., & Hamilton, W. (1985). Formative evaluation of gifted programs: A process and model. *Gifted Child Quarterly, 29,* 5-11.

Chinn, P., & Hughes, S. (1987). Representation of minority students in special education classes. *Remedial and Special Education, 8*(4), 41-46.

Clark, B. (1992). *Growing up gifted: Developing the potential of children at home and at school* (4th ed.). New York: Macmillan.

Cohen, J. (1988). *Statistical power analysis* (2nd ed.). Hillsdale, NJ: Erlbaum.

Cohen, J. (1990). Things I have learned (so far). *American Psychologist, 45,* 1304-1312.

Cohen, J. (1992). Statistical power analysis. *Current Directions in Psychological Science, 1,* 98-101.

Colangelo, N., & Davis, G. (Eds.). (1997). *Handbook of gifted education* (2nd ed.). Needham Heights, MA: Allyn & Bacon.

Cook, T., & Campbell, D. (1979). *Quasi-experimentation: Design and analytic issues for field settings.* New York: Holt, Rinehart, & Winston.

Cronbach, L., & Furby, L. (1970). How should we measure "change"—or should we? *Psychological Bulletin, 74,* 68-80.

Darlington, R. (1990). *Regression and linear models*. New York: McGraw-Hill.

Daurio, S. (1979). Educational enrichment versus acceleration: A review of the literature. In W. George, S. Cohn, & J. Stanley (Eds.), *Educating the gifted: Acceleration and enrichment* (pp. 13-63). Baltimore: Johns Hopkins University.

Duran, B., & Weffer, R. (1992). Immigrants' aspirations, high school process, and academic outcomes. *American Educational Research Journal, 29*, 163-181.

Edwards, A. (1985). *Multiple regression and the analysis of variance and covariance* (2nd ed.). New York: W. H. Freeman.

Elashoff, J. (1969). Analysis of covariance: A delicate instrument. *American Educational Research Journal, 6*, 383-401.

Enersen, D. (1993). Summer residential programs: Academics and beyond. *Gifted Child Quarterly, 37*, 169-176.

Feldhusen, J. (1991). Effects of programs for the gifted: A search for evidence. In W. Thomas Southern & E. Jones (Eds.), *The academic acceleration of gifted children* (pp. 133-147). New York: Teachers College Press.

Feldhusen, J. (1993). Talent development in education. *The Journal of the California Association for the Gifted, 23*(4), 34-38.

Feldhusen, J. (1993/1994, Winter). Talent development as an alternative to gifted education. *The Journal of Secondary Gifted Education*, pp. 5-9.

Feldhusen, J. (1995). Talent development during the high school years. *Gifted Education International, 10*, 60-64.

Ferguson, G. A., & Takane, Y. (1989). *Statistical analysis in psychology and education* (6th ed.). New York: McGraw-Hill.

Fetterman, D. (1986). Gifted and talented education: A national test case in Peoria. *Educational Evaluation and Policy Analysis, 8*, 155-166.

Ford, D., & Harris, J., III. (1990). On discovering the hidden treasure of gifted and talented black children. *Roeper Review, 13*(1), 27-32.

Ford, D., & Harris, J., III. (1994). Promoting achievement among gifted black students: The efficacy of new definitions and identification practices. *Urban Education, 29*, 202-229.

Frasier, M. M. (1997). Gifted minority students: Reframing approaches to their identification and education. In N. Colangelo & G. Davis (Eds.), *Handbook of gifted education* (2nd ed., pp. 498-515). Needham Heights, MA: Allyn & Bacon.

Gall, M., Borg, W., & Gall, J. (1996). *Educational research* (6th ed.). New York: Longman.

Gallagher, J., & Gallagher, S. (1994). *Teaching the gifted child* (4th ed.). Newton, MA: Allyn & Bacon.

Gardner, H. (1983). *Frames of mind: The theory of multiple intelligences.* New York: Basic Books.

Getzels, J., & Dillon, J. (1973). The nature of giftedness and the education of the gifted. In R. Travers (Ed.), *Second handbook of research on teaching* (pp. 689-731). Chicago: Rand-McNally.

Glass, G. (1977). Integrating findings: The meta-analysis of research. *Review of Research in Education, 5,* 351-379.

Glass, G. (1988). Quasi-experiments: The case of interrupted time series. In R. Jaeger (Ed.), *Complementary methods for research in education* (pp. 445-465). Washington, DC: American Educational Research Association.

Glass, G., Peckham, P., & Sanders, J. (1972). Consequences of failure to meet assumptions underlying the fixed effects analysis of variance and covariance. *Review of Educational Research, 43,* 237-288.

Griffin, J. (1992). Catching the dream for gifted children of color. *Gifted Child Quarterly, 36,* 126-130.

Guba, E., & Lincoln, Y. (1981). *Effective evaluation.* San Francisco: Jossey-Bass.

Guba, E., & Lincoln, Y. (1989). *Fourth generation evaluation.* Newbury Park, CA: Sage.

Haller, E. (1974). Cost analysis for educational program evaluation. In W. J. Popham (Ed.), *Evaluation in education: Current applications* (pp. 399-450). Berkeley, CA: McCutchan.

Harris, C. (Ed.). (1963). *Problems in measuring change.* Madison: University of Wisconsin Press.

House, E. (1983a). Assumptions underlying evaluation models. In G. Madaus, M. Scriven, & D. Stufflebeam (Eds.), *Evaluation models* (pp. 45-64). Boston: Kluwer-Nijhoff.

House, E. (Ed.). (1983b). *Philosophy of evaluation* (New Directions for Program Evaluation, No. 19). San Francisco: Jossey-Bass.

House, E., & Lapan, S. (1994). Evaluation of programs for disadvantaged gifted students. *Journal for the Association of the Gifted, 17,* 441-466.

Iverson, G., & Norpoth, H. (1976). *Analysis of variance. Quanitative applications in the social sciences* (No. 1). Beverly Hills, CA: Sage.

Judd, C., & Kenny, D. (1981). *Estimating the effects of social interventions.* Cambridge, MA: Harvard University Press.

Karnes, M., Shwedel, A., & Lewis, G. (1983). Short-term effects of early programming for the young gifted handicapped child. *Exceptional Children, 50,* 103-109.

Kerlinger, F., & Pedhazur, E. (1973). *Multiple regression in behavioral research.* New York: Holt, Rinehart, & Winston.

Khatena, J. (1982). *The educational psychology of the gifted.* New York: Wiley.

Khatena, J. (1992). *Gifted: Challenge and responses for education*. Itasca, IL: F. E. Peacock.

Kingsley, R. (1986). "Digging" for understanding and significance: A high school enrichment model. *Roeper Review, 9*, 37-38.

Kitano, M. (1991). A multicultural educational perspective on serving the culturally diverse gifted. *Journal for the Education of the Gifted, 15*, 4-19.

Kitano, M. K., & Perez, R. I. (1998). Developing the potential of young gifted children from low-income and culturally and linguistically diverse backgrounds. In J. F. Smutny (Ed.), *The young gifted child: Potential and promise, an anthology* (pp. 119-132). Cresskill, NJ: Hampton Press.

Klockars, A., & Sax, G. (1986). *Multiple comparisons. Quantitative applications in the social sciences* (No. 61). Beverly Hills, CA: Sage.

Kolitch, E., & Brody, L. (1992). Mathematics acceleration of highly talented students: An evaluation. *Gifted Child Quarterly, 36*, 78-86.

Kulik, J., & Kulik, C. (1991). Ability grouping and gifted students. In N. Colangelo & G. Davis (Eds.), *Handbook of gifted education* (pp. 178-196). Boston: Allyn & Bacon.

Light, R., & Pillemer, D. (1984). *Summing up: The science of reviewing research*. Cambridge, MA: Harvard University Press.

Linn, R., & Slinde, J. (1977). The determination of significance of change between pre- and posttesting periods. *Review of Educational Research, 47*, 121-150.

Maker, C. (1987). Quality education for gifted minority students. *Journal for the Education of the Gifted, 6*, 140-153.

Maker, C., & Schiever, S. (Eds.). (1989). *Critical issues in gifted education. Vol. 2. Defensible programs for cultural and ethnic minorities*. Austin, TX: PRO-ED.

Marsh, H., Chessor, D., Craven, R., & Roche, L. (1995). The effects of gifted and talented programs on academic self-concept: The big fish strikes again. *American Educational Research Journal, 32*, 285-319.

McCain, L., & McCleary, R. (1979). The statistical analysis of the simple interrupted time-series quasi-experiment. In T. Cook & D. Campbell (Eds.), *Quasi-experimentation: Design and analytic issues for field settings* (pp. 233-294). New York: Holt, Rinehart, & Winston.

Passow, A. (1972). The gifted and the disadvantaged. *The National Elementary Principal, 51*(5), 24-31.

Pedhazur, E. J., & Schmelkin, L. P. (1991). *Measurement, design, and analysis: An integrated approach*. Hillsdale, NJ: Erlbaum.

Renzulli, J. (1973). Talent potential in minority group students. *Exceptional Children, 39,* 437-444.

Renzulli, J. (1977). *The Enrichment Triad Model: A guide for developing defensible programs for the gifted and talented.* Wethersfield, CT: Creative Learning Press.

Renzulli, J. S., & Smith, L. H. (1979). Issues and procedure in evaluating programs. In A. H. Passow (Ed.), *The gifted and talented: Their education and development. The 78th yearbook of The National Society for the Study of Education. Part 1* (pp. 189-307). Chicago: University of Chicago Press.

Richert, E. (1987). Rampant problems and promising practices in the identification of disadvantaged gifted students. *Gifted Child Quarterly, 31,* 149-154.

Roscoe, J. T. (1975). *Fundamental research statistics for the behavior sciences* (2nd ed.). New York: Holt, Rinehart, & Winston.

Rossi, P., & Freeman, H. (1989). *Evaluation: A systematic approach* (4th ed.). Newbury Park, CA: Sage.

Scott, M. S., Perou, R., Urbano, R., Hogan, A., & Gold, S. (1992). The identification of giftedness: A comparison of white Hispanic and black families. *Gifted Child Quarterly, 36,* 131-139.

Scriven, M. (1967). The methodology of evaluation. In R. Tyler, R. Gagné, & M. Scriven (Eds.), *Perspectives of curriculum evaluation* (pp. 39-83) (American Educational Research Association Monograph Series on Evaluation, No. 1). Chicago: Rand-McNally.

Shapiro, J. (1985). Evaluation of a worksite program in health science and medicine: An application of Stake's model of contingency and congruence. *Educational Evaluation and Policy Analysis, 7,* 47-56.

Sowell, E. (1993). Programs for mathematically gifted students: A review of empirical research. *Gifted Child Quarterly, 37,* 124-129.

Stake, R. E. (1969/1973). Evaluation design, instrumentation, data collection, and analysis of data. In J. L. Davis (Ed.), *Educational evaluation.* Columbus, OH: Ohio State Department of Public Instruction. (Reprinted in B. Worthen & J. Sanders (1973). *Educational evaluation: Theory and practice* (pp. 303-316). Worthington, OH: Charles A. Jones Publishing).

Stanley, J. (1976) The case for extreme educational acceleration of intellectually brilliant youth. *Gifted Child Quarterly, 20,* 66-75.

Stone, E. (1992). *The Hunter Campus Schools for the gifted: The challenge of equity and excellence.* New York: Teachers College Press.

Stufflebeam, D., Foley, W., Gephart, W., Guba, E., Hammond, R., Merriman, H., & Provus, M. (1971). *Educational evaluation and decision making.* Itasca, IL: Peacock and the Phi Delta Kappa National Study Commission on Evaluation.

Taylor, C. (1968). Cultivating new talents: A way to reach the educationally deprived. *Journal of Creative Behavior, 2,* 83-90.

Torrance, E. (1969). Creative positives of disadvantaged children and youth. *Gifted Child Quarterly, 13,* 71-81.

Torrance, E. (1977). *Discovery and nurturance of giftedness in the culturally different.* Reston, VA: Council for Exceptional Children.

Torrance, E. (1986). Teaching creative and gifted learners. In M. Wittrock (Ed.), *Third handbook of research on teaching* (pp. 630-647). New York: Macmillan.

Vaugh, V., Feldhusen, J., & Asher, J. W. (1991). Meta-analysis and review of research on pull-out programs in gifted education. *Gifted Child Quarterly, 35,* 92-98.

Wampold, B., & Drew, C. (1990). *Theory and application of statistics.* New York: McGraw-Hill.

Wildt, A., & Ahtola, O. (1978). *Analysis of covariance. Quantitative applications in the social sciences* (No. 12). Beverly Hills, CA: Sage.

Willet, J. (1988). Questions and answers in the measurement of change. In E. Rothkopf (Ed.), *Review of research in education* (Vol. 15, pp. 345-422). Washington, DC: American Educational Research Association.

Willson, V., & Putnam, R. (1982). A meta-analysis of pretest sensitization effects in experimental design. *American Educational Research Journal, 19,* 249-258.

Winer, B., Brown, D., & Michels, K. (1991). *Statistical principles in experimental design* (3rd ed.). New York: McGraw-Hill.

Woods, S., & Achey, V. (1990). Successful identification of gifted racial/ethnic group students without changing classification requirements. *Roeper Review, 13*(1), 21-26.

Worthen, B., & Sanders, J. (Eds.). (1973). *Educational evaluation: Theory and practice.* Worthington, OH: Charles Jones.

Worthen, B., & Sanders, J. (1987). *Educational evaluation: Alternative approaches and practical guidelines.* New York: Longman.

Worthen, B. R., Sanders, J. R., & Fitzpatrick, J. L. (1977). *Program evaluation: Alternative approaches and practical guidelines* (2nd ed.). New York: Longman.

Author Index

A

Achey, V. H., 138, *145,* 219, *262*
Achter, J. A., 64, *77*
Adderholdt-Elliot, M., 128, 129, 134, *140*
Ahtola, O., 235, *262*
Albert R., 198, *210*
Aleman, N., 30, *41*
Alexander, C. M., 150, *158*
Algozzine, B., 128, 129, 134, *140*
Algozzine, K., 128, 129, 134, *140*
Aliotti, N. C., 94, *101*
Allan, S. D., 168, 169, 170, 172, *184*
Almeida, R., 195, 196, 209, *212*
Amaral, O. M., 90, *96*
Amodeo, L., 139, *140*
Anderson, S., 223, 233, 241, 244, 245, 251, *256*
Archambault, F. X., Jr., 168, 169, *184*
Armour-Thomas, E., 129, *140*
Arreaga-Mayer, C., 90, *96*
Arsenian, S., 84, 87, *96*
Asher, J. W., 236, *262*
Asher, J., 236, *256*

B

Bain, B., 91, *96*
Baker, C., 20, *26,* 84, 85, 88, *96*
Baker, S. A., 55, 56, *60*
Baker, S. R., 128, *144*
Baldwin, A. Y., 62, *77,* 128, 137, *140,* 165, 166, *184,* 218, 228, *256*
Ball, S., 223, 233, 241, 244, 245, 251, *256*

Baptiste, L., 167, 198, 203, 206, 208, 209, 210, *212*
Barkan, J. H., 30, *40,* 127, *140,* 160, 181, *184*
Barrera, I., 51, *59*
Baruth, L. G., 7, 10, *26*
Beattie, O., 199, *211*
Beaudry, J., 51, *59*
Bell, L. A., 63, *77*
Bellis, D. D., 161, *190*
Ben Zeev, S., 19, *26,* 34, *40,* 91, *96*
Benbow, C. P., 63, 64, *77, 80*
Benson, A. J., 133, *140*
Berk, R., 93, *100,* 241, 242, *256*
Bermudez, A. B., 30, *40*
Bernal, E. M., 30, 33, *40,* 127, 131, *140,* 160, 161, 162, 163, 166, 167, 170, 171, 172, 173, 174, 175, 176, 177, 178, 179, 181, 182, *184, 185, 187, 188,* 197, 198, *210,* 218, 244, 257
Bernstein, M., 119, *123*
Berry, J. W., 119, *122*
Betts, G. T., 67, 77
Bialystock, E., 17, 19, *26,* 95, *96*
Biasini, A., 150, *158*
Blatt, B., 206, *213*
Bloom, B., 224, *257*
Blum, L. A., 133, *141*
Borg, W., 227, 231, *258*
Borland, J. H., 132, 136, 138, *140,* 218, *257*
Boston, B., 169, 170, *186*
Boyde-Frankllin, N., 194, 195, *212*

Subject Index